PRESSURE GROUPS IN BRITAIN: a reader

edited by

Richard Kimber

and

J. J. Richardson

UNIVERSITY OF KEELE

DENT, LONDON
ROWMAN AND LITTLEFIELD, TOTOWA, N.J.

© Introduction and editorial matter
J. M. Dent & Sons Ltd, 1974

All rights reserved
Made in Great Britain
at the
Aldine Press · Letchworth · Herts
for
J. M. DENT & SONS LTD
Aldine House · Albemarle Street · London
First published 1974
First published in the United States 1974
by ROWMAN AND LITTLEFIELD, Totowa, New Jersey

This book is set in 10 on 11 pt Times New Roman 327
by The Lancashire Typesetting Company Limited

Dent edition
Hardback ISBN: 0 460 10199 4
Paperback ISBN: 0 460 11199 x

Rowman and Littlefield edition
Library of Congress Cataloging in Publication Data
Kimber, Richard, comp.

  Pressure Groups in Britain.
  (Rowman and Littlefield university library)
  CONTENTS: Lieber, R. J. Interest groups and
political integration: British entry into Europe.—
Self, P., and Storing, H. The farmers and the state.—
Harrison, M. Trade unions and the Labour Party. [etc.]

  1. Pressure groups—Great Britain—Addresses,
essays, lectures. I. Richardson, Jeremy John, joint
comp. II. Title.
JN329.P7K54   322.4'3'0942   74-1192
ISBN 0-87471-524-5

Preface

Our aim in this book has been to produce a reader on pressure groups in Britain, a central aspect of the British political process, which both offers enough material to provide some detailed information to complement the general accounts of group activity that may be found in many of the basic texts on British politics, and also gives a sufficiently wide selection of items to indicate the nature of that section of the literature concerned with the activity of British pressure groups.

In our selection we have tried to strike a balance between the well known and the less well known, the new and the old, and have included a number of articles which encapsulate or are taken from fuller studies. Inevitably we have had to compromise: considerations of length and cost have forced us to exclude some items which would otherwise be automatic selections (we have in mind particularly articles by S. H. Beer, S. E. Finer and J. P. Nettl—see bibliography). Since much of the theoretical literature on pressure groups is American in orientation, and in any event is so extensive that it could not be represented adequately by a few articles, we have omitted an overtly theoretical section but have endeavoured to indicate the basic issues and associated literature in our introduction. Thus we have adopted what is predominantly a case-study approach illustrating aspects of group activity in Britain.

We should like to thank Martin Harrison for agreeing to write the section on trade unions and the Labour Party especially for this book, and Leonard Tivey for revising his article on consumer politics. We are also grateful to Stuart Brookes for helping with the bibliography, to our wives (Jennifer and Anne) for helping with the proof reading, and to Mrs Arlene Holmes and Miss Marjorie Young for undertaking the typing.

University of Keele
July 1973

Richard Kimber
J. J. Richardson

iii

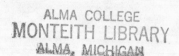

Contents

Contents

Part I
Introduction

Definitions

For a problem which lacks real intellectual depth it is remarkable how much terminological discussion has prefaced group literature. The tendency of different writers to espouse different terms is a source of confusion for many students approaching the subject for the first time. Even a cursory glance at the literature will reveal the following terms: political group, lobby, interest group, political interest group, special interest group, organized group, voluntary association, pressure group, cause group, sectional group, promotional group, attitude group, protective group, defensive group, anomic group, institutional group, associational group, non-associational group, formal-role group, exclusive group, and partial group.

The two main aspects of the debate on terminology have revolved, firstly, around the problem of finding a suitable collective term for the whole class of political phenomena of which organized groups are a part and, secondly, around how the class may best be sub-divided to provide a useful classification.

The principal contenders in the first case have been 'pressure group', 'interest group', and 'lobby'. Of these perhaps the term 'pressure group' has been used most widely in the British context. S. E. Finer has objected that this term implies that some sanction will be applied if a demand is refused and that most groups, most of the time, simply make requests or put up a case:[1] they are not always forced to bang upon a closed door—on many occasions the door may be wide open.[2] Finer's preference is for the term 'lobby'. Pressure need not be viewed quite so starkly however; applying a sanction is only one way of exerting pressure. There is a perfectly reasonable sense in which the simple articulation of a demand is equivalent to exerting pressure upon a part of the political system.

1

Finer further objects that groups are pressure groups only intermittently. This is strictly true according to his interpretation of 'pressure', but it is equally true that the lobby is not always lobbying nor an interest group always articulating an interest. Perhaps the word 'lobby' is best reserved for use as a verb indicating an aspect of group activity. The problem with the word 'interest' is that, in Britain at least, it has a rather narrow connotation, implying the selfish pursuit of one's own welfare or that of a particular section of society.

Thus it does not seem fruitful to search for a term which reflects all aspects of group activity and is entirely neutral. If the choice of terms matters at all, 'pressure group' is probably the most satisfactory for use in the British context. What, then, is a pressure group?

Demands are, of course, articulated both by people acting individually and by people acting through groups. A major difficulty lies in distinguishing these activities from one another, particularly when political science lacks an adequate definition of 'group'. David Truman's definition, though subjected to criticism, still has considerable utility however. In avoiding the inclusion of 'categoric' groups (i.e. 'farmers', 'blondes', 'mothers'), he places the emphasis on the relationships or interactions of the persons involved. A group is said to exist when two or more individuals interact, on the basis of shared attitudes, with a certain minimum frequency:[3] it is these shared attitudes which constitute an interest. Even so, it is clearly a weakness in this approach that the frequency of interaction remains unspecified and cannot, perhaps, be specified.[4] Also, it is misleading to equate a shared interest with shared attitudes. In a Parent-Teacher Association, for instance, the shared interest is the education of the children; attitudes concerning the furtherance of this interest, however, may be far from shared.

Some writers have restricted their attentions to *organized* groups.[5] While such groups do account for the bulk of group activity in Britain there is an element, and possibly a growing one, of more spontaneous and less formally organized group activity. For example, villagers have brought traffic to a standstill in Ditchling, Sussex, to draw attention to the stream of heavy lorries which thunder through it, while housewives have blockaded the United Carbon Black factory in Swansea, have manned picket lines at a site near Aberdare where natural gas storage tanks are being built, and have sponsored a petition against foul-smelling air pollution in Battersea. Although such groups may not be a prominent feature of British politics, clearly for comparative purposes a scheme must be used which takes account of their activity.[6]

Thus a pressure group may be regarded as any group (in the sense previously indicated) which articulates a demand that the authorities in the political system or sub-systems should make an authoritative allocation. In order to exclude from this definition political parties and other groups whose objective is to take over the government, it is usual to add a rider that such groups do not themselves seek to occupy positions of authority. It is also worth noting that some group behaviour may be in support of the system and may be oriented to its maintenance.[7]

Although this definition has narrowed the field, it is still an extremely large and diverse one, and many writers find it useful to subdivide pressure groups. Perhaps the most obvious method of classification is by means of the interests which the groups seek to promote or the causes they purport to foster.[8] It will become clear when we examine the range of groups which operate in Britain that, while this approach may be used to describe the many groups which exist, it has little analytical value. More useful is the distinction between 'sectional' and 'promotional' groups.

Sectional pressure groups seek to protect the interests of a particular section of society, while *promotional* pressure groups seek to promote causes arising from a given set of attitudes.[9] Even these terms are only a guide to categorization: many groups belonging primarily to one category partake of characteristics from the other. For example the National Smoke Abatement Society, primarily a promotional group, was found by J. B. Sanderson to receive financial support from the National Coal Board;[10] the membership of the Noise Abatement Society includes manufacturers of noise suppression equipment, and so on. Similarly, trade unions, primarily sectional groups, sometimes seek to promote causes.

The Group Theorists

Robert T. Golembiewski has emphasized that 'political science and the social sciences in general are characterized by a fantastic discontinuity—one of the unfortunate consequences (and causes) of the research fads which periodically sweep across them'.[11] It has been the misfortune of 'group theory' (insofar as there is such a 'theory') to have been out of fashion with most political scientists for a considerable period. Various attempts to revive it have found little support, often on the ground that it is far from a complete 'theory of politics'. Whether group theorists have really claimed that the group model offers a complete explanation in political science is perhaps open to question. Even at its minimum, group theory has a useful role to play in political analysis in that it attempts to explain one of the central features of at least Western political systems—namely the existence and activity of the multitude of groups in a society and their relationship to the authoritative allocation of values for that society. In fact it could reasonably be argued that, even though an analysis of group activity will not provide a complete explanation of the political process, it will at least give clear indications as to where authoritative allocations are made within a given political system or, to put it more simply, where power lies. For example an analysis of group activity under the Fourth and Fifth Republics in France illustrates quite clearly the shift in the locus of power which occurred as a result of the Debré Constitution of 1958.[12] As O. R. Young has argued, most group writers have accepted Bentley's view that the group approach provides 'a systematic orientation toward political phenomena and that it would be a useful aid in generating questions and hypotheses for detailed investigation'.[13] This is why, as he suggests, political scientists who have selected the group approach have a strong leaning towards empirical investigations.

Most contemporary writers attribute modern group theory to Arthur F. Bentley, whose book *The Process of Government* was first published in the United States in 1908. The group approach, however, has a much longer pedigree than this would suggest. For example, Plato in many ways adopted the group approach in his theory that justice was an equilibrium among groups in society imposed by the guardians.[14] Similarly, Marx, in concentrating on the class struggle, recognized the interplay of powerful groups in society, as did Ludwig Gumplowicz when he claimed that the social process throughout history has consisted in the relations and reciprocal actions between heterogeneous social groups.[15] It is not surprising of course that so many writers have been concerned with the importance of groups in society, for as Odegard has pointed out, the group phenomenon is so universal that it is tempting to say that 'life is "togetherness" and "togetherness" is life'.[16]

It is nevertheless in Bentley's work that the group approach is to be found in its most explicit form and he is still considered to be the 'tap root' of modern group theory.[17] Bentley, it should be stressed, did not think of his book as *the* theory of politics—he described it simply as 'an attempt to fashion a tool'. In the text, however, many of his statements do imply that he believed his 'attempt' would be proved successful by later empirical investigation.[18] For example, he argued that it was only when group activities had been isolated, when their representative values had been determined and when the whole governmental process was stated in terms of groups, that we would be able to approach a satisfactory knowledge of government. Thus 'all phenomena of government are phenomena of groups pressing one another, forming one another and pushing out new groups and group representatives (the organs or agencies of government) to mediate the adjustments'.[19] It is clear that ultimately Bentley was prepared to see the government as yet another group participating in the struggle between groups out of which policy emerged. Indeed he claimed that the interest groups actively create the government as well as working through it. The government as activity, he argued, works 'for' the groups and from the point of view of certain groups may at times be their private tool, whereas from the point of view of other groups it would appear as the deadly enemy.[20] In a similar way Earl Latham considered that the apparatus of the state exhibited many of the characteristics of groups outside the structure of government. However, he did concede that (to take one example) the Bureau of Internal Revenue was in a privileged position *vis-à-vis* non-governmental groups. These governmental groups 'are distinguished from others only in the characteristic of officiality. The designation "official" is the sign manifest that the bearer is authorized by social understanding to exercise against all groups and individuals certain powers which they may not exercise against him'.[21] In short, 'the difference between public and private groups is the officiality of the former'.[22] Perhaps the most famous statement of the efficacy of the group approach to the study of politics is, however, Bentley's much quoted passage where he claims that 'when the groups are adequately stated, everything is stated. When I say everything I mean everything. The complete description will mean the complete science, in the study of social phenomena, as in any other field'.[23]

One particular consequence of an acceptance of the primacy of groups in the political process is that it may lead to the notion of society being an equilibrium of the forces represented by the competing groups. Indeed, Bentley explicitly stated that, as he believed that the phenomena of government are from start to finish phenomena of force,[24] the balance of group pressures was in fact the existing state of society.[25] In the broadest sense he considered government to be a 'process of adjustment' of a set of interest groups. That theme was enlarged upon by Earl Latham who considered that every statute was a compromise 'because the process of accommodating conflicts of group interest is one of equilibrium and consent . . . what may be called public policy is the *equilibrium* reached in this struggle at any given moment, and it represents a balance which the contending factions of groups constantly try to weigh in their favour'.[26]

5

A more refined approach to the study of the role of groups in the political process, but still taking the group as its central unit, is David Truman's *The Governmental Process*. First published in 1951, it attempts to build-in various refinements to the group theorists' approach. His work is seen partly as an attempt to justify a political system in which groups play a key role. Indeed he is accused by Olson as being even more benign in his view of the effects of groups than Bentley.[27] Truman's is essentially a restatement of Arthur Bentley's thesis. For example he argues that '. . . the behaviours that constitute the process of government cannot be adequately understood apart from the groups . . . which are operative at any one point in time'.[28] And, in discussing the institutions of government, he follows Bentley by describing them as centres of interest-based power.[29] The particular contribution by Truman has been an attempt to show that the threats posed to democracy by the existence of groups have been greatly exaggerated. Thus he introduces two elements in his conception of the political process, designed to show that there are inherent checks in society which prevent an excessive concentration of power in any one group or set of groups. These elements are (1) overlapping membership and (2) potential interest groups.

The notion of overlapping membership is a function of Truman's view that a group is not a collection of individuals but is a 'standardized pattern of interactions'.[30] Because an individual's activities are diverse, he is bound to be involved in a variety of groups. Hence members of any one group '. . . will perceive the group's claims in terms of a diversity of frames of reference'.[31] He cites as an example members of a Parent-Teacher Association, who assess proposals in the light of the fact that some members will also belong to the Catholic Church, others to the local chamber of commerce and others to the local taxpayers' league. Thus, 'it is the competing claims of other groups *within* a given interest group that threaten its cohesion, and force it to reconcile its claims with those of other groups active on the political scene'.[32] The second factor suggested by Truman as acting as a restraint upon the excesses of the group system is the notion of the unorganized interest or the potential interest group. Any mutual interest or shared attitude, he argues, is a potential group. New organized interest groups will be formed as a result of a disturbance in established relationships and expectations anywhere in society.[33] The mere threat of the formation of another group may act as a restraint upon the existing groups in society— '. . . it may be this possibility of organization that alone gives the potential group a minimum of influence in the political process'.[34] Even though the formation of an organized group may be, for various reasons, extremely difficult, the possibility of the disturbance which would accrue from their formation necessitates that such latent interests should be taken account of and accorded 'at least a minimum of influence'. These unorganized interests may find expression in what Truman has described as the 'rules of the game', or, more explicitly, in the laws and constitution of the state. For example he cites '... the value generally attached to the dignity of the individual human being, loosely expressed in terms of "fair dealing", or more explicitly verbalized in formulations such as the Bill of Rights'.[35] Violation of these loosely defined rules of the game will both weaken a group's own cohesion and reduce its status in the community. It will also, more importantly, expose it to the claims of the other groups.[36]

Such a benign attitude towards the existence of group pressures in society has naturally provoked considerable criticism, and many writers have sought to discredit the 'group theorists', both in terms of principle and on many points of detail.[37] It is impossible to do justice to their criticisms in a limited space, but two or three common elements in the group approach have attracted almost universal criticisms from its opponents. For example a frequent attack is made on the de-emphasis of the individual in the group approach. This criticism stems from the writings of both Bentley and Truman. Bentley was quite categoric in claiming that the individual as such was unimportant in the process of government. He argued that 'the individual stated for himself and invested with an extra-social unity of his own, is a fiction. But every bit of the activity ... can be stated either on one side as individual or on the other as social group activity. The former statement is in the main of trifling importance in interpreting society, the latter statement is essential first, last and all the time'.[38] Truman similarly claimed that whenever we look at an individual, whether citizen or legislator, we cannot understand his activity in the governmental institution '... except in terms of the interests with which he identifies himself and the groups with which he affiliates and with which he is confronted'.[39] Stanley Rothman has, however, pointed out that on this principle if we are to understand, say, a Congressional decision, we would need 'to examine at least the history of group membership of *each* Congressman from infancy on, including all the various friendship groups of childhood'.[40] Other critics, notably Odegard, have suggested that the broad definition of group sometimes used by the proponents of the group approach leads to a meaningless statement. Thus he argues that '... when Congress and the Courts and the President and all other institutions and aggregations . . . are defined as interest groups, the term becomes synonymous not merely with politics but with human life itself'.[41] In England Bernard Crick has accused Bentley of sheer obscurantism in, for example, his discussion of the Supreme Court, and has argued that Bentley lacks historical discipline. It is, Crick suggested, 'the existence of Constitutional law and convention that is one of the greatest stumbling blocks to that view which seeks to understand politics purely as process'.[42]

An extremely common criticism is that the group theorists are said to have a simplistic view of the political process and that other factors, such as the role of reason and logic, play an important role in the decision-making process.[43] Rothman, whilst readily conceding the importance of groups in the political process, argues that the study of politics 'must also involve . . . the study of patterns of normatively oriented political action' and that 'changing conceptions of reality, the ideas of political theorists, changes in socio-economic structure may all be found to play a role in determining these patterns'.[44] However, group theorists would no doubt reply that groups would certainly play an important role in, for example, changes in the socio-economic structure and moreover that such changes could only be fully understood with reference to group pressures. The critics of the group approach are on less firm ground when they appear to be introducing value judgments concerning the morality of the group system in society. At one point Odegard appears to be approaching this position when he asks if the vogue for group theory reflected 'an escape from freedom and a nostalgia for a neomedieval corporate society'. Is the process of government as described by Bentley, he asks, 'substantially different from that described by Thrasymachus, Machiavelli and Hobbes? Does it in effect defend the principle that Might is Right?'[45] In Britain W. J. M. Mackenzie has also admitted that he feels unhappy about the group system—'I think my own answer is that I don't like it very much . . . if great problems are to be handled at all it must be by a government prepared to use its majority.'[46]

The most fundamental criticism of the traditional group approach has, however, been put forward by Mancur Olson in his seminal work *The Logic of Collective Action*. Olson has questioned the whole rationale of group membership and has argued that there is a fundamental inconsistency in the thinking of the group theorists. The suggested inconsistency is that the group theorists '. . . have assumed that, if a group has some reason or incentive to organize to further its interest, the rational individuals in that group would also have a reason or incentive to support an organization working in their mutual interest'.[47] This assumption is false because '... if the individuals in any large group are interested in their own welfare they will *not* voluntarily make any sacrifices to help their group attain its political (public or collective) objectives'.[48] To explain group membership Olson introduces the concept of 'selective incentives'. Thus an individual in a potential group will be stimulated to act in a group-oriented way, '... only through an incentive that operates, not indiscriminately, like the collective good, upon the group as a whole, but rather *selectively* toward the individuals in the group'.[49] Brian Barry, though conceding the force of Olson's position, has raised doubts as to whether, for example, his theory can explain the generally higher levels of unionism in Britain than in the U.S.A.[50] Nevertheless he readily concedes that Olson's work is 'the only book fit to rank with Downs' *Economic Theory of Democracy*, as an example of the virtues of the "economic" approach to political analysis'.[51] Even Truman has conceded that Olson's work sheds light on various group phenomena noted by himself and other group theorists.[52] It is unfortunate that Olson's work has been largely ignored by British political scientists, as it does focus attention on some fundamental problems concerning the existence and activity of groups in the political process.

The relevance of economic analysis to the problems of studying politics has not escaped the notice of contemporary supporters of the group approach. Charles Hagan, for example, has suggested that the authoritative allocation of values is roughly equivalent to the allocation of scarce resources and that the political scientist's equivalent to the supply and demand curves used by economists is the group struggle itself.[53] If, as he believes, we take the central problem of political science as the authoritative allocation of values, then 'the means by which these values are allocated is the group struggle'.[54] In contrast to Crick, he argues that a constitution 'is a behaviour that the dominant groups manifest in the operation of the community. If the groups change then the constitution changes with them'.[55] As proof of this he cites the Fourteenth Amendment to the U.S. Constitution which on paper has remained constant over the years, yet in practice has changed. Neither the words nor the institutions have changed but the interest groups have: the interests gaining representation in 1868 and 1896 have now been replaced by another set of interests. Hagan also tries to allow for the importance of the individual and goes on to claim that, by using the group as the basic unit of analysis, we can explain all that other approaches claim to explain with their 'reified categories'.[56]

Is, then, the group approach to the study of politics the universal model for analysis of the political process, or is it yet another 'theory of politics' which must be discarded in favour of more comprehensive theories? The answer is that it is probably neither and that it is what Bentley claimed originally, namely a 'tool' of analysis. Even critics such as W. J. M. Mackenzie have conceded that the group approach, like that adopted in Pendleton Herring's *Groups Before Congress* (1928), though '. . . thoroughly illogical', works and that it is 'one effective way to present the facts'.[57] Joseph La Palombara perhaps strikes the correct note in suggesting that although it would be wrong to consider the political process as being 'characterized exclusively by group behaviour . . . it is obvious that no political process . . . can be understood without according serious attention to the role of interest groups'.[58] Neither, he argues, does one need to claim that the group approach is *the* theory of politics ' . . . in order to derive empirical utility from the approach'. In the context of the British situation R. T. McKenzie, in his article reprinted in Part III (p. 276), has suggested that although groups do not play the role suggested by Bentley, the group system '. . . provides an invaluable set of multiple channels through which the mass of the citizenry can influence the decision-making process at the highest levels'. Even if we only take this limited view of the importance of pressure groups then the studies included in this volume would be fully justified. If we take the more ambitious group theorists' claims then the studies are essentially concerned with the central feature of the political system—namely the constant and shifting struggle between competing groups in society.

Pressure Groups in Britain

Almost every aspect of society has some associated group activity, and the number and range of pressure groups active in the British political system are enormous. It has been estimated that there are approximately 2,500 employers' associations alone, at least 1,600 of which are active.[59] Partly because the information about groups which is most readily available concerns 'business' or 'labour' groups, and also, perhaps, partly because of a tendency to see everything in economic terms, many students overlook the rest of the group spectrum and consequently are apt to underestimate the complexity of pressure group activity in Britain. For this reason it is worth sketching the range of groups, any or all of which may articulate demands from time to time.

The professions are particularly assiduous in protecting their interests, and are represented by organizations like the Royal Institute of British Architects, the British Medical Association (B.M.A.), or the Association of British Tree Surgeons and Arborists. Local government and its employees are represented by bodies such as the County Councils Association, the National and Local Government Officers Association (N.A.L.G.O) or the Society of Local Government Barristers. Local communities have spawned Ratepayers' Associations, Tenants' Associations and many other community action groups including Claimants' Unions and Squatters. There is a wide range of welfare organizations such as Alcoholics Anonymous, Aid for the Elderly in Government Institutions, Shelter, Christian Aid, and also of religious groups like the Association for Latin Liturgy, the Actors' Church Union, or the British and Foreign Bible Society. Many groups exist to promote recreational interests such as the National Playing Fields Association, the National Small-bore Rifle Association or the British Racing Tobogganing Association; while others concentrate on cultural matters, for example the Folklore Society, the Royal Academy of Arts, or the International Association of Art Critics (British Section).

The 1960s saw a considerable growth in the number of societies concerned to protect aspects of the environment, particularly at the local level; between 1957 and 1973 the number of societies registered with the Civic Trust grew from 200 to over 1,000. At the national level, the Conservation Society (founded 1966) and the Friends of the Earth (formed in 1970) have been added to the list of longer established groups like the Council for the Protection of Rural England, and the Ramblers' Association. Then there is a range of groups concerned about aspects of the operation of the political system, like the Electoral Reform Society or the Study of Parliament Group, and a number of groups associated with the main political parties (e.g. the Monday Club, or the Fabian Society); while others have at times assumed some of the characteristics of a political party (Edward Martell's Freedom Group, the Campaign for Nuclear Disarmament, or—at the local level—Ratepayers' and Tenants' Associations). All these and more exist in addition to the organizations connected with the business world (such as the Confederation of British Industry, the Cake and Biscuit Alliance, or the Society of Motor Manufacturers and Traders) and the various organizations of Labour (such as the Trades Union Congress, the Transport and General Workers' Union, or the Amalgamated Association of Beamers, Twisters and Drawers (Hand and Machine)).

In reviewing the range of British groups we have deliberately avoided presenting them in neat categories. Such classifications are often accorded a veneration which is unwarranted and, as Truman points out,[60] they may achieve simplicity of communication, but only at what may be a high cost. In particular, standard categories often seem to imply a cohesion within the category which does not exist. Furthermore, one may be tempted to ascribe an interest to a particular group *because* it has been classified in a certain way. There is also the more practical difficulty that there is no obvious principle of classification which avoids the problem of a group belonging to several categories. Indeed, the use of rigid categories tends to overlook the fact that the political process is a dynamic one, and that organizations which start in one category may evolve in such a way that their activity subsequently qualifies them for inclusion in other categories. For example, the Institute of Contemporary Arts, formed in 1948 with the objects of promoting the arts and providing a meeting-place for artists and the public, might have been classified as a cultural organization at its inception. Since then, however, it has nurtured a variety of political groups including All Change, the I.C.A. Transport action link (a clearing house for the exchange of information among transport reform groups). In this context it must also be remembered that the lives of some groups are limited to a single campaign, and that many *ad hoc* groups are organized to fight individual decisions, both at the national and at the local levels (e.g. the Wing Airport Resistance Association, formed to prevent London's third airport from being sited at Wing, Bucks.,[61] or the Friends of Truro School, formed to fight the Governors' decision to sell the school).[62] Of course, many of the groups mentioned above make demands of the system only very occasionally. Much of their activity is geared to providing services of one kind or another for their members. Only when they begin to articulate demands do they become pressure groups.

The pattern of activity of a pressure group is determined by its perception (usually its leaders' perception) of the nature of the strategic situation it confronts in relation to its own aims, and to its resources. Since it is more desirable, from a group's point of view, that it should play a part in the formulation of policy rather than have to wage a public campaign after policy has crystallized, much pressure group activity is directed towards the administrators, especially at the national level. At the local level it is probable that the disposition of elected representatives to regard themselves as the legitimate channels through which demands should be communicated tends to leave group contacts with administrators relatively unexploited.[63]

12

The importance of the administration as a focus for group activity at the national level should not, however, be exaggerated. The administration is indeed the prime focus for many business, labour and professional groups; many of them are represented on a wide range of Government committees [64] and have virtually continuous access to the formative stage of the policy process. In some cases (e.g. the National Farmers' Union) the relationship becomes almost symbiotic.[65] Ready access to Whitehall, together with the statutory provisions for consultation in some cases,[66] places some pressure groups in a quite different strategic situation from those lacking these facilities. It is therefore unwise to generalize about group activity as a whole from the activities of a professional organization like the B.M.A. or from those of the major unions or business organizations. Eckstein's comment, for example, that 'the public campaign has been replaced largely by informal and unostentatious contacts between officials,[67] and his tendency to regard the use of other channels as 'special cases' [68] look rather odd when set against the almost daily press reports of public campaigns. For similar reasons, Finer's suggestion that groups approach the various parts of the system in a sequence requires some modification. He has suggested that the characteristic activity of sectional groups (he refers to them as interest groups in this case) is that they work through the Executive. 'Then, in so far as these groups seek to go further than the Executive has suggested, their next line of attack will be Parliament, where their success or failure will be influenced by their relationship to Party. At this stage, they may also appeal to the public. But in Britain the "grass roots lobby" is infrequent and dubiously successful.'[69] This order of activity is reversed for promotional groups. It is our contention that pressure group activity is generally much more complicated than this and that such a straightforward scheme only applies in some cases. In many instances groups try to use several channels simultaneously. It is quite common for promotional groups to submit memoranda to the relevant Department, to lobby M.P.s, and to utilize the mass media concurrently (as was done in the National Parks Campaign, see pp. 164–90). The British Road Federation, to take a sectional example, wages a continuing public campaign on the need for more roads even though it and its members have good administrative contacts. Many groups also supplement these contacts with support from 'friendly' M.P.s. Indeed, this is bound to be the case since the administrative response in many situations is to indicate that a particular amendment to legislation would be acceptable if proposed in Parliament. The other side of this particular coin is of course that groups not having access to the

Executive sometimes use Parliament as a means of gaining access, by getting an M.P. to raise the matter (maybe privately) with the Minister. It was, for example, through the intervention of Terry Boston, M.P. for Faversham, that the Civic Trust gained consultative status over the construction and use regulations affecting 'heavy' lorries in 1969.[70]

The success or failure of groups in their dealings with Parliament is much more likely to be a function of factors other than party. For example, the Government's own strategy may play a decisive role; Government time may be set aside to aid the passage of a Private Member's Bill (as happened with the Bill to reform the abortion laws), or the Government may hold back a decision until a debate has been held, thus allowing time for a campaign to be mounted (as it did over the decision to build the third London airport at Foulness); though Finer is right to imply that the party complexion; of the Government is important, and that many groups (especially sectional ones) tend to work through the M.P.s of one particular party.

Looking at the relationship between pressure groups and parties at a more general level, some writers have overstated the importance of party in processing group demands. It is certainly not the case in Britain that 'the party system stands between the interest group system and the authoritative policy-making agencies and screens them for the particularistic and disintegrative impact of special interests' as Almond once suggested.[71] Nor is Beer's hypothesis that 'party does not merely aggregate the opinions of groups, it goes a long way toward creating these opinions by fixing the framework of public thinking about policy'[72] entirely convincing; it depends on the issues. The parties do not give their attention to every issue—they have had very little to say, for example, about environmental protection—and moreover there is no reason for thinking that the group opinions which are formed on a specific issue in the absence of a pronouncement from the parties are particularly restricted by the framework of thinking implied by party policies on other issues: compare, for example, the conflicting attitudes to economic growth implicit in the policies of the main parties on the one hand, and the opinions of many environmental groups on the other.

Overall, parties play a relatively minor role as channels of influence,[73] and relatively few groups utilize party machinery directly in order to have their policies adopted as party policy; most groups remain unaligned—though there are some major exceptions to this. Firstly, a number of groups exist, either within or on the fringes of the parties, which aim to influence party policy and to some extent public opinion. Groups such as the Bow Group, Pressure for Economic and Social Toryism (P.E.S.T.—The Progressive Tory Pressure Group), or the Monday Club attempt to influence Conservative policy, while the Fabian Society, the Tribune Group and others are active on the Labour side. Secondly, there are of course major sectional interests associated with each of the two main parties. On the one hand over seventy unions, Socialist and Cooperative societies are affiliated to the Labour Party;[73] on the other hand considerable industrial and commercial interests are aligned with the Conservative Party,[74] although none are actually affiliated. Despite this apparent polarization, both sets of interests normally cooperate with the government of the day regardless of party, though sections of the labour movement (e.g. the All Trades Union Alliance) would like to see a general policy among the unions of non-cooperation with Tory governments. While the Conservatives can expect little support from the unions, there are signs of some industrial and commercial support for Labour. Under the chairmanship of Lord Wilfred Brown the 1972 Industry Group has been formed to provide a channel of communication between those who hold senior positions in commerce, industry, the professions, public services, etc., and the Labour Party, with the objects of bringing about a greater understanding of the policies of the Labour Party within industry and commerce and of enabling those with useful knowledge and experience to give information and comment at a formative stage in the development of the Party's commercial and industrial policies.[75]

More important to most groups than party in this sense is the cultivation of public opinion, and the use of the public campaign. In this connection, the central role in the communication process occupied by the newspapers, radio and television makes coverage of their activities extremely valuable to pressure groups, especially in view of the propensity of governments to respond to the press and broadcasting media (cf. the response to dramatic news reports of cyanide dumping or to reports of the harmful effects of cyclamates). For their part the media find group activity to be convenient and sometimes entertaining or dramatic copy, and are often receptive to suggestions for stories from group publicity officers. In 1972 B.B.C. 2 took pressure group coverage a step further by offering free time to groups in its *Open Door* programme, particularly those which do not normally have the opportunity of putting their views on television. While this is a limited step, it does improve the position of some groups, though those advocating really extreme views are still likely to encounter obstacles.[76] Lastly, as is sometimes overlooked, pressure groups, such as Women in Media and Environmental Communica-

15

tors Organization, now exist within the media to propagate various causes.

Finally, it is worth re-emphasizing that not all pressure group activity is directed towards influencing *government* policy. Pressure groups feature more or less prominently in the operation of all other aspects of the political system. We have already noted the activity of groups in relation to local authorities, to the parties, and to the mass media. We should also note not only that institutions (such as universities) act as pressure groups, but also that there is often considerable group activity within these institutions (for example, an association of lecturers within a university) and that group campaigns are often directed at other groups or institutions.[77]

The complexity and subtlety of group behaviour in Britain which we have tried to emphasize is a factor which tends to be forgotten when we begin to examine individual case studies. It cannot be explained solely, or even largely (as Eckstein implies) by reference to the structural aspects of the system. The explanation must be in terms of the whole strategic situation in which groups are placed.[78]

Notes

1 S. E. Finer, *Anonymous Empire*, Pall Mall, 2nd ed., 1966, p. 3.

2 *Ibid.*, p. 22.

3 D. Truman, *The Governmental Process*, Alfred Knopf, 2nd ed., 1971, p. 24.

4 See J. La Palombara, *Interest Groups in Italian Politics*, Princeton University Press, 1964, p. 14.

5 For example G. C. Moodie and G. Studdert-Kennedy, *Opinions, Publics and Pressure Groups*, Allen and Unwin, 1970, p. 60; or Allen Potter, *Organised Groups in British National Politics*, Faber, 1961.

6 See, for example, Almond's fourfold classification in G. A. Almond and G. B. Powell, *Comparative Politics: a developmental approach*, Little, Brown and Co., 1966, pp. 74–9.

7 La Palombara, p. 17. Our definition is broadly based on David Easton's definition of politics. See *A Framework for Political Analysis*, pp. 49–50.

8 Potter, pp. 47–60 and 119–26, offers a classification on this basis.

9 *Ibid.*, p. 25.

10 'The National Smoke Abatement Society and the Clean Air Act (1956),' *Political Studies*, vol. IX (1961), reprinted in R. Kimber and J. J. Richardson (eds.), *Campaigning for the Environment*, Routledge and Kegan Paul, 1974.

16

11 ' "The Group Basis of Politics." Notes on Analysis and Development,' *American Political Science Review*, LIV (December 1960), p. 971.

12 For a discussion of this point see Bernard E. Brown, 'Pressure Politics in the Fifth Republic,' *Journal of Politics*, vol. 25, no. 3 (1963).

13 *Systems of Political Science*, Prentice Hall, 1968, p. 87.

14 See Peter H. Odegard, 'A Group Basis of Politics: A New Name for an Ancient Myth,' *Western Political Quarterly*, vol. 11 (September 1958), p. 692.

15 See H. E. Barnes, *An Introduction to the History of Sociology*, Chicago University Press, 1948, p. 192.

16 Odegard, p. 689.

17 See Golembiewski, p. 962.

18 The most useful edition of Bentley's book is edited by Peter H. Odegard and published by the Belknap Press (Harvard), 1967. An excellent general survey of the group approach is to be found in Mancur Olson, *The Logic of Collective Action*, Harvard University Press, 1965, Chapter V.

19 Bentley, p. 269.

20 *Ibid.*, p. 270.

21 Earl Latham, *The Group Basis of Politics*, Octagon Books, 1965, p. 35.

22 *Loc. cit.*

23 Bentley, pp. 208–9.

24 *Ibid.*, p. 258 (although Bentley preferred the term 'pressure' to the term 'force').

25 *Ibid.*, pp. 258–9.

26 Latham, pp. 35–6 (our emphasis).

27 Olson, p. 124.

28 Truman, p. 502.

29 *Ibid.*, p. 506.

30 *Ibid.*, p. 508.

31 *Ibid.*, p. 509.

32 *Ibid.*, p. 510.

33 *Ibid.*, p. 511.

34 *Loc. cit.*

35 *Ibid.*, p. 512.

36 *Ibid.*, p. 513.

37 See for example: Odegard, *op. cit.*; Stanley Rothman, 'Systematic Political Theory: Observations on the Group Approach,' *American Political Science Review*, vol. 54 (March 1960); W. J. M. Mackenzie, 'Pressure Groups: The "Conceptual Framework",' *Political Studies*, vol. III, no. 3 (1955); Roy C. Macridis, 'Interest Groups in Comparative Analysis,' *Journal of Politics*,

vol. 23 (February 1961), pp. 25–45; P. Moneypenny, 'Political Science and the Study of Groups: Notes to Guide a Research Project,' *Western Political Quarterly*, vol. 7 (June 1954), pp. 183–201.

38 Bentley, p. 215.

39 Truman, p. 502.

40 Rothman, p. 24.

41 Odegard, p. 695.

42 B. Crick, *The American Science of Politics*, Routledge and Kegan Paul, 1959, p. 128.

43 Odegard, p. 700.

44 Rothman, p. 32.

45 Odegard, p. 701.

46 W. J. M. Mackenzie, 'Pressure Groups in British Government,' *British Journal of Sociology*, vol. VI, no. 2 (1955), pp. 133–48, reprinted in R. Rose, *Studies in British Politics*, Macmillan, 1967, pp. 202–19.

47 Olson, p. 127.

48 *Ibid.*, p. 126. See also B. Barry, *Sociologists, Economists and Democracy*, Collier-Macmillan, 1970, pp. 23–9.

49 Olson, p. 51.

50 Barry, p. 29.

51 *Ibid.*, p. 24.

52 Truman, p. xxx.

53 C. B. Hagan, 'The Group in Political Science,' in R. Young (ed.), *Approaches to the Study of Politics*, Atlantic Books, 1958, p. 42.

54 *Loc. cit.*

55 *Ibid.*, p. 46.

56 *Ibid.*, p. 48.

57 Mackenzie, 'Pressure Groups: The "Conceptual Framework",' p. 252.

58 La Palombara, p. 13.

59 Report of the Commission of Inquiry into Industrial and Commercial Representation. Published jointly by the A.B.C.C./C.B.I., November 1972, pp. 24–5. For an extensive list of institutions and societies, see *Whitaker's Almanack*.

60 Truman, pp. 63–5.

61 For an account of this campaign see R. Kimber and J. J. Richardson, *Campaigning for the Environment*, Routledge and Kegan Paul, 1974, chapter 8.

62 *The Daily Telegraph*, 9 November 1972.

63 J. Dearlove, 'Councillors and Interest Groups in Kensington and Chelsea.' See p. 221.

64 See pp. 110–18.

65 P. Self and H. J. Storing remark: 'The relationship has been closer to a true partnership than its constitutional status of consultation would suggest.' *The State and the Farmer*. Allen and Unwin, 1972, p. 230.

66 The N.F.U., for example, is consulted over the annual price review. For further comments on consultation see: H. W. Clarke, 'Statutory Consultation Provisions,' *Local Government Chronicle* (13 April 1973); L. Dion, 'The Politics of Consultation,' *Government and Opposition*, vol. 8, no. 3 (summer 1973).

67 H. Eckstein, *Pressure Group Politics*, Allen and Unwin, 1960, p. 22.

68 *Ibid.*, p. 21.

69 S. E. Finer, 'Interest Groups and the Political Process in Great Britain,' in H. W. Ehrman (ed.), *Interest Groups on Four Continents*, University of Pittsburgh Press, 1958. p. 130.

70 See R. Kimber and J. J. Richardson (eds.), *Campaigning for the Environment*, Chapter 7.

71 G. A. Almond, 'A Comparative Study of Interest Groups and the Political Process,' *American Political Science Review*, vol. 52 (March 1958), p. 275.

72 S. H. Beer, *Modern British Politics*, Faber, 1965, p. 347.

73 Eckstein, p. 18.

74 See S. E. Finer, 'The Political Power of Private Capital,' *Sociological Review*, vol. 3, no. 2 (1955), and vol. 4, no. 1 (1956), (two parts).

75 Constitution and Rules of the 1972 Industry Group, May 1972.

76 For example the *New Statesman* modified an advertisement submitted by the British Withdrawal from Northern Ireland Group on the ground that parts of it were considered subversive. *The Daily Telegraph*, 9 June 1973.

77 For example the campaign waged by the parents of Thalidomide children was directed primarily at the manufacturers of the drug. Similarly in the controversy over mining in Snowdonia, much of the effort of Friends of the Earth was directed at the Rio Tinto-Zinc Corporation. Clearly it may be strategically advantageous for opponents of a group to persuade that group to modify, or even drop, its demands before the authorities are called upon to act.

78 A similar conclusion is reached by R. D. Coates on the basis of a study of Teachers' Unions. See *Teachers' Unions and Interest Group Politics*, Cambridge University Press, 1972, pp. 112–29.

Part II

CASE STUDIES

CASE STUDIES

Introduction

The investigation of case studies, both of the purely descriptive and of the analytical kind, is a prerequisite for the construction of generalizations about political behaviour. This section contains examples of both.

Robert Lieber's study of the involvement of interest groups in the formulation of British policy towards European integration from 1956 to 1967 is an example of the second, analytical, kind of case study, at a fairly general level. Taking two schools of thought—group theory and functionalism—he derives two hypotheses about political integration. He then tests these to determine which approach is more useful in the context of integration, and concludes that it is the theoretical perspective of group politics which is the more applicable of the two.

The remaining sectional studies are narrower in conception and are studies of aspects of particular interests. One feature of many sectional groups noted in the introductory chapter is that, in addition to other activities, they frequently have a close relationship with civil servants. In their study of the N.F.U., Self and Storing show just how close this relationship had become in the sphere of agricultural policy by 1957. It is arguable that the relationship has become even closer since their study was completed. To take only one example, the N.F.U. (working through the Ministry of Agriculture) was particularly successful in obtaining important concessions from the D.o.E. concerning the reorganization of water and sewerage services in Britain. As a result of N.F.U. pressure, the Ministry of Agriculture secured special provisions for the administration of land drainage (of prime importance to agriculture) contrary to the main principles embodied in the Water Act (1973). We are not, however, claiming that the N.F.U. hegemony is total. The Government's decision (after a Commons defeat) to suspend the export of live animals is an interesting example of promotional groups (the R.S.P.C.A. and the Animal Defence Society) defeating a sectional one. Even more interesting is the light the example sheds on how the N.F.U. sees its relationship with the political system. On learning about the suspension, the N.F.U. commented, 'We are very annoyed, because the Commons seemed to be going on evidence given by pressure groups and not on strong evidence' (*The Times*, 14 July 1973).

Space does not permit us to include studies of both the business community and the unions and so, apart from some general information about the C.B.I. included in our comments on the two major 'peak' organizations, we have concentrated on the unions. A particular advantage in doing this is that, while there is recent material available on the C.B.I. (e.g. W. P. Grant and D. Marsh, 'The Confederation of British Industry', *Political Studies*, vol. XIX, no. 4, December 1971), much of the material on the unions needs revision in the light of events in the 1960s. In a new essay analysing the relationship between the unions and the Labour Party, Martin Harrison reformulates and brings up to date the conclusions he reached in his study *Trade Unions and the Labour Party Since 1945* (Allen and Unwin, 1960).

Thus far our case studies are primarily concerned with the external relations of groups with other parts of the political system. However, the internal political processes of pressure groups, though given relatively little attention by political scientists, are an important determinant of their behaviour. W. Roy examines the participation of members of the N.U.T. in the normal processes of ballots and union meetings and analyses the membership response to the Durham crisis in the early 1950s.

Finally, in the context of sectional groups, we provide some information illustrating the position of the two major 'peak' organizations, the C.B.I. and the T.U.C., and the extent to which they have been integrated into the policy-making process at all levels.

The remaining studies are of promotional groups. In the first, H. J. Steck argues that the emergence of the C.N.D. represents the first signs of the birth of a new style of 'ideological politics'. He examines the relative absence of protest to atomic policies before 1957, the formation of C.N.D. and the political and social factors which allowed the group to grow so rapidly. Even when Steck was writing, C.N.D. had passed its heyday and since then it has been almost totally eclipsed. On the other hand the number of ideologically based groups has probably increased, and groups such as the Stop the '70 Tour (an anti-apartheid group which succeeded in preventing the South African cricket team from touring Britain) or the End the Alliance Group (urging the Government to end Britain's alliance with Portugal) and many others have continued C.N.D.'s pattern of ideological politics.

An accusation often made against sectional groups is that they achieve changes in public policy which are approved by only a minority. The abolition of capital punishment is interesting in this context since it illustrates how well-organized and determined promotional groups, given the right conditions, can succeed in persuading Parliament to pass legislation which is generally opposed by the majority of the electorate. In a section from his book on capital punishment, J. B. Christoph assesses the post-war role played by established pressure groups up to the 1957 Homicide Act, one of the landmarks on the road to complete abolition.

In their study of the abortion lobby, Hindell and Simms describe how the Abortion Law Reform Association succeeded in embodying a large part of its demands in legislation by means of a Private Member's Bill. Their study reminds us of the importance of chance factors (in this case the Thalidomide tragedy) in the development of many political issues.

Finally, we describe a relatively unsuccessful promotional campaign in a rather less emotionally charged policy area—namely the administrative structure to be adopted for Britain's National Parks. We have included an account of the National Parks Campaign partly because it is important to examine campaign failures as well as successes, and partly because the campaign was fairly typical of those being conducted by the rapidly increasing number of groups concerned specifically with the protection and improvement of the environment.

Interest Groups and Political Integration: British Entry into Europe*

Robert J. Lieber

I. Introduction

This paper [1] analyses the influence of interest groups in the formation of British policy toward successive European unity developments in the years from 1956 to 1967. Considerable attention has been given elsewhere to the subject of Britain and Europe, particularly through detailed accounts of the various negotiations and the development of official views,[2] but this study seeks to analyse the effect of the major interest groups upon the development of British policy toward Europe in order to test specific hypotheses regarding the relationship between interest groups and the process of political integration.[3]

Two important bodies of writing and theorizing can be brought to bear in analysing the relationship between group behaviour and political integration. One of these is the group politics approach, which is set out in a coherent body of interest group theorizing based on British and American politics.[4] The hypothesis that may be inferred from this approach will here be termed the *group politics hypothesis*. The second major approach is that of functionalism; it figures predominantly in much of the recent work on political integration. In this paper the functionalist approach is extended beyond the area to which it has hitherto been applied, and this extension gives rise to an alternative *functionalist hypothesis*. The following sections will set out the context of the two hypotheses, test them against the empirical evidence derived from the British experience, and then offer some conclusions regarding the theoretical implications of these results.

II. Collectivist Politics in Britain and the Group Politics Hypothesis

This study is placed in the context of the British political process,

* Reprinted with permission from the *American Political Science Review*, vol. 66, no. 1, March 1972, pp. 53–67.

which Samuel Beer has aptly described as one of 'collectivist politics'.[5] It differentiates two channels through which society and government interact. On the one hand there is the system of *party government*. Development of the welfare state and the realities of winning power have required that the political parties (each influenced by its distinctive conception of the common good) bid for the votes of consumer groups (blocs of voters), who thereby exercise their influence through the electoral process. The alternative channel linking society and government is that of *functional representation*.[6] Here, as development of the managed economy has involved the government in extending its control over the economy, the realities of governing in a free society have compelled the government to bargain for the active cooperation of the major interests involved.[7] Pressure groups embody these interests, and at least one prominent political scientist in Britain finds that they have become 'a far more important channel of communication than parties for the transmission of ideas from the mass of the citizenry to their rulers'.[8] Similarly, Harry Eckstein identifies a fading of major class and ideological contours and sees the emergence of a fundamental consensus on general policy matters which relegates conflict to points of detail. These trends lessen the intensity and importance of party competition and enhance the role of pressure groups in the political process.[9]

Several specific bases of group influence exist. To begin with, pressure group *advice* is essential in order for government to obtain basic information and technical knowledge without which economic regulation would be impossible. Next, *acquiescence* is a necessity if governmental programmes are to operate successfully. Finally, the *approval* of the groups concerned is required if particular governmental policies affecting them are to possess legitimacy.[10] This last consideration reflects a basic collectivist ethos which is shared by the Labour and Conservative Parties. In Labour's case it is expressed in terms of 'Socialist Democracy', and for the Conservatives it is embodied in traditions of 'Tory Democracy'. The collectivist theory of representation, which sets both parties apart from the nineteenth-century political individualism of the Liberals, is an intrinsic part of twentieth-century British political culture.

In the present context the term 'pressure group' is understood to follow the relatively straightforward conception of S. E. Finer. It designates those organizations which are 'occupied at any point of time in trying to influence the policy of public bodies in their own chosen direction; though (unlike political parties) never themselves prepared to undertake the direct government of the country'.[11]

More specifically, this paper will concentrate on *sectional* pressure groups, those types of organizations whose political task it is to reflect the interests of the economic or occupational sections they represent. Unlike promotional pressure groups, which are organized around attitudes and which generally seek to persuade people without regard to their sectional affiliation, the sectional groups do not direct their attention to the parties, Parliament, or the electorate, which make up the party government sphere. Instead, as a result of governmental structure, activities, and attitudes, they normally concentrate their efforts upon the administrative departments of government.[12] Thus they typically operate through the functional representation process. Their bargaining power ultimately rests upon their performance of crucial productive functions in the society, and to the extent that government commits itself to intervene in the economy, it must obtain their cooperation. This need can be minimized in a totalitarian system, but in a country with a system of representative government there is little choice but to secure a large measure of voluntary cooperation from the bodies being regulated.[13] The actual mechanisms for group operation via functional representation are both formal and informal. They include numerous advisory committees on which sectional groups are represented, as well as close personal contact between representatives of the interests and their opposite numbers in the Civil Service.[14]

While sectional pressure groups have a thoroughly economic basis, they do not function exclusively on the basis of a mechanistic economic self-interest for the following reasons: first, they seek to enhance their own legitimacy by identifying themselves with some conception of broader national interest which their actions are designed to advance. Thus the Confederation of British industry (C.B.I., and its precursor, the Federation of British Industries, or F.B.I.),[15] National Farmers' Union (N.F.U.), and Trades Union Congress (T.U.C.)—which are the three most important groups and the ones treated in this paper—all articulate their demands above the level of crude advantage for businessmen, farmers, and trade unionists, respectively, even though their particular conceptions of free enterprise, agricultural prosperity, or working-class advancement still fall short of a more or less universalistic public interest. A second restraint upon these bodies is that their role depends on competence in specialized areas. The sectional pressure groups thus focus more upon matters of a technical nature than on overall policy. A third limitation is that the groups devote much of their attention to organizational self-maintenance—providing information and services and seeking to hold together a huge and heterogeneous

29

membership with divergent interests. As a result of coping with internal stresses of this character, a group will often find it difficult to formulate a business, agricultural or labour view at the national level. Fourth, and finally, leadership constitutes a critical variable in the determination of group interest. A change in individuals can produce an entirely different organizational policy. In the present case, a nonactivist F.B.I. President, a staunchly anti-European N.F.U. President, and a pro-Common Market T.U.C. leader were personally responsible for organizational viewpoints which differed sharply from those adopted under leaders who immediately preceded or followed them in office.[16]

Despite such restraints, these groups do occupy positions of great power within the British political system How, then, can the amount of their power—particularly in specific policy matters—be assessed? In dealing with the Italian experience, Joseph La Palombara judged it impossible to measure the influence of groups over administrative decisions.[17] It is possible, however, to attempt such a judgment by utilizing the characterization of the pressure group role put forward by S. E. Finer. He finds that although organized capital and labour in Britain do not dictate public policy, their position in the economy makes it essential that their cooperation be won. Essentially, the relationship is such that 'they do not direct but they may veto'.[18] In Finer's terms, Britain has reached the position wished for by John C. Calhoun well over a century ago. Calhoun had dreaded the prospect of the 'numerical majority' gaining control of government by means of its majority status and then using its authority to oppress minority sections. To forestall this situation he sought to have government regard interests as well as numbers, allowing each a concurrent voice in the making of laws or a veto in their execution. Finer estimates that the major sectional pressure groups have attained exactly this 'concurrent majority' status in British domestic politics.[19] This notion of group veto power provides, in the present study, a means of determining whether and under what conditions the groups' position of power carried over into the formulation of Britain's policies toward European unity in the 1956-7 period.

As will be shown below (Part IV), the evidence from successive periods, 1956-60 (negotiations for a Free Trade Area and then a European Free Trade Association), 1961-3 (the Macmillan Government's attempt at Common Market entry), and 1966-7 (the Wilson Government's renewal of the Common Market application), indicates a progressive decline in the power of the sectional pressure groups over Britain's European policy making. This decline is caused by effective *politicization* of the European issue, that is, by the perception and treatment of European unity as a matter of major national importance rather than as a relatively specialized or economic question. The result of politicization is to transfer the subject from consideration by the processes of functional representation, in which sectional pressure groups are dominant, to the channel of party government, in which parties play the leading role. Politicization does not require that the issue be subject to partisan dispute, though it may be, for issues can be highly politicized even when there is bi- or tri-partisan accord.

It should be made clear that the term politicization is applied in this paper only when the overall *treatment* of policy merits the label. In one sense, to be sure, all the interactions analysed here are political in their content, as exemplified by the kind of argument which Almond and Powell offer in their definition of the political system:

> When we speak of the political system we include all of the interactions which affect the use or threat of use of legitimate physical coercion. The political system includes not only governmental institutions such as legislatures, courts and administrative agencies, but *all structures in their political aspects*. Among these are traditional structures such as kinship ties and caste groupings; and anomic phenomena such as assassinations, riots and demonstrations; as well as formal organizations like parties, interest groups, and the media of communication.[20]

As a result, the usage adopted in this study can be regarded as only a specialized case within Almond and Powell's all-encompassing framework.[21] It should also be understood that politicization applies here to the status of those issues which enter into the public domain. Thus, as alternative designations for politicization and nonpoliticization, respectively, we can make use of the terms 'publicization' and 'privatization', as suggested by Beer.[22]

To be more systematic, it seems useful to identify three necessary indicators of politicization. The *first* of these is the handling of an issue by a primarily political ministry (such as the Foreign Office) rather than by an economic one (such as the Board of Trade). The two types of ministry can be differentiated on the basis of what provision they make for group access. While the Board of Trade accords groups an intimate corporate role, so that extensive consultation occurs between civil servants and their opposite numbers in the sectional groups, the Foreign Office makes no such provision. Although it may receive deputations from groups such as the T.U.C., these are heard as bodies of substantial importance within the country rather than in their capacity as sectional representatives. Routinized consultation and bargaining are central to the functional representation process; the shift of attention away from the economic ministries tends to prevent their operation.[23]

The *second* indicator is the existence of involvement by the broader public. At a minimum it implies that an issue passes from the exclusive scrutiny of an élite or specialized audience to the notice of the attentive public.[24] This wider attention is reflected in the activity of promotional pressure groups and attention to the issue in the communications media (including the mass press) and in by-elections and opinion polls. The significance of such involvement is that it conflicts with the necessarily private process of bargaining between government and sectional pressure groups which makes up functional representation.

The *third*, and most important of the indicators, is the participation of the political parties. Since public opinion sets few limits on foreign policy[25] the crucial element in politicization, and in the limitation of group influence, becomes the political parties. Party involvement interferes with the exclusively technical consideration of an issue in a closed relationship between administrative department and sectional pressure group. It also provides the opportunity —though certainly not the assurance—that judgments may be rendered more often on the basis of an interpretation of broad national interest than on some kind of cost-benefit calculations important mainly to sectional interests. This impact of party involvement stems not only from the fact that parties are organized around some distinctive conception of the common good—no matter how vague or vestigial—but also because those interests which the parties do heed in their search for support and in bidding for votes have to be aggregated with numerous other interests. Inherently this aggregation implies dilution. For politicization to become *effective* in the limitation of group influence, one other dimension must be present: the issue involved must be treated as falling within the realm of diffuse or general-purpose politics rather than of functional or special-purpose politics. The distinction resembles that made by Stanley Hoffman between 'high politics' and 'low politics'.[26]

If the above factors are indicators of politicization, what are its causes? The onset of politicization appears to be determined by a combination of external events and conscious choices. Thus a pressing international situation may thrust a subject into the forefront of national attention, or at least make such treatment possible. What events do is to create a propensity toward politicization. They constitute the necessary, if not always the sufficient, condition. Internally, a conscious choice by political or governmental figures is almost always essential before politicization can occur. For example, despite the importance of the E.E.C., neither Conservative nor Labour leaders consciously chose to treat European unity as a salient political matter until 1961.

The importance of the above treatment of the circumstances in which pressure groups rather than parties can be expected to influence policy is that pressure groups are different from parties in ways that directly affect issues such as those involving European unity. Basically, pressure groups influence policy formation whenever the criteria for judgment are based more upon the foreseeable balance of economic gain and loss than upon broader conceptions of national interest or political benefit. As a result, policy initiatives which threaten identifiable costs to significant interests, even though these may represent a minority of the sector involved, are likely to be opposed. Comprehensive groups, such as the C.B.I. and N.F.U., will tailor their positions so as not to outrage important sectors of their membership; and in a setting which remains nonpoliticized, political parties will play little role in the policy process. The result, therefore, is likely to be that profound new ventures such as those involving European unity cannot be made so long as pressure groups provide the main constituency for policy makers.

While the group politics theorists do not deal with the phenomena of supranational integration per se, it does seem possible to extend their analysis in order to do so. Based on the above arguments, such an extension would logically imply that when an integration issue is nonpoliticized (i.e., treated as a technical matter), groups will tend to influence policy formation, because cost-benefit calculations become the criteria for judgment, and movement toward integration is likely to be hindered. Put more economically, this extension of the group politics position gives rise to an hypothesis: *If interest groups influence policy formation, then progress toward integration is likely to be impeded.*

By implication, progress toward any major new initiative in European unity (that is, obtaining a British decision to join an integrated European organization) will require that an issue become effectively politicized.

III. The Functionalist Hypothesis

Functionalism shares basic assumptions with group politics in the sense that it implies there will be group influence if an issue (specifically one involving integration) is nonpoliticized. But, unlike the group politics analysis, it finds nonpoliticization to be advantageous for integration.

The basic arguments of functionalism are most commonly associated with David Mitrany and Ernst Haas.[27] The essence of Mitrany's position is that the surest route to world peace is to organize a multitude of international organizations around functional tasks such as health, transport, and postal services.[28] As governments eventually cede more and more of their tasks to these worldwide organizations, a diminution of national antagonisms will result. Functional institutions will gradually bring about a sense of community; ultimately, peace, world government, and political integration will follow. Mitrany's thought is usually contrasted with that of the federalists, but he also stands apart from present functionalist theory in certain respects, particularly in his stress upon functional organizations which are universal rather than regional in their membership. Nonetheless, that aspect of the Mitrany thesis which is most relevant to the present discussion and which is shared by contemporary functionalists, is that the surest route to political integration is to depoliticize the subject by concentrating on technical or functional tasks.

For Ernst Haas, who has developed important modifications of Mitrany's approach, the essence of functionalism is that step-by-step economic decisions are superior to crucial political choices and that the operation of ever more controversial policies, starting from a shared interest in economic welfare, will, with a certain automaticity, bring about the establishment of a new central, supranational authority regardless of the wishes of individual actors. Haas's functionalism assumes that economic self-interest is more important than political commitment and that unintended consequences and incremental decision making are more effective in bringing about integration than are purposive behaviour or the construction of grand designs. Basing his analysis upon the Western European experience, Haas identifies a natural economic progression which has led the six members of the European Economic Community (E.E.C.) from their initial common community treatment of coal and steel (in the European Coal and Steel Community) to refrigerator tariffs, and then to chickens, to monetary policy, and ultimately to a mutual interest in the operation of the business cycle.

Initially, Haas argued that in modern democratic industrial society, particularly that of Western Europe, there was no longer a distinctly political function, separate from economics or welfare or education, that existed in the realm of foreign policy, defence, and constitution making. He also viewed the advent of supranationality within the E.E.C. as symbolizing the 'victory of economics over politics', thus signalling the demise of the ethnocentric nationalism which preferred guns to butter, passion to reason, and excited demands to statistical bargaining.[29] During the past decade, Haas has modified his dismissal of the political function. He acknowledges that *The Uniting of Europe* erred in assuming the permanent superiority of step-by-step economic decisions over crucial political choices, and takes the position that while integrative decisions based on high politics are more durable, in the absence of a statesman with the vision to weld disparate publics together 'we have no alternative if we wish to integrate a region, but to resort to gradualism, to indirection, to functionalism'.[30] In sum, he maintains that subject to amendments, the expansive logic of functionalism remains valid.[31]

Yet Haas does characterize the relationship between economic and political union as a 'continuum'.[32] And his functionalism continues to imply that a kind of benign invisible hand will operate to bring about supranational integration in a nonideological, depoliticized economic setting. Since government concentrates increasingly on technical questions of an economic nature, political life more and more revolves around interest groups seeking narrow advantages, and public policies are regarded as the outcome of these manœuvrings along with other economic and political forces.[33] Haas stresses the growth of interest groups across frontiers, and a chief conclusion of his main work is that group pressure will shift from a national to a community level and have the effect of stimulating integration as groups organize across national boundaries to influence policy.[34] His pluralistic thesis holds that in advanced industrial democracies a larger political community can be developed if crucial expectations and behaviour patterns of key groups can be refocused on a new set of central symbols and institutions; and over time, political loyalties, following economic interests, will gradually become attached to new supranational institutions.

It is true that functionalism has been more concerned about integration within existing communities, where processes such as spillover do in fact seem to take place, than about the geographic expansion of integration or the construction of new communities.[35] Leon Lindberg and Stuart Scheingold have characterized the former type of integration, to which Haas's expansive logic of functionalism has been applied, as 'forward-linkage growth'. This process involves primarily incremental change and the projection of well-established trends. They label the latter type of process as 'systems transformation'. This category includes not only the adherence of new

35

members to an established community, but also other large changes which mean the introduction of new constituencies such as those involving a notable increase of integrated activities within an existing community.[36] In fact, the functionalists generally have not sought to extend their argument to deal with the adherence of a new member such as Britain to an established supranational entity. But in seeking to analyse the British case, we nonetheless may find it worth the effort to extend the functionalist approach in order to determine whether it could also account for this kind of effort at systems transformation. Such an extension would logically imply that whenever an integration issue is nonpoliticized, groups will tend to influence policy formation, because cost-benefit calculations become the criteria for judgment, and movement toward integration is likely to be facilitated. Put more economically, this extension of the functionalist position gives rise to the following hypothesis: *If interest groups influence policy formation then progress toward integration is likely to be facilitated.* The difference between the hypotheses here imputed to the group politics and functionalist approaches is that, while both agree upon a significant role for interest groups in the absence of politicization, the first hypothesis asserts that this role will hinder integration, while the second predicts the opposite—that it will facilitate integration. The difference of orientation is evident in the notion of group veto power identified by the group politics analysis, as compared to the stress on technocratic politics and the attribution of an integrative group role by the functionalists.

With these two hypotheses in mind, it is now appropriate to see how each one holds up against the British experience. The period concerned begins with Britain's effort to come to terms with the newly established European Economic Community by means of the ultimately abortive Free Trade Area during the years from 1956 to 1958. It then continues with the establishment of the European Free Trade Association during 1959–60, the effort of the Macmillan Government to join the Common Market beginning in 1961 and vetoed by President de Gaulle in January 1963, and—following a hiatus of more than three years—the similarly fruitless renewal of Britain's application by the Wilson Government in 1966–7.

IV. Pressure Groups and British Policy: 1956–67

A. The Free Trade Area and the European Free Trade Association.
During the years from 1956 to 1960, the period of policymaking for the Free Trade Area and the European Free Trade Association, the

European issue remained almost completely nonpoliticized. Neither external events nor the choices of party or governmental leaders compelled a political treatment. The three indicators reflected this lack of politicization. First, at the administrative level, policy formulation and international negotiations were conducted by the Board of Trade with some participation by the Treasury. The Foreign Office did not take part. Second, generalized debate and involvement by the broader public were largely absent. The mass press gave little coverage to the F.T.A. and E.F.T.A., particularly in comparison with its later handling of the Common Market question, and there was no mobilization by promotional pressure groups. Third, the parties remained largely uninvolved, particularly because they shared similar official attitudes and because the subject of European unity was widely perceived as economic in content.[37]

Interest groups enjoyed concurrent majority power during this period; they succeeded in maintaining a political position similar to the one they customarily occupied in domestic politics. That is, they exerted influence because the executive found it necessary or desirable to bargain for their cooperation. Though the groups paid more attention to technical aspects than to overall policy, this was consistent with their usual pattern of operation on domestic matters.

Throughout this period, all three of the major groups were hostile to the idea of outright Common Market membership. For example, the T.U.C. was completely opposed, fearing that the Common Market would constitute a first step toward complete integration and the development of a central authority which could overrule national governments on important economic matters. T.U.C. leaders felt such a change would be undesirable since they viewed most governments of the Six as having less favourable ideas on economic and social policy than the British government, albeit a Conservative one. Even more important for the T.U.C.—as for the other sectional interest groups—was the structural change involved. A transfer of authoritative decision-making power to a supranational body would drastically weaken the effective influence of the T.U.C. In a new European Community, the sectional veto which British trade unions often hoped to exercise upon their own government's policies would no longer be so significant. That is, even though operation of a concurrent majority might persist at the national level, its existence would be far less important because the determination of economic policies would have been removed to a supranational authority upon which the British government—and the British public—would have only partial influence.

During the years from 1956 to 1958 Britain unsuccessfully sought to negotiate establishment of a wide Free Trade Area linking the six members of the newly formed Common Market with the other Western European members of the O.E.E.C. What is noteworthy about this period is the extent to which the pressure groups not only resisted any thought of membership in a supranational E.E.C., but also took a very cautious position toward even the very limited European arrangements in the proposed Free Trade Area. Thus, in the case of the Federation of British Industries, while the larger business firms and the F.B.I. leadership were favourable to European free trade, many of the smaller firms expressed concern about meeting increased competition; given the nature of the F.B.I. as an organization, this apprehension meant that its policy had to remain a cautious one. As for the National Farmers' Union, it categorically refused to consider any European agreement which would include agriculture. By its success in delaying until October 1957 a governmental move to meet demands by the Common Market countries for some provision for increased agricultural trade, it played a significant role in hindering European agreement on the F.T.A. Even the T.U.C.'s policy toward the F.T.A. concentrated almost entirely on safeguards for full employment instead of on the opportunities for economic growth offered by the proposed trading arrangements.

There is every reason to judge, as Miriam Camps does, that the government felt its main task lay in defeating internal opposition to free trade and in winning over business and labour, rather than concentrating on gaining agreement with the Six.[38] The government's decision to exclude agriculture from the initial F.T.A. proposals prompted a very explicit acknowledgment of the groups' importance from a Labour M.P.:

> The only really effective argument which I have heard for excluding food-stuffs from the scheme is that if we are going to have trouble with pressure groups and with the F.B.I., why should we have trouble at the same time with the N.F.U.? From a tactical point of view, there is much to be said for taking on these pressure groups one at a time.[39]

Most of the European countries wanted Britain in Europe for political reasons, but France was unwilling to pay Britain's price and later vetoed the F.T.A. in November 1958. The question, then, is why the U.K. required such a price, which was ultimately to preclude the successful establishment of a Europe-wide F.T.A. The answer is to be found in the requirements of British pressure-group politics. The groups were highly active participants in the formulation of British policy, by virtue of their concurrent majority powers, yet they played a role that directly opposed European integration and emphasized sizeable economic safeguards, even upon the quite limited F.T.A. arrangements.

In 1959–60 (the period during which the European Free Trade Association, or E.F.T.A., was formed), the sectional pressure groups again played an intimate role in the shaping of policy, one which went well beyond a mere veto power. In fact the Federation of British Industries, through meetings with its Scandinavian counter-parts during the winter of 1958–9, played a substantial part in moving the British government toward the establishment of the E.F.T.A.[40] The F.B.I., in close cooperation with the N.F.U., overtly worked to secure the establishment of E.F.T.A. at a time when government probings were still without commitment. F.B.I. activities gave prominence to the E.F.T.A. option, and at the very least this advocacy made it possible for the government to proceed with E.F.T.A. in the knowledge that such a course of action would benefit from firm F.B.I. support. In the face of industrial disapproval, the E.F.T.A. choice would have been unlikely.

As in the case of the Free Trade Area, the E.F.T.A. issue remained almost entirely nonpoliticized. Because of the economic and com-mercial treatment of the European issue throughout 1959, the F.B.I.'s involvement and importance came naturally. To describe the government as having taken the more narrowly economic view is no idle generalization. In their failure to adopt a wider outlook, British leaders paid little attention to the political dynamics behind the Common Market; they seldom displayed awareness of the Common Market countries' sense of building Europe and of laying to rest the antagonisms which had caused two World Wars.

While the interest groups played a significant role in a depoliticized setting, their participation was not such as to contribute to integra-tion, particularly in terms of Ernst Haas's definition, widely em-ployed by the functionalists, which sees integration as:

> the process whereby political actors in several distinct national settings are persuaded to shift their loyalties, expectations, and political activities toward a new and larger centre, whose institutions possess or demand juris-diction over the pre-existing national states.[41]

But the merely intergovernmental arrangements of the E.F.T.A. did not begin to provide a setting in which institutions or arrangements existed toward which previously national loyalties might be trans-ferred. By continuing to oppose British participation in genuine integration of the E.E.C. variety, interest-group activity impeded integration. Indeed, the groups contributed to the formulation of a policy and to the establishment of an organization which actually hampered British efforts to come to terms with the Six. The existence of E.F.T.A. complicated Britain's task in seeking Common Market membership, both technically and—as it contributed to the Six's suspicion of British motives—psychologically.

It thus becomes clear in looking at the 1956–60 period that a non-politicized treatment of European policy would not suffice to move Britain into an integrated European arrangement. As long as the setting remained nonpoliticized, interest groups would play a significant role in policy making, at least to the extent of preserving veto power, but this role would be in opposition to rather than in the direction of genuine integration. The contrast with 1960–1 is dramatic, for no British movement would be possible until the European issue became politicized.

B. Common Market I: 1961–3. In the case of Britain's first Common Market application, during the period 1961–3, the key decision was taken by Prime Minister Macmillan when he decided to abandon Britain's aloofness from European integration and to seek membership in the European Economic Community. The overwhelming preponderance of views by élite respondents interviewed for the present study was that political motivations (both short- and long-run) predominated. To a slightly lesser extent, these respondents also concurred in the observation that once the decision was made, Macmillan presented the European choice to the British public as though Common Market membership were primarily an economic matter. The result was that there were really two distinctly different phases to the British approach, the first being that of the initial decision to seek entry, the second consisting of the period of actual negotiation. Treatment of the European issue, the role of pressure groups, and the nature of the policy process differed sharply between these two phases.

As for the initial decision, its aims corresponded with the conclusions of an early 1960 report by the Economic Steering Committee under the chairmanship of Sir Frank Lee (then newly appointed as Joint Permanent Secretary to the Treasury). This interdepartmental group of senior civil servants had been assembled to study possible association with the Six, but concluded that Britain should seek outright membership in the Common Market, for primarily political reasons.[42] The Committee regarded the economic arguments as at best balanced; for them, entry was a political, not an economic question. They expected Britain to exert leadership within a united Europe, thus regaining a certain measure of world influence and even improving her transatlantic ties.

In short-range political terms, European integration offered a novel issue on which to set the Conservatives apart from the Labour Party, following a period in which the two major parties had drifted toward the political centre as factors of ideology and class diminished. Finally, Macmillan himself, seeking a lasting contribution with which to cap his political career, had long been favourable toward European unity.[43] Macmillan had become Prime Minister in early 1957, and having disposed of the urgent tasks of liquidating the Suez venture, assuming control of the Conservatives, and rallying his dispirited Party for an overwhelming victory in the 1959 election, he felt that circumstances in 1960–1 at last seemed appropriate for seeking Common Market entry.

The available evidence indicates that the Prime Minister made his decision in late December 1960. It is quite clear—especially in comparing the chronology of public statements and private documents of the sectional interest groups—that Macmillan's decision antedated group advocacy of Common Market membership. This finding offers no comfort for the functionalists. The distinctly political function is evident; its existence is a prime requisite for the critical transformation of British policy from opposition to European integration to participation in it. The key point here is that the July 1961 announcement that Britain would seek E.E.C. entry reflected a political judgment, made by political authorities before pressure groups had strongly articulated their own interests. In particular it meant that considerations of broad national interest, construed in terms of Britain's overall international position, took precedence over cost-benefit calculations about the effects of Common Market membership on individual economic interests. It also reflected the existence of policy powers held by the Prime Minister and Cabinet which could be exercised relatively free of the constraints that interest groups typically imposed on lesser domestic issues. But because Macmillan would not or could not make the case to the British public in grandly political or Churchillian terms (as opposed to less ambitious commercial ones), the subsequent formulation of Britain's negotiating position offered the opportunity for a powerful pressure-group role.

Politicization of the issue of European unity was evident throughout the period of the first Common Market application, and the three indicators reflect this fact: first, the negotiations were no longer handled by ministers with primarily economic departmental responsibilities, but by Edward Heath, then number two man at the Foreign Office. Second, the broader public was drawn into the debate. Promotional pressure-group activity became widespread; mass

41

circulation papers such as the *Daily Mirror* and *Daily Express* launched strident campaigns for and against entry; and polls and by-elections reflected the Common Market's position as a highly visible subject of debate. Third, the political parties became deeply involved and even made European unity a matter of partisan contention. Yet while there was full politicization of the European issue, in the sense of publicization, during the actual negotiation period, politicization did not become *effective* because Macmillan chose to treat the Common Market as an economic issue. He operated, in the words of Richard Neustadt, 'by disguising his strategic choice as a commercial deal'.[44] The Prime Minister's decision to deal with the issue as one of functional politics rather than of general purpose politics, facilitated the persistence of functional representation and hence assured a significant pressure-group role in shaping the practical terms of entry to be sought by Britain.[45]

The increasing opposition to Common Market entry by the Labour Party also enhanced the significance of sectional demands because, lacking bipartisan reinforcement for a policy which he had described in economic terms, Macmillan needed to assure himself of the fullest possible support within his governing Conservative Party. In this case, because the Tory constituency was composed very considerably of the agricultural, industrial, and commercial portions of the society, sectional groups such as the N.F.U. and F.B I. actually were able to exert influence via the Prime Minister's own party.

The relationship between domestic and international forces is especially visible in the 1961–3 period, with Macmillan becoming increasingly trapped between domestic political needs and the necessities of the Brussels negotiations. An easier domestic situation would have allowed the Government to accept the E.E.C.'s Rome Treaty more unreservedly. This acceptance in turn would have facilitated mutual concessions by the Six and a speedier course for the negotiations. As Kenneth Waltz has observed, however, Macmillan failed publicly to confront the European issue as one which challenged long-existing national notions.[46] Instead, in order to gain domestic approval for Common Market entry, he pledged to obtain safeguards which were virtually incompatible with full British membership in the E.E.C. The British reservations were not dictated by public opinion; they were established on the basis of consultations with the major interests.[47] The consequences of this approach were to hinder the negotiations at Brussels, and then to undercut the Government's domestic position because the necessary retreat from the initial conditions was interpreted at home as a series of surrenders. These difficulties facilitated the subsequent de Gaulle veto.

Once again, interest groups exerted an influence which cannot be said to have promoted integration. The case of the F.B.I. is the most interesting. During 1956–60, British business had perceived the trend toward European unity more as a threat than an opportunity, though near the end of 1959 a number of larger business firms became more favourable toward Europe because of their concern with stagnating British Commonwealth trade as contrasted to growing opportunities within the E.E.C. Smaller firms remained more hostile, whether because of vulnerability in the home market or less imaginative leadership, but they sometimes expressed their fears in political rather than economic terms. By the spring of 1961, the heads of giant firms such as Imperial Chemical Industries, General Electric Corporation, and British Motor Corporation had begun to advocate outright entry into the Common Market rather than some more limited form of association. The F.B.I., caught between conflicting views, issued a major report in July 1961, two weeks before the Government's announcement. This report stressed the need for Commonwealth and E.F.T.A. safeguards, termed many of the E.E.C.'s agricultural arrangements unacceptable, expressed a preference for intergovernmental cooperation rather than common European institutions, and also took note of numerous 'negotiable' lesser problems.[48] While the F.B.I. had taken one important step in its willingness in principle to accept a common external tariff, even this declaration was negatively phrased.[49] The whole tenor of the F.B.I. report was legalistic and parochial; the terms it stipulated remained quite irreconcilable with Common Market membership—especially because of the position on agriculture and common institutions. At the same time, however, a survey of 130 large firms found more pro-E.E.C. sentiment.[50] The leaders of some of Britain's largest industries were clearly moving toward European unity faster than the F.B.I. was, though even these industrialists moved no more rapidly than Prime Minister Macmillan.

During the actual period of negotiation for Common Market entry, the role of the F.B.I. vis-à-vis the government and its own membership shifted somewhat. The F.B.I. maintained a close relationship of sustained consultation with the government, expressing concern over vulnerable sections of industry and also offering technical advice. Because outright hostility on the part of business would have prevented the Common Market application altogether, the British government needed to devote considerable care and attention to entertaining the representations and occasional protests of the F.B.I. (and of the T.U.C. as well) in order to insure that they continued to provide support, or at least acquiescence, for entry.

43

With the passage of time, and following the lead of the larger industries, the F.B.I. became increasingly pro-E.E.C. and directed substantial effort at educating and persuading its own membership as to the benefits of entry.

It was the National Farmers' Union, having the most to lose, which exerted the greatest influence upon the British position. The farmers may not have been able to veto entry itself, but they did succeed in shaping the conditions under which Britain sought that entry. The N.F.U. first obtained a governmental pledge, in a January 1961 White Paper, that the government would be concerned to see whether closer European unity could be achieved 'without sacrificing the vital interests of U.K. farmers and horticulturalists'.[51] Next, in the official July 1961 announcement, the Prime Minister incorporated safeguards for British agriculture as one of three essential British conditions in negotiations with the Six.[52] Finally, and perhaps more importantly, agriculture received its most specific pledge in the speech made by Edward Heath in submitting Britain's application to the Ministers of the Six at Paris on October 10, 1961. In a speech otherwise regarded as one of wholehearted commitment to Europe, Heath enumerated three necessary safeguards for the vital interests of British farmers: a transition period of 12–15 years, British retention of the ability 'to use such measures as are necessary to safeguard our farmers' standard of living', and special arrangements for horticulture.[53] Eventually, the problem would be that the Six would find each of these elements largely unacceptable, and Britain would have to retreat from them if she wished to reach agreement.

Thus, from July 1961 to the January 1963 de Gaulle veto, the British government was seeking to placate specific economic objections of the major interest groups in order to insure that Common Market entry would have domestic political support. The groups could not assert their inherent involvement in the central political issue of whether Britain should merge her destiny with that of the Europeans; but because the issue was incompletely politicized (i.e., treated as functional or economic, despite publicization), these groups still could claim direct concern with portions of the European issue involving trade, full employment, and agricultural arrangements. The groups thus retained an approximate concurrent majority role in the formulation of Britain's negotiating position.

C. Common Market II: 1966–7. The orientation of the Wilson government toward Europe provides some useful contrasts to the 1956–60 and 1961–3 periods. During the 1966–7 attempt at Common Market entry,[54] the effectiveness of politicization rendered group interests relatively insignificant. Unlike Macmillan, Harold Wilson was thoroughly political in the way he handled the European negotiations and the way he presented them to the British public, as well as in his decision criteria.[55] Wilson's effort was thus virtually unimpeded by the requirements of pressure-group politics.

This difference of approach resulted from a combination of external events and conscious choices. The urgency of events, particularly the collapse of alternatives, resulted in a strong propensity toward politicization; and the nature of Wilson's choices, most notably the decision to treat the European commitment as a major national departure (i.e., as a matter of general, or high, politics rather than of functional, or low, politics), resulted in an effective politicization.

Sectional pressure groups therefore found themselves in a position of unprecedented weakness. Effective politicization had closed the channel of functional representation, and a number of conditions, including the existence of bipartisan agreement over European policy, discouraged group access through the channel of party government. Unlike Macmillan, Wilson made no pledges to pressure groups; he also sought entry with far fewer conditions.[56] Moreover, Wilson centred the work of his negotiating team in the Cabinet Office, where he himself would be in control. The sectional interests found themselves fobbed off upon a consultative committee operating through the (short-lived) Department of Economic Affairs and providing them with occasional briefings and only *pro forma* consultation rather than genuine bargaining. Groups might still influence lesser technicalities, but they were left without a vestige of concurrent majority powers.

One lesson suggested by the 1966–7 period is that the perceived precedence of external international factors dictated that the European approach would be unimpeded by the stipulation of conditions. In its Common Market approach, the Macmillan government had acknowledged no such predominance of external concerns and had consequently devoted more attention to domestic 'consensus' than to international 'compatibility'.[57] But Prime Minister Wilson's desire to avoid presenting President de Gaulle with a genuine pretext for another veto required a de-emphasis of domestic considerations, which, in turn, meant the demise of functional representation. Labelling the changed treatment as effective politicization implies that a broadly construed national interest had become the dominant concern; this heightened national interest transcended the previous pattern in which sectional pressure groups had exercised effective bargaining power in the absence of a

45

clear-cut invocation of Britain's national interest. As in the case of the 1961 Common Market application, political authorities had again made the crucial decision in advance of, or without real regard for, the sectional pressure groups' strong articulation of their positions. But unlike the earlier period, during 1966–7 effective politicization continued beyond the initial decision phase and thus shaped the context in which the actual terms of the application were formulated.

V. Conclusions

The evidence of these successive periods is that group influence in foreign policy is inversely proportional to effective politicization. The sectional pressure groups' domestic corporatist role, as expressed by the concurrent majority notion, appears to carry over into the realm of foreign policy making unless the issue becomes effectively politicized. The relationship between group influence and politicization, however, may be somewhat more complex than either the group politics or functionalist hypothesis implies. The evidence of the period following Macmillan's July 1961 announcement that Britain would seek Common Market entry is that if political authorities do not consciously choose to treat an issue as broadly political, so that considerations of general national interest take precedence, then the sectional interests are likely to reassert their involvement in a situation where cost-benefit calculations become important criteria for judgment. The question of bipartisanship also assumes some importance in the limitation of group influence. As we have seen, Macmillan's hand was weakened by the absence of Labour Party backing in 1961–3. This lack forced him to seek additional support by making a succession of pledges, and it facilitated a measure of pressure-group access via the party government process (as opposed to the usual concentration of these groups on the administrative departments of government by means of functional representation). In contrast, Prime Minister Wilson's position was strengthened by opposition support for Common Market entry in 1966–7. Nonetheless, it would be wrong to conclude that simple bipartisanship, rather than the more complex phenomenon of politicization, best accounts for restricted pressure-group access. The simpler explanation proves inadequate when applied to the entire 1956–60 period, during which bipartisanship in a completely nonpoliticized setting coincided with an exceedingly high group access.

How then do the suggested group politics and functionalist

hypotheses compare in terms of their prediction of the role of interest groups in the integrative process? The results indicate a confirmation of the group politics hypothesis—at least within the confines of the British case. During the F.T.A. and E.F.T.A. phases, and again during the first set of negotiations for Common Market entry, pressure groups did influence policy, and they functioned to restrain Britain's movement toward participation in integrated European ventures. They exercised this role first by means of direct veto powers, then indirectly by operating to influence and qualify the terms of British association or membership.

Why were these groups generally opposed or at best guardedly favourable toward integration throughout a period when British membership of the E.E.C. offered economic prospects ranging from breaking even[58] to clear and substantial advantages? Evidently, these group orientations reflected organizational rather than strictly economic considerations. While the C.B.I., N.F.U., and T.U.C. are powerful and important bodies, as the peak organizations in their fields, they are amorphous and unwieldy. Group leaders lack the centralized authority which exists within an individual corporation, and policies tend to be developed on the basis of a lowest common denominator.[59] The groups' political muscle is consistently employed to protect sectors which could be sacrificed as uneconomic, even though the resultant balance of gain and loss might leave businessmen or farmers or trade unionists, on the whole, much better off.[60] An appropriate example is the operation of the National Farmers' Union during the 1961–3 negotiations for Common Market entry: British agriculture in general stood to gain from Common Market membership, but the N.F.U.'s considerable powers were employed to secure governmental pledges of safeguards for the horticultural sector, which by virtue of Britain's climate and geography was simply not in a position to compete successfully within an expanded E.E.C.

Another set of group considerations which is not exclusively economic involves the status of interest groups within the British political process. The groups explicitly claim a veto power within a setting of collectivist politics, and they are prone to resist any shift which, while promising material benefits, might threaten this status. Integration theorists have celebrated the phenomenon of Community-wide pressure groups emerging to press their common interest upon the E.E.C. Commission at Brussels, as the Community organs have taken on decision-making functions once exclusively the province of national governments.[61] This process is regarded as offering a new channel for sectional groups to influence policy out-

comes, but even in some future federal Europe with effective trans-
national interest groupings, a single national organization still
would have considerably less influence than in a domestic context.
It is thus readily understandable that during 1956–60 a group such
as the T.U.C. preferred that European cooperation proceed on the
pattern of the intergovernmental O.E.E.C. rather than on the basis
of supranational integration. During 1961–3, the N.F.U. expressed
a similar concern in its orientation toward the Common Market.

Finally, in assessing the reluctance of British interest groups to
support European integration, one must consider the background
variable of political culture. These groups have been characterized by
a resistance to innovation, a distrust of complex written constitutional schemes, an insularity, and a sense of national self-reliance
that in Britain—unlike the Continental countries—had not been
discredited by occupation or defeat during World War II. In all these
respects, the groups shared an orientation inherent in British life as a
whole.

Taken together, their organizational nature, their position in
corporatist politics, and perhaps the background effects of political
culture, make interest groups highly complex and autonomous in
their operations. To the extent that the functionalist view defines
interest groups as representing more or less a mechanical vector
sum of economic forces, it clearly needs modification.

As for the suggested hypothesis based on an extension of functionalism, the results of the British case require a rejection. Rather
than facilitating integration, the weight of sectional pressure group
influence was almost always opposed or equivocal. Functionalist
theory holds that interest groups will favour integration, particularly if economic benefits are involved, but in the British experience,
so long as the country did not belong to a supranational grouping,
this generally was not the case.

More broadly, functionalist theory, from its origins in Mitrany's
writing, has viewed depoliticization, along with a functional or
technical treatment of issues, as the most likely route to integration.
But to the extent the British operated this way in their relationship
to Europe (in 1956–60, and again following the Macmillan decision
in 1961–2), the approach simply did not work. Political judgments
were indisputably the sine qua non for any significant British
movement toward participation in European supranational integration. The fact that political authority, moved by considerations
going well beyond material advantage or cost-benefit calculations,
exercised the ultimate responsibility for such a step, implies a further
difficulty for any extension of functionalist theory. For one thing,

these results indicate that policy formation in an industrial democracy, even one that has corporatist politics, is not reducible to a mere interplay among organized interests. For another, it implies that movement toward such integration cannot be achieved simply by leaving matters on a technical level where interest groups are a leading policy influence. The problem is that the functionalist view may imply the operation of a benign invisible hand which will guide nations toward supranational integration in a nonideological, depoliticized, and overwhelmingly economic setting. But no more than in the realm of economics can the suitability of such a laissez faire process be taken for granted. In other words, what functionalism conceives of as a 'painless transcendence of the nation-state'[62] is unlikely to come about without conscious political intervention.[63]

Moving beyond the confines of the British case, one can generalize about the importance of the distinctly political function.[64] At least in the task of enlarging a geographic area of integration—if not in expanding that integration once a grouping already exists—a conscious political decision must first be made. Just as the political leadership of Macmillan and Wilson was essential in moving Britain to seek Common Market entry, so the intervention of Chancellor Adenauer in carrying Germany through the transformation from the European Coal and Steel Community to the E.E.C., and the role of President de Gaulle in vetoing British entry in 1963, were major instances of national political leadership for which functionalist theory had made no place.[65]

This perspective and that of the functionalists need not conflict totally, in that (as noted earlier in this article) the functionalists have been primarily concerned with integration within existing communities, rather than with the geographic expansion of integration or the construction of new communities. Indeed, when Britain does become a member of the E.E.C., circumstances will then exist in which the functionalist hypothesis is likely to apply. Major portions of functionalist theory do in fact remain valid and theoretically fruitful, but it is clear from testing the functionalist hypothesis against the British case, as well as in considering the criticisms raised by other recent writings,[66] that the functionalist theory of supranational integration would seriously overreach itself if applied to this major kind of problem. Thus at least in the case of Britain's approach to Europe, another theoretical perspective, specifically that of group politics, seems to be in order.

[*Editors' note:* Britain became a member of the E.E.C. on 1 January 1973.]

Robert J. Lieber

Notes

1 The study is based on data drawn from pressure group materials and o fficia publications, and from sixty élite interviews with civil servants, former cabinet ministers, party leaders, and officials of the major pressure groups. The major part of the interviewing was conducted in London during the spring of 1967. Subsequent work took place in Oxford and London during 1969–70. For support, I wish to express my appreciation to Harvard University for a Knox Travelling Fellowship, to the Social Science Research Council for a postdoctoral Research Training Fellowship, and to the University of California for a Faculty Research Grant.

This is a revised version of a paper presented at the Annual Meeting of the American Political Science Association, Los Angeles, September 8–12, 1970. For their comments and criticisms on the original and later drafts, I wish to thank Kenneth I. Hanf, Alexander J. Groth, Donald Rothchild, Richard L. Merritt, Nelson W. Polsby, and Nancy I. Lieber. For a more comprehensive treatment of the data on which the analysis is based, see Robert J. Lieber, *British Politics and European Unity: Parties, Élites and Pressure Groups* (Berkeley: University of California Press, 1970).

2 See, for example, Miriam Camps, *Britain and the European Community, 1955–63* (Princeton: Princeton University Press, 1964), and her subsequent work, *European Unification in the Sixties: From the Veto to the Crisis* (New York: McGraw-Hill, 1966); Nora Beloff, *The General Says No: Britain's Exclusion From Europe* (Baltimore: Penguin, 1963); Uwe Kitzinger, *The Second Try: Labour and the E.E.C.* (Oxford: Pergamon Press, 1968); Pierre Uri, *From Commonwealth to Common Market* (Harmondsworth, Middlesex: Penguin, 1968).

3 This effort also differs from previous British pressure group case studies in that it examines neither an important piece of legislation nor the administration of an existing programme, but rather the formulation of a policy, and one which is concerned with foreign rather than domestic matters. Cf. James B. Christoph, *Capital Punishment and British Politics: The British Movement to Abolish the Death Penalty, 1945–57* (Chicago: University of Chicago Press, 1962); H. H. Wilson, *Pressure Group: The Campaign for Commercial Television in England* (New Brunswick, New Jersey: Rutgers University Press, 1961); and Harry Eckstein, *Pressure Group Politics: The Case of the British Medical Association* (Stanford: Stanford University Press, 1960).

4 See, for example, Samuel H. Beer, *British Politics in the Collectivist Age* (New York: Knopf, 1965); S. E. Finer, *Anonymous Empire*, 2nd ed., rev. (London: Pall Mall Press, 1966); and Eckstein, *Pressure Group Politics*. For the United States, see also Raymond A. Bauer, Ithiel de Sola Pool, and Lewis A. Dexter, *American Business and Public Policy: The Politics of Foreign Trade* (New York: Atherton, 1963); and Lester W. Milbrath, 'Interest Groups and Foreign Policy', in *Domestic Sources of Foreign Policy*, ed. James N. Rosenau (New York: Free Press, 1967), pp. 231–61.

5 Beer, *British Politics in the Collectivist Age* (see especially Chapter 12). Collectivist or corporatist politics are not confined to Britain: Joseph La Palombara describes in Italy 'a vast network of quasi-corporatve relationships between certain interest groups and the administrative agencies.' See La Palombara, 'The Utility and Limitations of Interest Group Theory in Non-American Field Situations,' in *Comparative Politics*, ed. Harry Eckstein and David E. Apter (Glencoe: Free Press, 1963), p. 427.

6 As Beer defines it, the notion of functional representation is one which 'finds the community divided into various strata, regards each of these strata as having a corporate unity, and holds that they ought to be represented in government' (p. 71).

7 Beer, p. 321.

8 R. T. McKenzie, 'Parties, Pressure Groups and the British Political Process,' *Political Quarterly*, 29 (January–March, 1958), 10.

9 Eckstein, pp. 18–19.

10 Beer, pp. 321–31.

11 However, Finer actually prefers the term 'lobby' to the term 'pressure group'. (See Finer, p. 3.) In this paper, the terms 'pressure group' and 'interest group' will be employed interchangeably. There is, however, considerable—and occasionally tedious—treatment of the definitions elsewhere. See Gabriel Almond and G. Bingham Powell Jr., *Comparative Politics: A Developmental Approach* (Boston: Little, Brown, 1966), p. 75; Allen Potter, *Organized Groups in British National Politics* (London: Faber and Faber, 1961); Peter Self and Herbert J. Storing, *The State and the Farmer* (Berkeley: University of California Press, 1963); and Wilson, Christoph, and Eckstein.

12 Eckstein, pp. 16–17.

13 Beer, p. 321.

14 For a detailed treatment, see Political and Economic Planning, *Advisory Committees in British Government* (London: Allen and Unwin, 1960).

15 In 1965, the Federation of British Industries merged with two smaller organizations, the National Union of Manufacturers and the British Employers' Confederation to form the Confederation of British Industries.

16 These limitations on British pressure group activity are similar to those found by Bauer, Pool and Dexter in their analysis of American groups. Thus in the United States, the role of a trade association leader may be more that of 'arbitrator' among forces within his organization than of 'statesman'; he also finds himself in a position of mediating between his organization and the outside world and is often caught in a web of conflicting forces (p. 331). In addition, groups are reluctant to take stands on issues unless there is near unanimity within the organization (p. 337). However, British groups do not suffer from the serious lack of money, skills and information which Bauer, Pool and Dexter find characteristic of their American counterparts (p. 349). The parallels are further limited because the British groups operate within a corporatist political culture so that their legitimacy is enhanced. They also

51

enjoy far greater 'density' (percentage of potential membership actually belonging) and 'amalgamation' (extent to which the organized have been brought into one body) than do the American pressure groups. See Beer, p. 332.

17 La Palombara, p. 425. For an alternative conception, based on Dahl's criteria for the measurement of power as the capacity to shift the power of outcomes, see Lieber, Chapter 10.

18 Finer, p. 27.

19 Finer, p. 133.

20 Almond and Powell, p. 18. Italics in original.

21 Politicization is also used in different contexts, but with related meanings, by Karl Deutsch *et al.*, *Political Community and the North Atlantic Area* (Princeton: Princeton University Press, 1957), pp. 46–7; and by Ernst B. Haas and Philippe C. Schnitter, 'Economics and Differential Patterns of Political Integration: Projections About Unity in Latin America,' in *International Political Communities: An Anthology* (Garden City, N.Y.: Anchor, 1966), pp. 261–2.
   According to the P.E.P. study, a nonpolitical subject 'is merely one about which politicians do not feel strongly for the time being' (p. 106).

22 This is also akin to the distinction drawn by E. E. Schattschneider between 'socialization' and 'privatization' of conflict. Expanding the scope of a previously privatized conflict brings the public, or 'audience', into involvement, thus changing the coalition possibilities and decisively affecting the outcome. *The Semi-Sovereign People: A Realist's View of Democracy in America* (New York: Holt, 1960), pp. 2–8.

23 One listing of 700 central advisory committees presented to the House of Commons in 1949 included only two attached to the Foreign Office and both of these were highly specialized. (The two committees were in the Foreign Office's German Section: The Book Selection Committee and the Scientific Committee.) See Allen Potter, pp. 223–5.

24 'Élite' and 'attentive public' are here used in the manner of Gabriel Almond's basic approach. The attentive public is 'informed and interested in foreign policy problems, and ... constitutes the audience for the foreign policy discussions among the élites'. The 'policy and opinion élites' are 'the articulate policy-bearing stratum of the population which gives structure to the public, and which provides the effective means of access to the various groupings'. *The American People and Foreign Policy*, rev. ed. (New York: Praeger, 1960), p. 138.

25 British voters tend to be bi-partisan on foreign policy, and concentrate their attention on domestic matters. Their tendency to vote on the basis of domestic issues is analysed in Max Beloff, *New Dimensions in Foreign Policy: A Study in British Administrative Experience, 1947–1959* (London: Allen and Unwin, 1961), p. 15; Jean Blondel, *Voters, Parties and Leaders* (Harmondsworth, Middlesex: Penguin, 1966), pp. 75–9. 81–3, 87; and Kenneth Younger,

'Public Opinion and British Foreign Policy,' *International Affairs*, 40 (January, 1964), 22–3.

26 See, e.g., 'European Process at Atlantic Crosspurposes,' *Journal of Common Market Studies*, 3 (February, 1965), 92.

27 See especially Mitrany's *A Working Peace System: An Argument for Functional Development of International Organization* (London: Oxford University Press, For the Royal Insitute of International Affairs, 1943); also Haas's *The Uniting of Europe: Political, Social and Economic Forces, 1950–1957* (Stanford: Stanford University Press, 1958), and his *Beyond the Nation-State: Functionalism and International Organization* (Stanford: Stanford University Press, 1964).

28 For a useful summary of Mitrany's functionalism and its differences from later interpretations, see Andrew Wilson Green, 'Review Article: Mitrany Reread with the Help of Haas and Sewell,' *Journal of Common Market Studies*, 8 (September, 1969), 50–69.

29 'Technocracy, Pluralism and the New Europe,' in *A New Europe*, ed. Stephen Graubard (Boston: Houghton Mifflin, 1964), p. 71.

30 '*The Uniting of Europe* and the Uniting of Latin America,' *Journal of Common Market Studies*, 5 (June, 1967), 327–8.

31 Haas, '*The Uniting of Europe* . . . ,' p. 321.

32 Haas and Schmitter, 'Economics and Differential Patterns of Political Integration . . .' p. 261. For Haas's revisions to his original theorizing, see '*The Uniting of Europe* . . .' and his 1968 Preface to the reissued edition of *The Uniting of Europe*.

33 See Michael J. Brenner, *Technocratic Politics and the Functionalist Theory of European Integration* (Ithaca, New York: Cornell University Center for International Studies, 1969), p. 5.

34 According to Haas, perhaps his 'chief finding is that group pressure will spill over into the federal sphere and thereby add to the integrative impulse'. *The Uniting of Europe*, 1968 edition, p. xxxiii.

35 Brenner discusses this on p. 8.

36 *Europe's Would-Be Polity: Patterns of Change in the European Community* (Englewood Cliffs, N.J.: Prentice-Hall, 1970), p. 244.

37 E.g., Edward Heath told the 1960 Conservative Conference that the government had sought to create the F.T.A. and E.F.T.A. 'for economic reasons'. National Union of Conservative and Unionist Associations, *79th Annual Conservative Conference* (October 12–15, 1960), p. 61.

38 *Britain and the European Community*, pp. 104–5.

39 Fred Mulley in Hansard, *Parliamentary Debates* (Commons), 561 (November 26, 1956), c. 80.

40 The original seven members of E.F.T.A. were Sweden, Norway, Denmark, Switzerland, Austria, Portugal and Britain. The arrangements resembled those which Britain had sought for the abortive F.T.A., namely freer intra-

group trade, a minimum of institutions and of integration, and no harmonization of external tariffs.

41 'International Integration: The European and the Universal Process,' in *International Political Communities*, p. 94.

42 Camps, *Britain and the European Community*, pp. 280–1.

43 Macmillan later wrote in his memoirs, 'About Europe, regrets still haunt me,' and he recalled that he had written Churchill in protest when the newly elected Conservative government of 1951 failed to move Britain toward the European Coal and Steel Community. *Sunday Times* (London), July 31, 1966.

44 'Whitehouse and Whitehall', Paper delivered at the 1965 Annual Meeting of the American Political Science Association, Washington, D.C., September 8–11, p. 9.

45 The negotiations also became mired in detail, a prime area of group operation, because the Government sought to negotiate *à sept* (rather than regard the Six as a single group with a coherent position), because it felt obliged to negotiate on behalf of the Commonwealth, and because the openness of the negotiations frequently involved Edward Heath in an embarrassing dialogue with the groups.

46 *Foreign Policy and Democratic Politics: The American and British Experience* (Boston: Little Brown, 1967), p. 266.

47 This point is emphasized by Lord Windlesham in *Communication and Political Power* (London: Jonathan Cape, 1966), p. 158.

48 Federation of British Industries, *British Industry and Europe* (London, July 1961).

49 'In principle we do not oppose the suggestion for a common or harmonized tariff put forward by H.M.G.' Federation of British Industries, p. 3.

50 *Sunday Times* (London), July 16, 1961.

51 Cmnd. 1249 (Her Majesty's Stationery Office, December 19, 1960), paragraph 37, cited in *British Farmer*, No. 163 (January 7, 1961).

52 Hansard, *Parliamentary Debates* (Commons), 645 (July 31, 1961), c. 1483–8.

53 *The United Kingdom and the European Economic Community*, Cmnd. 1565, Vol. 36 (H.M.S.O., November, 1961), pp. 14–15.

54 The Labour government's approach to the E.E.C. began in November 1966 with exploratory talks. The application was formalized in May 1967, then vetoed by de Gaulle in November 1967. Prime Minister Wilson initiated a renewal of the application in 1969–70, and Labour was then defeated in the June 1970 General Election. The incoming Heath government continued with the negotiations and reached agreement with the Six in June 1971. The later phase is beyond the scope of this paper.

55 This political emphasis was quite obvious. See, e.g., Kitzinger, *The Second Try*, pp. 9–10.

56 The unconditional nature of the Labour government's application is particu-

larly visible when its terms, as set out by George Brown at The Hague on 3–4 July, 1967, are contrasted with those outlined by Edward Heath in Paris on 10 October, 1961. Thus, for example, on agriculture, Brown accepted the E.E.C.'s Common Agricultural Policy without safeguards, while Heath sought to retain Britain's existing safeguards for her farmers. On the Commonwealth, Brown cited only New Zealand and the need to avoid defaulting on the Commonwealth Sugar Agreement; Heath listed each country, requested 'comparable outlets', and said Britain could not join if trade was cut with a severe loss to the Commonwealth. On E.F.T.A., Brown asked only one year's standstill for its members 'to make their own arrangements', while Heath said Britain could not join unless all seven members 'could participate, from the same date, in an integrated European market'. On collective action, Brown accepted the Rome Treaty and all 'regulations, directives and ... decisions taken under it'; Heath accepted the Treaty but proposed to negotiate over agreements reached among the Six since then. See Nora Beloff, 'What Happened in Britain After the General Said No'. in Uri, *From Commonwealth to Common Market*, pp. 81–3.

57 The terms are those of Wolfram Hanrieder, 'Compatibility and Consensus: A Proposal for the Conceptual Linkage of External and Internal Dimensions of Foreign Policy', *American Political Science Review*, 61 (December, 1967), 971–82.

58 Almost no serious assessment of the economic prospects of membership reached conclusions more pessimistic than these.

59 This is not to imply that even fully centralized authorities can not make irrational or dysfunctional decisions.

60 In this regard, they resembled American trade associations, which Bauer, Pool and Dexter found reluctant to take stands on issues on which unanimity was absent. (*American Business and Public Policy*, p. 337).

61 E.g., see Leon N. Lindberg, *The Political Dynamics of European Economic Integration* (Stanford: Stanford University Press, 1963).

62 Brenner, *Technocratic Politics and the Functionalist Theory of European Integration*, p. 1.

63 There is also a normative implication here. It is that parties ought to play a greater role than pressure groups in the policy-making process. Unlike pressure groups, parties provide at least the opportunity for political leaders to make independent judgments on the basis of some broad interpretation of the national interest. But during the nonpoliticized phase of European policy making, those intimately involved in the process were nonelective, not responsible to the public, and concerned to maximize values less broad than those of the country as a whole. More generally, the functional representation process tends to manifest a static bias. It provides bargaining advantages for those interests which are better organized, while minimizing more diffuse considerations of public benefit. See Andrew Shonfield, *Modern Capitalism* (New York: Oxford University Press, 1965), p. 389. For other critical views, see Finer, *Anonymous Empire*, pp. 126–9; Sigmund Neumann, 'Toward a Comparative

Study of Political Parties,' in *Modern Political Parties*, ed. Neumann (Chicago: University of Chicago Press, 1956), p. 397; and Bernard Crick, *Observer* (London), October 23, 1966. But for views which question the ability of parties to promote the broader interest, see J. R. Pennock, ' "Responsible Government", Separated Powers, and Special Interests: Agricultural Subsidies in Britain and America,' *American Political Science Review*, 56 (September, 1962), 621 and 633; also Wilson, *Pressure Groups*, pp. 210–11.

64 Stanley Hoffmann's argument also seems applicable here. He has indicated the importance of an irreducible political core of 'high politics', which is not susceptible to gradual erosion through step-by-step functional or spillover processes. See 'European Process at Atlantic Crosspurposes,' p. 92.

65 Lindberg and Scheingold find, directly contrary to Haas in *The Uniting of Europe*, that the successful transformation leading to the establishment of the Common Market itself was not due to functional spillover: 'The transformation of the European Community cannot be adequately described within the context of the standard neofunctional model with its heavy emphasis on supranational institutions and functional linkages.' *Europe's Would-Be Polity*, p. 243.

66 E.g., Lindberg and Scheingold; Brenner, *Technocratic Politics;* and Roger D. Hansen, 'Regional Integration: Reflections on a Decade of Theoretical Efforts,' *World Politics*, 21 (January, 1969) 242–71.

The Farmers and the State*

Peter Self and Herbert Storing

Post-war agricultural politics in Britain have been remarkable for
two developments. One is the creation of a comprehensive system
of state support and control for agriculture, operated in close partnership with the main agricultural organizations. The other, related
development, is the emergence of a strong, politically neutral
farmers' union occupying a close and privileged position in the
counsels of government. This article cannot deal in any detail with
the evolution of agricultural policies, nor does it consider the activities of the organizations representing agricultural landlords and
agricultural workers. It concentrates upon the activities of much
the most powerful agricultural organization, the National Farmers'
Union of England and Wales. There are separate Unions for
Scotland and Ulster, but on all main issues they tend to follow the
lead of the principal Union.

The Numerical Weakness of Farmers

Politically and economically, British farmers have always suffered
from their numerical weakness. Something like 250,000 full-time
farmers in England and Wales among a population of 44 million
have been impelled to speak with one voice that they might be
heard at all. The Union has always attempted to compensate for
this weakness with organizational strength. Founded in 1908, the
Union appeared at the right moment to exploit the shift in rural
farms and influence from the big landlords to the general mass of
working farmers, whether owner-occupier or tenants. It was in fact
the first organization to speak equally for both groups. Its claim to
speak for farmers was firmly established during the first world war,
and by the early 1920s its membership was more than 100,000. It

* Reprinted with permission from *The Political Quarterly*, vol. 29, no. 1, 1958.

managed to conserve its strength during the difficult depression years and entered the second world war with a membership of 125,000. By 1945 this had grown to 165,000, a growth which continued during the post-war decade. Membership now stands at about 210,000 and probably includes between 80 and 90 per cent. of the full-time farmers in the country.

In spite of this steady organizational progress, the Union has emerged with a clear political strategy only during the post-war period. An unsuccessful search for this strategy is the main theme of its pre-war history. While rejecting proposals for an independent agricultural party, the early leaders had sought to establish in Parliament an independent agricultural bloc consisting of members from all parties pledged to support the Union's programme. Substantial numbers of Members of Parliament gave their support and joined an all-party agricultural committee in the House of Commons, but the group never became an independent, disciplined holder of the parliamentary balance on agricultural questions, as the Union had hoped.[1]

A Tory Tradition

Concurrently the Union was sponsoring and giving financial support to certain farmer candidates. This was a second line of defence, intended to ensure at least that the views of practising farmers were put forward in parliamentary debates. Several Independent candidates were sponsored, as were a few Liberals, but with no success. The farmers' traditional Tory loyalties held fast, and the only Union candidates to be elected were Conservatives. There were usually one or two Union-sponsored Conservative Members sitting in the House of Commons from 1922 to the second world war. Throughout this period, the Union continued to insist on its neutrality in purely party matters and its willingness to work with the Government of the day. But its failure to find any but Conservative spokesmen in Parliament together with the Conservative predominance during the thirties made it easy for the Union to drift into an unofficial alliance with that party. Thus, as Sir Ivor Jennings has said, the Union's politics during the thirties consisted of 'discriminating support to the Conservative Party'.[2] It never wavered in its non-partisan claim, but this was little more than an expression of hope for the future and anxiety about an alliance which, however necessary under the circumstances, was felt to be basically unsound.

The second world war, with party politics on holiday and the country desperately in need of food, saw an immense increase in the prestige and influence of the Union. Whether this would continue after the war was another matter. In the hurried election of 1945, the Union sponsored no candidates, but there is little doubt where most farmers' sympathies lay. The Labour Party had agreed to the post-war agricultural programme planned under the Coalition Government and supported by the Union, but farmers were not happy about the election of a strong Labour Government. The Union's leaders wore their neutrality with little enthusiasm. They were highly suspicious of a party which stood (at that time) for land nationalization and which drew its main support from the urban workers, having few links with the countryside.

Sympathy from the Left

In the end, Labour proved far and away more tractable than the Union had dared to hope. The new Minister of Agriculture, Mr Tom Williams, had been Parliamentary Secretary to the Ministry during the war. An ex-miner and trade unionist, he was predisposed to view farmers (another group of primary producers) and their Union sympathetically. Labour's very inexperience in agriculture worked strongly to the Union's advantage during a period in which it seemed urgently necessary to expand food production. Where better to go for information, opinion, even policy, than to the farmers' own organization? Capitalizing on this inexperience, and helped by their fast friend in the Cabinet, the Union achieved during these years an unprecedented peak of influence in the making of agricultural policy.

When the Conservatives took office in 1951 the organized farmers maintained their political neutrality. Although one of its leaders became a Parliamentary Secretary to the Ministry of Agriculture, there was by now no question of the Union's attaching itself to a political party. The same attitude was maintained in 1955. Few Union leaders imagine that their slogan, 'Keep agriculture out of politics', means that agricultural policy can be uncontroversial or non-political. Its practical meaning is that agriculture should, so far as possible, be kept out of party politics and parliamentary politics. The Union prefers where possible to exert its influence through the private offices of Whitehall, where its strong organization and the post-war machinery for consultation give it a favoured place, rather than through influence in Parliament.

Peter Self and Herbert Storing

Of course the Union cannot disregard party and parliamentary politics altogether. Its representatives meet occasionally with the party agricultural committees in the House of Commons. Memoranda stating its position on current issues are distributed (in a surprisingly haphazard manner) to Members known to be interested in agricultural questions. But the Union tends to deal with Parliament in a respectful, cautious, and distant manner. It no longer sponsors candidates, nor does it have even quasi-official parliamentary spokesmen, though there are always Members willing to take account of its point of view. It supplies backbenchers and members of the Opposition with questions and material for debates, but this is always a subsidiary part of its strategy. On any major issue the vital negotiations will have occurred privately between the Union and the Government, and once having given its agreement (however reluctantly) the Union does not go 'behind the Government's back' to press its case in Parliament.

Neutrality Towards the Parties

As part of this general strategy the Union's headquarters sedulously avoids any activity that might be interpreted as showing partisan preference. The county branches generally pursue a similar neutrality. Most branches maintain some contact with their Members of Parliament, and they are encouraged by headquarters to do so. A committee in each branch usually interviews candidates at the time of each election, but the object is to stimulate a broadly favourable attitude towards farming opinion rather than to seek support for a specific programme. There is thus a curious stopping short in the branches' election-time activities. The results of these interviews are seldom published, and branches do not advise members how to vote. It is said that 'word gets around' and 'members draw their own conclusions'; but in the absence of any organized or official mobilization and direction, this source of political power remains (deliberately) potential.[3]

While politicians give weight to the views of the Union's branches, as they would to any substantial bloc of opinion, there is no doubt that the Union could take more effective action if its object were to influence the selection of candidates and the speeches and votes of Members of Parliament. Such action, however, would tend to undermine the special relationship with the Government on which it mainly relies. Party and parliamentary activities take an unobtrusive second place. They are an indirect means of keeping alive the notion that the farmers' vote is crucial, and they stand in readiness should circumstances once again force the Union into direct political activity.

The N.F.U. and the Government

It is now time to examine briefly this 'special relationship' between the Union and the Government of the day which has grown up during and since the war. Its legislative basis lies in the Agriculture Act of 1947, which rested on principles agreed to by both main parties as well as by all the principal agricultural organizations. The theory of the Act was that agriculture should enjoy a permanent degree of 'security' in return for measures designed to raise its 'efficiency'. Parliament was, however, deliberately vague as to the concrete meaning of these terms. It was feared that specific statutory provisions might prove too rigid to withstand changes in economic conditions (as they had after the first world war) and the Act provides only a broad framework of objectives and standards whose actual efficacy depends upon their administration.

In practice, the main instrument of 'security' has been the annual price review which since 1945 has taken place every February between Government and Union. This review is a highly complex affair which determines guaranteed prices and associated subsidies for all the principal agricultural (except horticulture) commodities and which absorbs a large part of the energies of both the Union and the Ministry of Agriculture. Based originally upon an agreement between the wartime Minister of Agriculture (Lord Hudson) and the Union, the review's character has been shaped by a series of 'understandings' (written or unwritten) arrived at by the two participants. The most significant if least admitted of these is that the final settlement (which, constitutionally, is of course the Government's sole responsibility) shall be broadly acceptable to both parties. In the earlier years most settlements won a clear endorsement from the Union; subsequently, its concurrence was often given grudgingly or was hedged with reservations, but only in one year (1956) did it actually dissociate itself from the result.*

The Annual Price Review

The price review has been the forum for numerous tussles between Government and Union which cannot be related here. Suffice it to note that the main proceedings and purposes of the review have so

* See note on p. 68.

far successfully survived all political and economic vicissitudes, although there was a time (the period during which food was being decontrolled) when the most cherished assumptions of the Union were shaken and it almost wavered in its political impartiality. Most of the bickering goes on in private, but on occasions it has erupted into a fierce public controversy. The best examples are the special price review row between Tom Williams and the Union in 1946, and the breach over the price settlement of 1956. The latter even marked one of the rare irruptions of the Union into parliamentary politics, with county branches severely castigating their Conservative M.P.s. In both cases the Union's indignation produced gratifying results, with the Government demonstrating its unwillingness to accept a complete break with its well-established agricultural practices. Yet the essence of such tactics is that they can be deployed only rarely. The breakdown of the partnership, however unpopular it might make the Government, would destroy still more certainly the foundations of the Union's policy.

The promotion of agricultural efficiency (the other half of the 1947 Act) has been mainly in the hands of County Agricultural Committees. These bodies have close links with the National Agricultural Advisory Service, they administer numerous subsidies and regulations, and they wield the sanctions of supervision and dispossession over the heads of inefficient farmers and landlords. Recently their work has been cut down and the use of penal sanctions is about to be scrapped—a change which hits at the wide original conception of the 1947 Act. Three of the members of each Committee are selected from nominations made by the Union, but the actual number of Union members is generally greater than this. The Union scrupulously refrains from 'controlling' in any way its members on the Committees, which act as the Minister's agents, but any split between Union and Government would affect these members' attitudes and might even cause their wholesale resignation —an event which would have had serious repercussions at the time of the food production drive.

A Unique Monopolistic Position

The Union has not only secured a unique position *vis-à-vis* the Government, its position is also close to being a monopoly one. When the Agriculture Act was being debated in the House of Commons, the Minister of Agriculture, Mr Tom Williams, made it clear that he presumed the Union to be adequately representative of farmers' interests and that he would refuse to admit other organizations into the annual price negotiations.[4] Despite some grumbles from other bodies, he and his successors have adhered to this policy.

The Union's participation in public policy-making for agriculture has become almost automatic. Its untouched position at the price review strengthens its claims in other fields. On one occasion (the decontrol of eggs) when it was *not* consulted, it declined to take part in the next annual review until it had secured a promise that the omission would not be repeated. Since the war, the preparation of marketing schemes has been a joint product of Union and Government. Union representatives sit on numerous advisory committees, such as the Agricultural Improvement Council, the Hill Farming Advisory Committee, and the Myxomatosis Advisory Committee. Its leaders, and more particularly its bureaucracy, are connected by dozens of informal ties with all kinds of agricultural policy-making and administration. The habits and attitudes engendered by the annual price reviews are all pervasive. While the farmers sometimes complain of lack of consultation by other departments, such as the Board of Trade, complaints of this kind about the Ministry of Agriculture are extremely rare.

The Leadership of the N.F.U.

The Union's post-war strategy has required changes in its internal organization. Its rules and traditions frown on continuity in the elected leadership, but in 1945 the National Council elected Mr (now Sir James) Turner to the Presidency, and he has been re-elected in each succeeding year. At the same time, the unusual step was taken of appointing Turner's predecessor as President, Mr William Knowles, to the position of General Secretary, which he still occupies. The next year the Council recognized the virtual professionalization of its leadership in its decision to pay the President a salary of £5,000 a year.

Dominant personalities are the usual pattern in some organizations; but in the old National Farmers' Union, once Colin Campbell had set it on its way, there had been a seemingly endless chain of nameless men moving regularly into and out of the positions of national leadership. Sir James Turner will be remembered, and the end of his tenure is not yet in sight. Urbane enough to put the countryman's case in Whitehall, the President is rustic enough to assure members that his loyalties are sound. His speeches, riddled with *clichés* and dripping with righteous indignation and heavy patriotic sentiment, achieve a remarkable response; and he is almost universally admired by farmers. The 'sacred bull of agriculture', as he has been jokingly called, is nicely complemented by the astute Mr Knowles. Aside from personal qualities, this team now has more experience of high level agricultural policy-making than almost any public servant holding responsible office in this field.

Its Internal Organization

Inevitably, this has its effect on the Union's organization. The top-heavy national council is the policy-making body only in form. The ordinary council member is not at the centre of decisive deliberations—however much, back at his county branch, he may pretend the contrary. Policy-making positions in the Union are primarily matters of personal relations with the President and General Secretary. Over the years, indeed, the calibre of council members has tended to decline. Farmers who would seek the honour and prestige of the top position see it closed to them; those who would share leadership see little prospect of breaking into the inner group and will very likely prefer a position on their county branch executive to one on the national council. Partly for this reason the atrophy has not spread to the local units. As a rule discussion there is free and critical, and the branches retain considerable vitality.

One final corollary of the Union's post-war strategy must be noted: an emphatic and sometimes ruthless pressure towards comprehensiveness. Because it has had no competition from another general farmers' organization, the Union's activities in this respect have been mainly at the periphery. It grants the legitimacy of specialist and commodity organizations, so long as they recognize its over-all pre-eminence in dealing with government. (The relationship, in the Union's view, is rather like that between suzeraine and protectorate.) But it tends to define the jurisdiction of the smaller bodies ever more narrowly. It wants no area of general interest to farmers and no area, however specialized, of potential political importance, to lie outside its own control.

The Union has found the co-operative movement difficult to digest, and there are rumblings elsewhere as well. Its grip on the horticultural side of the industry, which does not share the guarantees of the 1947 Act, is uncertain. In poultry and egg production the Union has extended its control and absorbed a number of small organizations in recent years, but there remains at least one substantial independent organization. Finally, a group of dissenters has established a new farmers' organization in Wales, now almost two years old. This revolt, fired by Welsh nationalism and fed with the grievances of small farmers, is unlikely to succeed in throwing the Union out of Wales, but it has shown a surprising tenacity in the face of the Union's vigorous counter-attack.

The Need for a United Front

Given their weak numerical position, the advantages to agricultural producers of a comprehensive organization are obvious enough, so long as their leaders do not neglect one or another section of the membership. Particular groups do periodically complain that their interests are overlooked, but discontent has not risen to the point where it outweighs the disadvantages of an isolated independence. Generally speaking, farmers have good reason to be satisfied with the Union's achievements on their behalf.

The public also benefits by this arrangement, but the issue here is more complex. The Union has to sift and adjust the various and competing claims of its members before the claims of farmers as a whole are put to the public. Farmers (and more particularly their local and national leaders) have become accustomed to seeking some basis of compromise broader than their own immediate interests. This tendency is reinforced by the Union's special consultative relationship with the Government, a relationship requiring the Union to moderate sectional demands with a share of responsibility for public policy. The farmers' leaders now tend to begin their utterances, and to some extent their thoughts, with 'the nation needs', rather than 'we want'. Obviously what they think the nation needs is prosperous farmers. There is a good deal of sectional bias in their public interest claim. But this discovery must not be— as it so often is in the literature on interest groups—the beginning and end of an evaluation. Many non-farmers too believe that the nation needs prosperous farmers. Moreover, the leaders of the Union can and do give reasons for their proposals and try to justify them in terms of the public interest. This implies an obligation to listen to reason in return. Leaving aside all other considerations, if the farmers demonstrated no willingness at all to engage in reasonable deliberation about the public interest they would soon lose the ear of the Government; they would thus destroy the basis for one of their important sources of 'access', the power of a good argument fairly heard. The farmers are not so rich in the cruder forms of political power that they can afford to neglect this one.

Having said that, it remains true that the leaders of the Union are, quite properly, not primarily concerned with the public interest. Sectional leaders can be taught to be statesmanlike, but they are not statesmen. Their first responsibility is to maintain a strong organization through which their members' opinions and interests can be expressed and to see to that expression. Thus the Union usually begins its negotiations with the Government by pressing almost all of the claims of its members equally hard. Making the expected retreat under Government pressure, its next object is to spread the effects of any change in policy equally among its membership. 'No change of emphasis' is an expression of the Union's rule of thumb standard of distributive justice and, at the same time, of its shrewd attempt to avoid rocking the organizational boat.

Competing Interests among the Farmers

So long as conditions change, however, Government policies will require changes in emphasis. Whether the aim is to achieve certain production targets or to get more value for each subsidy pound spent, the Government is likely to want some changes in the distribution as well as in the total amount of its support. This is one of the points where the advantages of dealing with a single comprehensive organization—rather than one representing arable farmers, another representing milk producers, etc.—might be expected to come into play. But, until recently at any rate, Governments have been extremely unwilling to risk the Union's disagreement with the final 'settlement'. The result has been a series of *ad hoc* bargains satisfying no one. The Union has managed to prevent any drastic changes in emphasis, but there have been frequent, relatively small shifts which farmers find irritating and upsetting. They criticize the Government for its lack of consistency, and they call for a long-term policy. But to a considerable extent the absence of such a policy is due to the very success of the Union's pressure on short-term objectives. Any reasonable long-term policy would involve some unpalatable adjustments and it would be unpopular with certain sections of farming opinion. While it is true that the Union's leaders might have been more flexible—in addition to a desire to avoid organizational upheaval they have an almost morbid fear that any changes will lead to a complete withdrawal of support—the post-war Governments (and, in particular, their Ministers of Agriculture) bear the main responsibility. It was they who, concerned with the need to secure farmers' co-operation, drifted into the habit of taking no major decision for which the Union could not or would not share the responsibility.

Recently there have been some signs that the ties of partnership are loosening, but they have not yet been thrown off. As already noted, in 1956 the Union refused, for the first time in a decade, to agree to the annual price settlement. Fortified by the declining importance of home food production and a Minister (now responsible for food as well as agriculture) less awed by the Union than his predecessors, the Government stood fast in its determination to reduce considerably the wastefully high guarantees on milk and eggs. The reaction was more violent than the Government (or, indeed, the Union leaders) had anticipated. After a parliamentary storm, talks were opened with the Union which led to a new long-term settlement, now embodied in the Agriculture Act of 1957. The Act makes the economic guarantees to agriculture a good deal more precise, by restricting the extent to which the Government may reduce their value—both collectively and for each commodity—in any one year. By implication, the Union has accepted in return the probability of some gradual reduction in the level of Government support. Essentially, the Act is a renegotiation of partnership within more definitive limits.

A Too-Close Embrace ?

It is possible to arrive at one tentative conclusion. 'Partnership' in agriculture, whatever its specific advantages, has on the whole been much too close to be really healthy for either partner. The Union has steered clear of most of the more obvious abuses of its privileged position, but inevitably its leadership has been strengthened and to some extent insulated from its rank and file. For example, some marketing schemes have provoked legitimate criticism on the grounds that Union members had no real chance to debate them. More seriously, perhaps, the effect of 'partnership' has been to divert all the energies of the Union (and too much of the interest of farmers) into close political bargaining and away from those schemes of enlightened self-help which have done so much to improve the status of agriculture in many other countries. For the Government and particularly for the agricultural department, 'partnership' has come to mean an excessive sensitivity to Union views, combined with a tendency to adopt an over-defensive attitude on agricultural issues. The development of new public policies is inhibited by fears either that they will be unacceptable to the Union or alternatively that they

67

will 'give away' rather more of what the Union would like than (on strategic grounds) is initially wise. Government by anxious compromise is not an inspiring process.

Notes

1 The object was similar to that of the American farm bloc operating at about the same time, but the constitutional and numerical position of American farmers was of course far stronger.

2 W. Ivor Jennings, *Parliament* (Cambridge: Cambridge University Press, 1939), p. 178. The emphasis Jennings lays on the farmer-Tory alliance, however, leads him to miss the ambivalence of the Union's strategy during these years. He is not correct, for example, when he asserts that 'the Union cannot pretend and does not pretend that it is impartial in the party sense' (p. 212). The Union never abandoned precisely this claim.

3 It should be noted that there are still close informal connections between the Union branch and the Conservative local organization in some counties, where prominent Union leaders sit on the Conservative selection committee; but these branches too avoid any official action that might compromise their neutrality.

4 *Hansard, Standing Committees* (1946–7), Vol. 2, Cols. 78–9.

[*Editors'* note: There are now 168,000 full-time farm businesses in England and Wales in a population of nearly fifty millions. The N.F.U. claims a membership of approximately 85 per cent of full-time farmers.

Since 1956 the N.F.U. has dissociated itself from eight price reviews (1958, 1960, 1962, 1963, 1965, 1969, 1970, 1971) and it 'noted' the 1968 price review.]

Trade Unions and the Labour Party *

Martin Harrison

After more than seventy years the alliance between Labour and the unions still rouses impassioned and contradictory assessments. On paper there would seem little room for doubt: the unions if they chose to do so could hold the Party in their grasp. At Labour's annual policy-making conference—that Parliament of the Labour Movement, as Attlee called it—almost ninety per cent of the votes are in union hands. The Transport and General Workers' Union (T.G.W.U.) and the Amalgamated Union of Engineering Workers (A.U.E.W.) alone *each* cast more votes than all the constituencies combined, and the National Union of General and Municipal Workers (N.U.G.M.W.) only a little fewer. On the National Executive Committee, whose twenty-nine members have prime responsibility for drafting policy statements and the election manifesto, twelve seats are assigned to trade unionists elected by the unions, which also have a preponderant weight in electing a further six. The unions also stand between the Party and bankruptcy or organizational collapse, providing over half its regular income (including over eighty per cent of the cost of the national headquarters), and a comparable proportion of the general election fund. In the House of Commons itself, no fewer than 137 of the 287 Labour M.P.s returned in 1970 had union financial backing.

Against this background one is scarcely surprised to hear complaints of union domination, as much from aggrieved internal factions as from opponents seeking to depict Labour as subject to the whims of militant unionism.[1] 'The outstanding fact is that the Labour party is dominated utterly by the trade unions', Aneurin Bevan once lamented during one of his spells of disaffection, and complaints about the tyranny of the union block votes formed a leitmotive of the Bevanite quarrels of the fifties.[2] Those were the days when Mr Shinwell was thanking the Deity for 'keeping the Party steady'[3] and the 'Praetorian Guard' of Arthur Deakin of the T.G.W.U., Tom Williamson of the N.U.G.M.W. and Will Lawther of the

* © J. M. Dent & Sons Ltd, 1974.

Miners provided the Party leadership with an almost unshakeable
position at the annual conference, to the chagrin of the Tribunite
wing. But as the T.G.W.U. and the A.U.E.W. cast their votes
increasingly often with the Left during the sixties, it was men like
Woodrow Wyatt who began talking of Frank Cousins of the
T.G.W.U. as 'the bully of the block vote ... moulding the Labour
Party to his will',[4] and the turn of Lord Kennet to echo Aneurin
Bevan's complaint from the moderate wing: 'We are nearly captive
to a sectional interest; we hardly any longer express the will of the
electors in the place where their power is exercised, but are well on
the way to being a mere emanation of part of the will of some of the
electors.'[5] The Left was now as silent on the 'undemocratic' block
vote of the unions as the Right had been in the fifties, apparently
accepting the altered complexion of union voting as proof in itself
that the process was now democratic.

However sceptically one views such manifestly self-interested
polemics, they at least illustrate the diversity of assessments of the
balance of power between Labour and the unions, and the characteristic tensions within their alliance. Yet the picture has always
been more complex than these simple stereotypes of dominance and
subjection suggest. For although a certain strand of union thought
has tended to see the Party as merely the political expression of trade
unionism, in practice in the period since 1945 one would be hard put
to produce examples of the unions dictating Labour policy on a
non-industrial issue. Even on the economic and industrial questions
where the unions tend to exercise their power more effectively and
unsentimentally there appear to have been remarkably few major
matters on which the union attitude alone was conclusive.[6]

There has in fact always been a considerable margin between the
unions' apparent capacity to dominate party policy and their actual
influence. This relates in part to the long-standing discrepancy
between theory and reality in Labour policy-making. This is not the
place for an exhaustive examination of the conflict between the
traditional characterization of the party conference as the 'final
authority' which 'lays down the policy of the Party and issues
instructions which must be carried out by the Executive, the
affiliated organizations, and its representatives in Parliament',[7] and
the opposing view that conference is merely 'an opportunity for the
ardent partisans who belong to the mass organization to meet
together to debate questions of national or party policy, and to
offer advice on these matters to the leaders of the Party in Parliament'.[8] The authority of conference is even today a painfully live
issue within the Labour Party. While Attlee's classic description now

looks simply grandiloquent, McKenzie's cavalier dismissal shows insufficient historical sensitivity. Nevertheless, there can be little doubt that for all the efforts to reassert the authority of the Party conference, the past two decades have broadly confirmed McKenzie's assessment of the parliamentarians' ascendancy over the mass party in the final effective determination of Labour policy.

But the unions are usually weakest at this parliamentary level. Despite its numerical strength, the influence of the trade union group of M.P.s is limited by its heterogeneity and its tradition of quiet loyalism. While the attitude of the group was a major factor in the rejection of the Wilson government's industrial relations proposals in 1969, its interventions in party battles are rarely either as cohesive or decisive.[9] Wherever possible the individual sponsoring unions usually prefer to speak directly to Whitehall and Downing Street rather than work politically through their M.P.s, to whom they assign the useful but secondary functions of prodding ministers, moving detailed amendments, eliciting information and lamenting lost causes. It is not unknown for union M.P.s to be instructed not to 'rock the boat' by intervening while delicate negotiations are under way or by challenging agreed compromises. Far from acting as disciplined agents of a trade union high command, many have felt frustrated at being held on the sidelines. The chairman of the group once sourly remarked, with at least one prominent loquacious union leader in mind, 'Others outside may publicly opine on every subject under the sun from the H-Bomb to education without regard to the impact on the wider movement, but we must never bring industrial issues to the chamber even though our cumulative knowledge and experience are impressive.'[10] Some unions make a determined effort to keep their M.P.s briefed, but in others the relationship is more distant, and even frankly antagonistic. The notoriously embattled relationship between Aneurin Bevan and the N.U.M., and George Brown and the T.G.W.U. are just two of the better known examples of deep-rooted disaffection. During 1964–70 there was particular exasperation among left-wing unions at the support some of their sponsored M.P.s gave to incomes policy and to British entry into E.E.C. This brought dark threats of withdrawal of financial support. But such threats have rarely led to action in the past, partly from fear of falling foul of parliamentary privilege, and partly because at bottom the unions sponsor M.P.s less as a means of achieving any precise policy objectives than of maintaining a distinctive trade union and working class presence on the Labour benches. It is a way in fact of keeping the Labour Party a labour party.

Traditionally the unions fight shy of undue involvement at

Westminster. The belief that 'politics' is best left to the politicians, combined with a certain conception of loyalty to elected leaders, leads them to stand aloof from the infighting of the parliamentary party. During the industrial relations quarrel of 1969 union leaders reacted coldly to a 'disloyal' bid for their support by Mr Callaghan, and later they were reported to have refused to have anything to do with intrigues to topple Mr Wilson from the leadership, though their hostility to the government's proposals was so strong as to lead them to contemplate direct industrial action against it.[11]

The unions' long-standing unreadiness to allow their officials to sit in the House or to incorporate parliamentary service into their career structure has further limited their influence at Westminster. The modest calibre of the union representation in parliament has meant that while every Labour government or shadow cabinet must contain a judicious sprinkling of men with union backgrounds, since the death of Ernest Bevin none of them has had the stature to interpret unions to Party and Party to unions authoritatively. Hopes that Mr Cousins might play such a role in the Wilson government were cruelly dashed. His departure left as the senior trade unionist Mr Gunter, who was handicapped in T.U.C. eyes by coming from a white collar union, the Transport Salaried Staffs Association, and by making no secret of his disillusionment with the General Council. When he went in turn, the only candidates for the mantle of Ernest Bevin were men like Mr Robert Mellish and Mr Roy Mason. With the memory of Mr Cousins' brief and unfortunate translation to the Cabinet still lingering it seemed unlikely that a future Labour government could contain a senior trade unionist who had either come up from the backbenches or would be prepared to move from a general secretaryship to the government. Increasingly the unions are therefore experienced by the Labour Party less as the industrial wing of a Labour Movement which is either understood instinctively or interpreted authoritatively in the highest levels of the Party, than as one of the many groups with which Labour must seek some modus vivendi.

Indeed, Labour leaders are more constantly aware of the unions as an external force acting through the T.U.C.—which is of course independent of the Party, drawing much of its strength from that independence—than of union demands reaching them internally through the normal policy-making processes.[12] If the unions are going to disagree with the Party's policy or attempt to turn it in a fresh direction, they normally prefer talks between representatives of the Party and the General Council or individual unions to moving resolutions at conference. Indeed, their negotiations with Labour are very similar in terms of formal structure if not of tone to those they have with Conservative governments. Thus although it would probably not be seriously contested even within the Labour Party that the unions sometimes get more than their strict due, we should recall that from Sir Walter Monckton's period at the Ministry of Labour through to the miners' strike of 1972 and beyond, employers' organizations and a section of the Conservative Party, *inter alia*, have complained repeatedly that Tory ministers were 'too soft' with the unions. To the extent that such criticisms are founded, they underline that the unions' impact on Labour policy is not due solely to their implantation in the Party's decision-making processes. One further element in the explanation must be that trade unionists and their families make up roughly half the electorate. It may well be that at times the unions fight for their own organizational vested interests rather than their members', that they sometimes voice the demands of unrepresentative militants, and that they are unpopular with the public at certain periods; and it is still not completely certain how far they can influence their members' voting at a general election. Nevertheless, it is easy to see why boldness in the face of the unions comes more readily to leader-writers than to practising politicians of either big party.

Since the War the unions have consolidated their position among the major sectional groups. While they have rarely proved capable of imposing their demands on either party against its will, on matters about which they are determined and united they may be able to cast an effective veto. Here again, the Conservatives have not been immune. In the 1950s they dropped their proposed Industrial Charter and their pledge to restore contracting-in to the political levy, and they also turned a deaf ear to backbench pressure for legislation curbing union power. Although they pressed the 1971 Industrial Relations Act through against union opposition, when the unions succeeded by a variety of means in neutralizing many of the Act's more distasteful provisions, the Conservatives showed little appetite for further measures to force their will on the unions. Rather, they tended to feel the need for some kind of olive branch to court the unions' co-operation on incomes policy.

Thus the problem of Labour's alliance with the unions must not be seen in isolation. Uncertainty about the relationship is part of a wider uncertainty about the role and functions of unions. And concern about the unions' power involves the more general issue of the weakness of British governments in the face of large, determined groups. Nevertheless, with its greater dependence on the votes of trade unionists, and its long-standing ties with the unions, based not only on cash and card votes but doctrine and sentiment, personalities and shared experience, Labour is naturally less inclined than the Conservatives to feel that electoral advantage or ideology counsel opposition to union wishes. On these grounds alone it is hardly surprising that Labour is so often receptive to the demands of the unions, even if its behaviour not infrequently stems as much from a prudent solidarity as from any intimate conviction.

In a sense it is misleading to speak of 'the demands of the unions'. Particular unions press their needs with energy and persistence, but there are remarkably few on which the movement is united. Its very heterogeneity and the widely varying degrees of politicization within its ranks hamper the formulation of any distinctive union catalogue of demands. The unions' impact has been to a remarkable degree negative. They expected the Attlee government to repeal the 1927 Trade Disputes Act, and it did. They were largely instrumental in the defeat of Gaitskell's proposal to revise Clause IV of the Party's constitution dealing with public ownership. They fought the Wilson government's Industrial Relations proposals, and they have tried to commit Labour to foreswear any future statutory incomes policy and to repeal the Industrial Relations Act of 1971. Thus beneath the popular stereotype of union militancy, politically the unions have often been surprisingly defensive and cautious—even conservative. Instead of pressing a programme of positive proposals on the Party, they have a more generalized expectation that it will maintain an expansionist economic climate in which they can operate success-fully in the manner to which they are accustomed, their traditional prerogatives protected from unwelcome incursions by the courts or the State. They have often been reluctant to solicit the intervention even of a friendly government in wide areas of economic and indus-trial policy. Although their demands are in a sense few, their impreci-sion makes them harder to satisfy completely, particularly in a period when the traditional prerogatives of the unions have become an increasing focus of political controversy.

While the unions have made very limited positive demands, and have usually preferred to pursue these through the T.U.C. rather than through strictly Party channels, they remain implanted in Labour's policy-making processes. With so massive a vote they are inevitably drawn into the controversies of the political wing when these move—as all the big issues do—from Westminster to the annual conference. In fact the unions' strength at conference is almost never cast in one direction. On all the great controversies like nationalization, German rearmament, nuclear weapons, membership of E.E.C., and even incomes policy they have been divided. There have actually been only a handful of occasions since the War when union and constituency majorities at conference have come down on opposing sides, and these do not add up to any coherent, consistent line of cleavage.[13] Given their overwhelming share of the vote it is striking how rarely in practice they have been the final arbiters. However, the distribution of union voting has not been by any means constant. From 1945 to the late fifties the union vote clearly favoured the Right, and men like Arthur Deakin and Will Lawther became the scourge of the Bevanites. But while the Left railed bitterly at the tyranny of the union bosses, its failure owed at least as much to the largely unnoticed strength of moderate views in the constituencies, its weakness in the parliamentary party, and the absence of public enthusiasm for red-blooded socialism of the *Tribune* variety. In any case the advent of Frank Cousins to the general-secretaryship of the T.G.W.U. in 1956 eroded the old right-wing predominance, although it was only in the sixties that a new balance in union voting became firmly established. At the close of the forties about sixty per cent of union votes was almost invariably moderate. By 1970 a slight majority (including those of the two largest unions) were fairly consistently favouring the Left. It was this changing disposition of the union vote rather than any change of heart in the constituencies, the parliamentary party or public opinion that brought such a shift in conference's attitude to questions like incomes policy and public ownership.[14]

The changing balance of union voting left its mark in other ways. In the fifties the support of its trade union 'Praetorian Guard' had helped moderate leaders withstand the shock of defeat and the onslaughts of the Bevanites. From the middle sixties the new disposition of union votes meant that party leaders more often went to conference facing an uphill fight for their policies, or even certain defeat—and once they lost the aura of office in 1970 such defeats were not quite so easily brushed aside.[15] Convinced that hopes of returning to power depended on clinging to the 'middle ground' of politics, and sceptical of many of the nostrums pressed upon them, Labour leaders did their best to contain the leftward tilt of the conference and the N.E.C. Though they could not prevent occasional lurches to the Left, they were to have considerable success in containing the substantive impact on party policy. But they paid a price. Many of their most energetic constituency workers felt cheated of their conference victories—though these paper victories gave ample ammunition to opponents seeking to picture Labour as in the grip of the wild men and selfish union bosses. The moderate line was more often held than not, but this often involved tortuous

75

attempts to face both ways. This was one of those periods when Labour often had to be held together rather than led, and it suffered both in internal morale and public esteem.

Yet over the years the unions' relationship with Labour has rarely subjected the Party to intolerable pressure. Not only for the semi-institutional reasons already outlined, but because so many issues leave the unions divided or indifferent, and their leaders have usually been ready to leave the brunt of the political battle to the politicans. The wisest have usually seen that the alliance might not survive an unduly forceful assertion of union power inside the political wing. From time to time leaders of major unions have been inclined to discount the dangers of asserting their strength. Thus Arthur Deakin's interventions in the early fifties did much to give the Bevanite controversy the appearance of a union-Party split. Later, in moving from defence of specific union interests to seeming the spearhead of attempts to shift the Party more generally to the Left, Messrs Jones and Scanlon created similar problems in the seventies. Such incursions not only heightened the perennial tensions within the Party,[16] but underlined the anomalous character of the unions' claim to use their prerogatives to the full. For ultimately the claim of the T.G.W.U. to one sixth of the nominal power to deter-mine Labour policy, outstripping the entire constituency movement, has rested under both Arthur Deakin and Jack Jones on its capacity to pay the appropriate affiliation fees rather than any more politi-cally significant measurement of its role in the Party. This not only drew attention to the shaky basis of the claim of conference to make 'democratic' decisions, but emphasized that while the unions claimed a share in Party policy-making as members of a 'Labour Movement', the unions have never been prepared to allow the Party a corresponding say in their decisions. Thus Labour has an oddly lopsided and anachronistic constitution. It cannot change this, and so must try to live with it. One essential condition of doing so tolerably is that those who carry the big stick must learn to talk softly.

The Labour Movement was envisaged as an alliance of unions, Party and Co-ops sharing an identity of interests and purposes. This was perhaps, on any coldly objective analysis, always in some sense a sentimental fiction. The alliance has in fact never been free of tension between the industrial and political wings, and the Move-ment's main institutional expression, the National Council of Labour, has long been moribund. Yet the myth was both powerful and in important respects 'true'. The Party was always described as the 'child' of the trade unions, and rows between the partners had the specially intimate violence of a family quarrel. There were many men of earlier generations for whom the Movement was a deeply experienced reality, and to whom any fundamental discord seemed to fly in the face of nature. As late as 1947 the trade union M.P. Sam Viant could declare with patent sincerity that 'it is impossible to draw a distinction between the interests of the members of the A.S.W. and the interests of the working people I represent in Willesden'.[17]

Nevertheless, it has long been clear that there cannot be a total identity of aims and purposes between an ostensibly radical party with responsibilities to the electorate generally, and a congeries of defensive sectional interests. It would be a distortion of reality to focus wholly on conflict to the exclusion of the areas of substantial harmony, yet the crucial problem of the alliance is its response to disagreement. For long periods this was effectively contained by a tacit division of labour. Attlee expressed it in these terms: 'It is useless and harmful to look on the trade unions purely as a revolutionary force to be subservient to the demands of political leaders It is equally dangerous for the trade unions to regard politicians merely as an agency for obtaining particular advantages for organized labour.'[18] In slightly different terms, the unions were usually prepared to leave political matters to the politicians and would refrain from throwing their weight about within the political movement; in return the politicians would leave trade union matters to the trade unionists. Thus Arthur Deakin once told the conference that political parties 'should leave industrial policy to the unions to determine', while 'questions of wages and conditions of employment are questions for the trade unions'.[19] Sam Watson of the N.U.M. said as bluntly, 'this conference has not the right to deal with strikes', and another union secretary, Sir Tom O'Brien, observed, 'this is the national conference of the Labour Party, not the Trades Union Congress', as if that automatically disposed of the issue.[20] The division was quite explicitly accepted by Frank Cousins: 'I told you last year not to tell the unions how to do their job, and I am certainly not going to tell the Labour Party how to do its job.'[21] The terms in which Mr Jones of the T.G.W.U. opposed constituency supporters of an incomes policy in 1970 had this in common at least with the hostility of his predecessor Arthur Deakin to constituency opponents of wage restraint twenty years earlier: these were union matters in which the political wing should not intrude. In deference to union susceptibilities, discussion of industrial issues was for many years severely inhibited at conference, to the frequent irritation of constituency representatives.[22] During the attempt to rethink policy in the fifties, documents like *Personal Freedom* emerged shorn of even the mildest reference to problems in relation to the unions. When taxed with the issue of trade union reform Mr Gaitskell felt obliged to answer lamely that 'we can safely leave it to the unions to take the necessary action'. Despite such embarrassments while Labour was in opposition it was usually not unduly difficult to maintain the traditional demarcation, though at the price of avoiding really candid exploration of such problems as incomes policy. Thus the Party has tended to build up a capital of goodwill in opposition in a way which contributed to the strains in the relationship when it came to power.

Once in power Labour has at times drawn heavily on this capital of goodwill. The Attlee government sought to involve the T.U.C. in the wage freeze of 1948–9 and took tougher action against unofficial strikers than subsequent administrations. The Wilson government taxed its relationship with the unions in a variety of ways, but most notably with the stagnation in real wages of the late sixties and its attempt to push through a reform of industrial relations against the wishes of the T.U.C. Indeed it can be argued that if Labour is sometimes too 'soft' with the unions, it has also shown a recurring disposition to be tougher with its ally than is either customary or politically prudent. As Mr Wilson said, looking back on 1968, 'I had . . . to tell my own supporters they had got to do things totally opposed to them and everything they had been brought up to believe'.[23] An earlier generation of union leaders never forgot that its close identification with the Cripps wage freeze of 1948–9 had undermined their domestic authority. Their successors would long nurse the scars of the battle over *In Place of Strife*.

Looking back, it would seem that each experience of Labour government has tended to deepen the partners' awareness of the inhibitions their alliance imposes, and weakened their sense of mutual advantage. The 1968–9 crisis was more than the product of misguided policies and faulty political management. It was aggravated by the fact that there was nobody like Ernest Bevin to hand to hold the alliance stable. But it went beyond questions of personality—and at all events the Party is unlikely to have another Bevin. The real gravity of the crisis was that it both confirmed that the old division of labour had irretrievably broken down, and revealed that even after seventy years unions and Party had an imperfect and immature understanding of their partnership.

In a sense the problem was a circumscribed one: the handling by a Labour government of that narrow range of issues which are of central concern to the unions. Thanks largely to its programme of social reform and its lifting of the stigma of the 1927 Trade Disputes

Act the Attlee government had some success in eluding or transcending these problems—though, as we have seen, even then there was a cost. But by 1964 Labour had less to offer in theory (and less still in practice) as a basis for a bargain with the unions. More important, those issues which had always been recognized as potentially the most disruptive were now the centre of political controversy. The mounting importance of questions like planning, incomes policy and union reform shattered the protective demarcation between the 'industrial' and the 'political'. In the event the politicians' incursions into the unions' former *chasse gardée* were to prove irrelevant, inept and unsuccessful. Nevertheless, Labour had made clear beyond all doubt that it would not contract-out its industrial policy to the T.U.C. What was perhaps not so immediately recognized was that the Party's invasion of the traditional prerogatives of the unions, through wage controls and industrial relations legislation, pointed logically to an erosion of the unions' restraint in political matters. Indeed, not only did they set about barring the route to any return to a statutory incomes policy or to intervention in collective bargaining but it may not be coincidental that both in conference and the N.E.C. several major unions showed few inhibitions about promoting militant policies in areas unrelated to their industrial concerns.[24]

Without building too much on a possibly transitory phase in union attitudes, the logic of the relationship is clear. The more the politicians intervene in areas of central concern to the unions, the more the unions will be driven to a greater politicization and an erosion of their former restraint within the political movement. As long as such issues as incomes policy and the social role of the unions remain unresolved the union-Party alliance will be under special tension. The position of the unions is simpler than the Party's. Over the years they have succeeded in demonstrating their independence beyond all doubt. Attlee did once argue that conference issues 'instructions which must be carried out by . . . the affiliated organizations', but today it is recognized that no union will be bound by adverse conference decisions on any matter of vital domestic interest to it. While Labour leaders at times presume too greatly on the unions' loyalty none of them harbour any illusions that they can be treated as political satellites.

The same is not true for Labour. Partly because the Party has spent eighty per cent of its life in opposition, where the occasions to assert its independence were fewer, and partly because it is conventionally treated as the 'child' of the trade union movement, its claim to comparable autonomy is less fully accepted. Many on the union side still think in terms of the T.U.C. declaration of 1931, 'The primary purpose of the Party should not be forgotten. It was created by the trade union movement to do those things in Parliament which the trade union movement found ineffectively performed by the two-party system.'[25] The tradition persists, Mr Cousins notwithstanding, that the unions do have the right to 'tell the Party how to do its job' in industrial matters. This contrasts sharply with the view of bargaining between equals advanced by Lord Wright: 'I hardly think that the Government even expects the trade union movement to say that we are going to give up our birthright for a mess of pottage. It is for the Government to govern, though this apparently offends some of my friends in the audience today. Nevertheless, it is for the Government to govern; but they must not expect the trade union movement always to acquiesce in the decisions that they have to take.'[26] But the critical reception his remarks received showed that many still saw the Party as essentially 'an agency for obtaining particular advantages for organized labour'.

Yet the Labour Party has never been exclusively a trade union party, and has never considered itself simply the political arm of the industrial movement. Its electoral centre of gravity has been firmly working class, but from birth it has aspired to a wider appeal. It has never committed itself to an acceptance that on matters concerning the unions its responsibility to either the community generally or the working class specifically would invariably be discharged by accepting the wishes of the T.U.C. which, with its disproportionate catchment of male industrial workers and underweighting of women, non-manual workers and the retired, is by no means always a faithful representation of the aspirations of working people. Nevertheless, on both wings there remains a powerful feeling that it is unnatural and perverse for Labour to run counter to union wishes on industrial questions. In some ways the Labour Movement has been a prisoner of its own rhetoric, which both encourages mutual expectations which tend to be disappointed when Labour is in power, and inhibits changes which might put the alliance on a secure and mature footing.

In their very differing ways both the 1931 and 1969 crises showed that if stretched too far the alliance would collapse. In both instances the Party presumed too heavily on union loyalty, and the unions saw the Party as simply their political instrument. Both crises underlined that if the alliance were ever pushed to breaking point there would also be a major convulsion within the Party; if the unions went a section of the political movement would surely follow. Quite apart from the threat of bankruptcy arising from the loss of union funds, the resulting convulsion would almost certainly shatter

Labour as a governmental party for some time, if not permanently. Awareness of these considerations is reflected in the common union view that the Party needs the unions nowadays more than they need it.[27] Though a plausible deduction, in view of the unions' greater industrial strength, it may underestimate the value to the unions of having a major national party basically well disposed toward them.

As yet the apocalyptic view of the Labour Movement has always proved unfounded. Somehow the alliance has survived early disappointments, syndicalism, the general strike, the 1931 débâcle, the Cripps wage freeze and the Bevanite split. Deep though the scars of 1968–9 were they could also heal. Indeed, relations between the two wings have been either tense or downright bad at least as much as they have been good. Yet the link has somehow survived, though not unchallenged. In the Bevanite period several trade union knights were tempted by an American-style independence. But a rupture never really seemed likely. As Arthur Deakin said, 'there is no trade union affiliated to the Party which would for one moment consider any disaffiliation or divorcement'.[28] It was not altogether certain the same could have been said in the late sixties; although no substantial moves were taken towards disaffiliation, for the first time the traditional motions of loyal support at the T.U.C. were opposed by manual unions refusing to endorse more than a qualified backing for Labour.[29] (The T.U.C. has not, in fact, issued a general appeal to trade unionists to vote Labour since 1951.) Without the abandoning of the Industrial Relations Bill pressures to cut financial support or to withdraw might well have gathered momentum rapidly. In the event Labour was given a spell in opposition in which it could mend its political fences and reconstruct the alliance. The problem was not just one of survival. Since the war the relationship has generally become more tenuous. There are fewer trade unionists in the highest counsels of the Party, and fewer senior men who retain a close involvement in the Party at any level. Indeed, several leading trade unionists, as ex-Communists, are more experienced in fighting the Labour Party than in working within it; at the very least they have little instinctive feeling for 'the Movement'. We have seen already the unwillingness of the unions to make special efforts to send more able spokesmen into the House. And while union money is the dominant factor in Party finance, it has not been sufficient to keep Labour at anything above a threadbare subsistence. The unions have also done little to involve themselves more fully in constituency work of grass-roots discussion of policy. By and large, confident in their industrial strength, they have not valued the political link sufficiently highly to make any real material sacrifices for it. The alliance is threatened at least as much by slow decay as by a dramatic collapse.

In present circumstances it is highly improbable that either partner would seek to create an alliance in anything approaching its present form; many on both sides would prefer somewhat less institutionalized arrangements not wholly dissimilar from those between the Conservatives and industry. Yet barring the sort of ultimate confrontation which skilful political management should avoid, the partnership will continue through a blend of conviction, mutual advantage and sheer inertia. But with issues which are so potentially disruptive to the relationship apparently certain to figure prominently on the agenda of politics, survival may depend on putting it on a less anachronistic basis. Labour may be the 'child' of the unions, but a 'child' of seventy might reasonably be granted full adult status. Within the existing constitution (which is hardly likely to be revised) full symmetrical equality is not in fact possible, since the unions' participation in Labour policy-making is not paralleled for the Party. (Labour's financial dependence on the unions might not inconceivably be eased by the introduction of state support for political parties on lines already operated by several continental countries.[30]) Nevertheless, institutional reform is perhaps less important than a general recognition that the logical corollary of the independence asserted and practised by the unions is an equal independence for the Party. At no time has the classic conception of 'the Labour Movement' operated with complete reciprocity, and it would certainly not constitute an acceptable basis for the alliance today. The soundest and most realistic relationship would seem to be a marriage of convenience on a basis of equality and autonomy embodying a much franker recognition of the limits of what one partner can do for the other than has operated hitherto. Over the years the relationship between Labour and the unions has been fruitful, but it has also had a cost for both. For more than a decade perception of these costs has tended to be sharper than awareness of the benefits. Yet a basis of substantial mutual advantage did remain if the partners could move forward from an immature relationship which both had outgrown. As Hugh Gaitskell once said, 'Either we change the attitude of the Party and the unions now, or in the end the Labour Movement will break up because of the inability to adapt to changed circumstances.'[31] Like so many British institutions the alliance between trade unions and the Labour Party was in danger of being the prisoner of its past. It remained to be seen whether it could accept the need for change, or whether it would move on to either some final confrontation or gradual degeneration

in which the Movement lingered like some ageing elm—outwardly
sound but dead at the heart.

Notes

1 While Conservative critics have usually alleged that Labour is too deferential
to the unions, this has not prevented them, on occasion, from accusing union
leaders of setting political loyalty before their members' interests during
periods of wage restraint. Compare, for example, E. H. C. Leather, *Advance*,
August 1950.

2 *Tribune*, 23 July 1943.

3 *Report of the Labour Party Conference* (hereafter, *Report*), 1952, p. 105.

4 *The Times*, 11 June 1960.

5 *Guardian*, 24 April 1973.

6 This point, like others in this essay, is more fully argued in my *Trade Unions
and the Labour Party Since 1945*, Allen & Unwin, 1960.

7 C. R. Attlee, *The Labour Party in Perspective and Twelve Years After*,
Gollancz, 1948, p. 93.

8 R. T. McKenzie, *British Political Parties*, Heinemann, 1955, p. 488.

9 Cf. particularly P. Jenkins, *The Battle of Downing Street*, Charles Knight,
1970; also E. S. Heffer, *The Class Struggle in Parliament*, Gollancz, 1973.

10 C. Pannell, quoted *The Times*, 4 November 1959—which also recalls the storm
when Mr Roy Mason, an N.U.M. M.P., described union M.P.s as 'gagged
men' in an article in *The People*.

11 Jenkins, *op. cit.*, pp. 116, 136.

12 About half the unions affiliated to the T.U.C. are also affiliated to the Labour
Party (though the proportion of members is much higher). Custom and
practice rule out dual membership of the General Council and the N.E.C.

13 Cf. Harrison, *op. cit.*, ch. 5, and K. Hindell and P. M. Williams, 'Scarborough
and Blackpool', *Political Quarterly*, 33(3), July–Sept. 1962.

14 Conferences in the early fifties regularly rejected nationalization 'shopping
lists'; the 1971 conference both supported a wide extension of public ownership and renationalization without compensation of denationalized companies. The 1963 conference carried with almost no dissent a motion favouring
a planned economy including an incomes policy. The diffidence of Mr Ted
Hill (Boilermakers) in opposing the motion was particularly striking: 'I hope
the platform will satisfy the trade unionists of this country that before ever they
had that thought [a wage freeze] in mind they would at least consult the trade
unions and get agreement with them . . . I sincerely hope the Labour Govern-

ment will respect the part that we play in the economy of this country. If you are in trouble, come to us, and as long as you do not humiliate us we will assist you.' (*Report*, p. 195.) Compare with the rejection of motions favouring an incomes policy in both 1970 and 1971. In 1970 Mr Scanlon declared it 'incomprehensible' that such a motion had been brought forward, and Mr Urwin (T.G.W.U.) said that if it were carried the resulting divisions would be so deep as to prejudice Labour's hopes of returning to power. (*Report*, pp. 222, 224.)

15 When the 1968 conference carried several unwelcome motions Mr Wilson stated that these were accepted as 'a warning, not an instruction. No one has ever seriously claimed that a Government which must be responsible to Parliament can be instructed'. (*Report*, p. 299.) (But this is precisely what a significant fraction of Labour activists did claim.) The 1970 conference carried a motion calling on the leadership to frame 'their policies on annual conference decisions', and deplored 'the P.L.P.'s refusal to act on conference decisions'. Mr Wilson said Labour governments would 'seek to act in accordance with the general policy, and indeed wishes of this Movement', but claimed the P.L.P.'s right to settle matters of timing and prerogatives, asserting that it was not 'required automatically to carry out each and every decision of each and every annual conference'. (*Report*, pp. 180–5.) Several unions showed some sympathy with proposals to subordinate the P.L.P. more effectively to the will of conference.

16 The hostility of many trade unionists to 'intellectuals' needs no further documenting. The unions' thrusting behaviour at the 1970 conference provoked an attack from a constituency delegate of a type which is rarely voiced openly. Referring to some union leaders as 'hard-faced men who have done well out of the class war', he concluded, to applause, that 'the trade union movement . . . is full of some of the biggest snobs in our society'. (*Report*, p. 24.)

17 *Report of the A.D.C. of the A.S.W., 1947*, p. 157.

18 *Op. cit.*, p. 62. Cf. R. Briginshaw (N.A.T.S.O.P.A.), 'We were on the scene before the political party. We cannot and must not be in their pockets.' *T.U.C. Report 1968*, p. 598.

19 *Report, 1947*, p. 144.

20 *Report, 1955*, pp. 132, 153.

21 *Report, 1956*, p. 82.

22 Cf. *Report, 1968*, p. 293 and *1971*, p. 172. At the 1967 T.U.C. the T.G.W.U. simultaneously supported legislation to implement a £15 minimum wage and equal pay, and opposed all governmental intervention in collective bargaining (*Guardian*, 2 September 1967). Speaking on incomes policy in 1966 Mr Cousins argued that 'you cannot have a social democracy and at the same time control by legislation the activity of a free trade union movement which is an essential part of the social democracy.' (*T.U.C. Report*, p. 462.) Compare this with the argument of Mr J. Peel (Dyers and Bleachers) that it would be 'inconsistent under a Labour Government to argue for

socially just forms of planning in every sphere of economic life except incomes' (*Report*, *1971*, p. 224), and Lord Cooper's view that 'unless we
appreciate that in the planning of the whole economy there has to to be some
planning about industrial relations and the behaviour of trade unions we are
not going to get very far' (*Report*, *1972*, p. 129); but these were unfashionable
pleas in the early seventies.

23 Jenkins, *op. cit.*, p. 99.

24 For example, unions were among the most energetic proponents of boycot-
ting the institutions of the E.E.C. A further sign of the breakdown of earlier
restraints was the A.U.E.W.'s 1968 motion of support for Labour 'subject to
the reservations involved in the policy decisions of the T.U.C.'. This was no
verbal slip. In 1969 the same union moved a comparable motion 'subject to
the policy decisions of the affiliated trade unions', and refused to accept an
amendment (which nonetheless succeeded) to delete the phrase on the ground
that 'the decisions of the Party could not be subordinated to those of outside
bodies'. (*Report*, *1968*, p. 293.)

25 Quoted, *Guardian*, 18 April 1969.

26 *Report*, *1968*, p. 265.

27 Cf. Heffer, *op. cit.*, p. 246: 'Labour is nothing without the trade unions, but
the trade unions can survive without the Labour Party.' Also H. G. Nicholas
of the T.G.W.U. acting as Labour Party fraternal delegate to the T.U.C.:
'It [the Labour Party] could not exist as a Party in its present form and strength
were it not for the support of its affiliated unions.' (*T.U.C. Report*, *1970*,
p. 604.)

28 *Report*, *1953*, p. 194.

29 *T.U.C. Report*, *1968*, pp. 598 ff. and *1969*, pp. 648 ff. Note the remarks of
general secretaries Woodcock and Feather on such motions, *T.U.C. Report*,
1967, p. 615; *1968*, p. 600, *1969*, p. 648.

30 It has usually been considered indelicate for unions to link their financial
contributions to policy considerations. There was quite a flurry when Arthur
Deakin did so obliquely at the 1953 Conference, but cf. Jack Jones' indication
that trade union funds might be at stake in the row over *In Place of Strife*,
Tribune, 25 July 1969. Later Mr Jackson of the Postal Workers asserted
quite categorically, 'Let the P.L.P. know that our support, both financial and
physical, depends upon the repeal of that Act'—the 1971 Industrial Relations
Act. (*T.U.C. Report*, *1971*, p. 449.)

31 Quoted *Tribune*, 27 June 1969. Cf. Cousins at the 1963 conference, '[Mr
Wilson] is wanting to be part of a team that is going to change the system,
and the function of a trade union will change along with a change in political
function.' (*Report*, p. 198.)

Membership Participation in the National Union of Teachers *

W. Roy

The purpose of this article is to examine the institutional behaviour of members of the National Union of Teachers. The N.U.T., by far the largest and most influential teachers' organization in England and Wales, is one of an important group of employee associations that is not affiliated with the Trades Union Congress. Teachers, with doctors, lawyers, higher civil servants and local government officers, think of themselves as belonging to a profession; they see their status as different from that of manual and clerical employees and they regard the N.U.T. as approximating more closely to a professional association than to a trade union. However, the gap between the N.U.T. and the traditional trade unions appears to be narrowing, and it is possible that the teachers and perhaps some of the other associations will eventually decide to affiliate to the T.U.C. So far all attempts to secure a vote of the National Union of Teachers in favour of this step have failed, but it is believed by some that opinion within the union is moving in the direction of affiliation.† Whether or not ultimately the N.U.T. along with N.A.L.G.O. and the other unaffiliated associations joins the T.U.C., it is likely that non-manual workers' organizations will become more influential as the proportion of clerical, administrative and technical employees grows larger; it is therefore of interest to examine the institutional behaviour of the members of one of this group.

The professional associations have often been at pains to point out that their functions are different from those of the traditional 'blue-collar' unions, and that their response to critical situations is not the same. As the following study of the N.U.T. will show, there are important differences in behaviour patterns. The differences are especially apparent when the membership is faced with specific threats to its professional status. However, the institutional behaviour of the members of professional associations is also in many respects

* Reprinted with permission from the *British Journal of Industrial Relations*, vol. II, no. 2, July 1964. The author is Headmaster of a Comprehensive School.

† See editors' note, p. 106.

markedly similar to that of manual workers. This clearly emerges not only from the study of attendance at branch meetings and of the participation of teachers in union elections,[1] but also from their behaviour in the superannuation and salaries struggle of 1956.

A recently completed investigation[2] of the internal political life of the N.U.T. showed that the members were influenced by conflicting desires. On the one hand, the rank and file member joins the N.U.T. for the same reason that other workers join a trade union: first and foremost, the teacher expects his union to obtain for him better salaries, improved conditions of work, and to protect him in any dispute he may have, either with his employers, the Local Education Authorities, or with the parents whose children he teaches. On the other hand, he sees the N.U.T. as an essentially 'respectable' organization, which keeps aloof from any involvement in party political issues, provides a forum for the discussion of educational topics, and paves the way for professional self-government as enjoyed by doctors and lawyers.

These conflicting desires arise partly from the nature of the N.U.T.'s membership, the bulk of which consists of the two- (now three-) year-trained non-graduate teacher, practising in the primary and secondary schools, for which the Local Education Authorities are responsible. Out of a total teaching force of 304,046,[3] 206,630 (68 per cent) of teachers are N.U.T. members; and the heaviest concentration of the membership is found in the primary schools (113,700 out of a total of 143,507, i.e. 79·2 per cent). The remainder of the membership consists almost entirely of secondary school teachers, and of these the vast majority teach in the secondary modern and comprehensive schools. Two-thirds of all N.U.T. members are women teachers, but it is the head teachers of both primary and secondary schools who, though numerically a much smaller group, dominate the National Executive of the Union and also play a leading part in Local Association politics. The drive towards 'trade union' tactics, and towards militancy, comes mainly (though not exclusively) from assistant masters who comprise an important section of the union, while the insistence on 'professionalism' and respectability stems largely, though by no means entirely, from those enjoying the highest status in the profession—the headmasters and headmistresses. This is as far as broad generalization can go; to obtain a more accurate picture of membership participation, a more detailed study of voting behaviour, attendance at meetings and response during a crisis situation is necessary.

87

W. Roy

Voting Patterns

Voting in the elections for the union's leaders—the Senior and Junior Vice-Presidents, the Treasurer, and the forty-three members of the National Executive—takes place at the teachers' place of work, in the schools. Printed ballot papers are supplied by headquarters to each of 690 local association secretaries, who send these to the school collectors or school representatives for distribution to individual members.

The following table shows the extent of membership participation in the election for the National Executive, on an area basis:

Table 1   Voting for Members of National Executive: Percentage of Eligible Membership Voting

District	1945	1948	1951	1954	Average for years sampled
North England	52·4	53·6	54·3	54·8	53·8
Lancashire	45·2	45·6	40·6	No contest	43·8
Yorkshire	50·2	55·2	No contest	47	50·8
North Midland	57·7	53·8	51·3	50	53·2
South Midland	No contest	49·8	48·3	No contest	49·1
East Anglia	38·3	35·2	34·6	37·9	36·5
South England	No contest	No contest	45·6	40·5	43·1
West England	41·8	47·3	43·6	44·5	44·3
Wales	70·7	70·6	67·2	62·1	67·7
Metropolitan	22·3	28·6	28·8	25·1	26·2
Extra-Metropolitan	35·2	44·1	42·2	38	39·9

Source: Compiled from N.U.T. Annual Reports for 1945, 1948, 1951 and 1954.
Note: The figures for 1957 correspond closely to the above; in 1960 there was a slight fall in most areas.

Although there are considerable variations in the percentages of votes cast in the various electoral districts, the general picture that emerges shows a concentration within the 40–45 per cent range, with an average over the years of 46·2 per cent for the country as a whole.

An analysis of votes cast for the vice-presidency of the union, over a ten-year period, yielded the following results:

88

Table 2   Voting for Vice-President: 1946–56

Year	Percentage of Eligible Members Voting
1946	43·4
1947	45·4
1948	47·3
1949	44·3
1951	42·7
1952	42·7
1953	42·4
1954	48
1955	36·8
1956	39·6
Average vote	43·3

Source: Compiled from N.U.T. Annual Reports, 1946–56.

Factors Influencing Voting

The significant part played by the school collector emerges at election times. It is he who is responsible for distributing the ballot papers, and if he were content to leave it to the individual members to post them, the poll in union elections would be abysmally low. Every collector worth his salt knows that the average member just will not bother to return the ballot paper by post, and needs a fair amount of urging and reminding before he completes it and gives it back to the collector, who usually parcels up those voting papers which have been returned to him, and posts them off to headquarters himself.

The vast majority of members voting ask the collector's advice for whom to vote, and it is not unknown for the school collector to be asked to complete the ballot paper, the individual member merely adding his signature. A minority of N.U.T. members simply 'plump' at the time of election, and many are influenced in their choice by the district from which the candidate originates, especially if this happens to be near their home district. As in any other large organization, the majority of N.U.T. members in the school do not know personally the candidates for the vice-presidency or for the National Executive, and many members give this as a reason for not casting their votes. Those who do vote are very frequently influenced by their

89

school collector, who often bases his opinion of the candidate on reports of meetings and discussions appearing in *The Schoolmaster*; if he attends local association meetings regularly, the chances are that he will most probably have made the personal acquaintance of the National Executive candidates for his district, as they make a practice of visiting local association meetings from time to time.

The distribution of election literature may play some part in influencing the vote, though, more often than not, such literature is lost in the general maze of notices on the Staff Notice Board or, if supplied to each member of staff individually, is hastily glanced at and finds its way either to the back of the register or straight into the wastepaper basket. Teachers generally take little notice of such communications because their lives are beset by papers—mountains of exercise books waiting to be marked, notes from parents, memos from the Head, circulars from the Local Education Authority, catalogues from educational publishers, and a hundred and one other things. It is therefore up to the collector, if he desires a good poll, to be thoroughly efficient in the distribution and collection of the ballot papers. Some collectors ask the headmaster for an extended tea-break and try to get the voting done on the spot, in the staff-room. Others send round for the completed ballot papers after a few hours or a few days, though the longer the matter is left over, the fewer the number of ballot papers that will be returned. However, there is no doubt that the extent to which members participate in elections depends largely on how efficiently the school collector organizes the election, rather than on the desire of the rank and file to exercise its democratic right to vote for its leaders.

How does this degree of participation compare with industrial unions employing a similar system of voting at the place of work? Table 3 opposite shows some comparative figures.

It will be noted that the figures for the N.U.T. occupy a midway position in the table; compared with the industrial trade unions, including one white-collar union—the Transport Salaried Staffs' Association—the teachers do not show either exceptionally great interest or very marked lethargy when electing their leaders.

The picture that emerges confirms Professor Roberts' conclusions [4] that the way in which union elections are conducted is the outstanding factor in determining membership participation. Professor Roberts found this to be the case for all the industrial unions listed in Table 3, e.g. in the National Union of Printing, Bookbinding and Paper Workers, the branch secretaries send the ballot papers to the Fathers of the Chapel, who in turn distribute them to the individual members; the Steel Workers and the Transport Salaried Staffs'

Table 3   Voting for Executive Councils or Committees at the Place of Work—A Comparison between N.U.T. and Certain Industrial Unions

Union	Percentage of Members Voting
British Iron, Steel and Kindred Trades Association	69·3
Transport Salaried Staffs' Association	64
National Union of Tailors and Garment Workers	49·7
National Union of Teachers	46·2
Transport and General Workers' Union	20–40
National Union of Printing, Bookbinding and Paper Workers	36·7
National Union of Railwaymen	32
Electrical Trades Union	30·4

Sources: *For Industrial Unions:* B. C. Roberts, *Trade Union Government and Administration in Great Britain* (Bell, 1956), pp. 230–7 (the highest figures have been taken in each case).
For N.U.T.: Average for years 1945, 1948, 1951 and 1954, compiled from Annual Reports for these years.

Association, like the N.U.T., use their branch secretaries to distribute ballot papers to individual members, either by post or through stewards and collectors. It is reasonable to conclude that in voting for their leaders, the teachers' behaviour pattern is not markedly different from that of many blue-collar and white-collar workers in industry.

Taking attendance at local association meetings as another criterion of membership participation, a questionnaire circularized to eighty-seven branches yielded the following information:

Table 4   Average Attendance at Local N.U.T. Meetings*

Membership of Association	No. of Local Branches Investigated	No. of Local Branches in N.U.T.	Attendance at Ordinary Meetings	Attendance at Annual General Meetings
			%	%
0–100	10	153	34	38
101–250	11	269	23	26
251–500	24	181	14	20
501–750	19	38	11	13
751–1000	6	14	6	8
Over 1000	17	26	6	7
National averages (based on statistical sample among 681 Local Associations)	87	681	21	25

* During the year of investigation—1955.

The steady decline in the attendance figures as the size of the union branch increases is at once obvious: the larger the branch the smaller the proportion of members who attend. The feeling of remoteness from the centre of decision-making, the greater difficulty of individual contact between the members of the larger branches and between local officers and rank and file members, the lack of opportunity for personal involvement in union affairs, all tend to depress attendances in the case of larger local associations. The same relationship between branch size and attendance at local meetings, which investigations of similar phenomena in industrial unions have revealed, also exists within the N.U.T. Roberts has shown that there is a progressive decline in voting performance in industrial union branches exceeding 1,000 members, and that members in the smaller branches, when they participated, did so in greater numbers than their fellow members in the large branches;[5] Goldstein found the same relationship in a study of the Transport and General Workers' Union.[6] The larger the branch, the greater the percentage of normally apathetic members. But on the whole, teachers show a somewhat better attendance at their branch meetings than industrial trade unionists and, indeed, than certain other white-collar workers, notably members of the Civil Service Clerical Association, the Union of Post Office Workers and the Transport Salaried Staffs' Association, whose attendance is between 5 and 7 per cent.[7] This is partly because their working day, at least in school, is shorter, and teachers have therefore greater opportunities to get to meetings, which are usually held at 5 p.m., soon after the end of the school day. The fact that meetings are held in the familiar environment of the school, and that most schools are easily accessible, also contributes to a better attendance, and the average of 21 per cent of all N.U.T. branches compares favourably with the average branch attendance for industrial unions, which seems to fall within a range of 3 to 15 per cent, with a concentration at the low end of the scale.[8] The slightly higher attendance at Annual General Meetings appears to be due to two factors: firstly, many members make a practice of attending at least this meeting—if no other—at which in most branches the election of officers takes place, and school collectors often make a special effort to get members to come; secondly, it is customary to elect a new local president every year and it is a fairly well established convention in the union that at least some members of the school staff on which the local president serves should support him on this occasion, and so share in the prestige which the president's position brings to a school.

However, active members and officials in the N.U.T. do not

regard attendance at local meetings as good, and the same complaints about apathy and lack of interest which are heard so frequently with regard to industrial unions and certain professional associations, are certainly echoed within the N.U.T.—in the absence of a crisis when, as will be shown, attendances rise to three or four times the usual average.

Membership Response to a Crisis Situation

One such crisis situation arose during the dispute between the Durham County Council and the N.U.T. on the issue of the 'closed shop', when a group of convinced and passionate trade unionists, in control of a local authority, attempted to force the teachers into compulsory union membership.

In November 1950, the Durham County Council passed a resolution requiring all its employees to be members of an appropriate trade union, stating that 'notice will be given to all those persons in the employment of the County Council who are not members of a trade union and, at the same time, the persons concerned will be offered re-employment on their existing terms, with an overriding condition that they become members of an appropriate trade union before being re-engaged'.[9]

Special instructions were given to all head teachers to satisfy themselves that all members of their staff belonged to a trade union and Heads were told to inspect current membership cards. The leader of the Durham County Council stated clearly that the achievement of the 'closed shop' was the policy of the Council: 'The Durham County Council have decided to make trade union membership a condition of employment—and why not? . . . if it is morally right for trade unionists to urge employers to adopt the "closed shop", then it cannot be wrong for us to enforce the same policy when we ourselves control the public authority . . . in Durham, we will not tolerate a non-unionist under any circumstances, and what Durham does today, the rest of the country will do tomorrow'.[10]

The reaction of the teachers was immediate. The Council of the Durham County N.U.T. Association unanimously agreed to tell its members to ignore this request for information as to union membership; the N.U.T. solicitor sent a strong letter of protest to the Clerk of the Durham County Council; the National Executive of the union advised teachers in Durham not to comply with the County Council's resolution, and promised full support; *The Schoolmaster* roundly condemned the County Council in a leading article entitled 'The

New Despotism', and accused it of coercion, regimentation and dictatorship. Whilst the N.U.T. was anxious to improve its membership, its members up and down the country were violently opposed to the 'closed shop', seeing in it a threat to the freedom of the individual, an involvement in party politics wholly repugnant to them, and a challenge to the teachers' conception of their professional status. When the matter reached the House of Commons, the Minister of Education made it clear that the Labour Government did not support the Durham County Council's attempt to coerce the teachers into joining a union.

Notwithstanding the teachers' opposition and the Government's statement, the Durham County Council reaffirmed its decision and began to implement the policy of the 'closed shop' by asking teachers called for interview for senior teaching posts and for headships, to state whether or not they belonged to a union. Miss Florence Horsbrugh, moving an opposition motion in the House of Commons, quoted the case of six applicants for a headmastership, all of whom were asked if they belonged to a teachers' union. Only one answered the questions, and he obtained the appointment.

Sir Ronald Gould, the General Secretary of the N.U.T., said that the issue was not political, but professional. Should a teacher, as a condition of employment, disclose membership of a professional organization? For him, and he spoke for the union, this involved a question of principle of vital concern to the teacher's status as a professional person, and he roused the National N.U.T. Conference to a memorable demonstration of enthusiasm when he paid tribute to the loyalty and the unity of the teachers of Durham: 'Teachers everywhere should pay tribute to their colleagues who, at great personal cost, have placed principle before personal advantage and loyalty to the Union before promotion. I am proud to state that Durham teachers are united and there is ample evidence that even those who are not seeking new posts view with abhorrence this infringement of personal liberties, this violation of professional self-respect . . . for the union, there can be no deviation from the principle I have enunciated.'[11]

In the meantime, the union had contacted the other teachers' organizations with a view to concerted action. On 30 March 1951, representatives of the N.U.T., the Association of Teachers in Technical Institutions, the Incorporated Associations of Headmasters, Headmistresses, Assistant Masters, and Assistant Mistresses met an Emergency Committee of the Durham County Council and requested that candidates for promotion should not be questioned by Appointing Committees as to their union membership. The

County Council blankly refused to give the requested undertaking. The N.U.T. next decided to call on 850 teachers in the East and East Central Divisional Executive areas of Durham to hand in notices terminating their appointments. The union stated that, if necessary, similar action would be taken throughout the county, and that members would receive full pay if no settlement were reached.

At this stage, whilst notices of resignation were still being collected, the Minister of Education intervened in the dispute and issued a directive to the Durham County Council instructing them to refrain from asking the offending question. This directive was subsequently accepted by the Labour group controlling the Local Authority and it looked as if the storm had blown over.

But the greatest test was still to come. Less than twelve months after agreeing to accept the Minister's directive, the County Council made another more subtle attempt to enforce the 'closed shop' by issuing the following regulation: 'That future applications for extension of sick payments be considered only if they are made by or through a trade union or other appropriate organization.' Other regulations laid it down that applications for leave of absence for other purposes, e.g. attendance at council or committee meetings, also had to be made through such channels. These new regulations were clearly an indirect method of applying the 'closed-shop' policy. First, the Local Authority had attempted to make membership of a union a condition of employment; next, there was the offending question about trade union membership at interviews for promotion, and now there was this new threat, which the teachers regarded as a vindictive method of forcing the issue.

The new regulations applied to all employees of the County Council and were opposed not only by the N.U.T. but also by the British Medical Association, the British Dental Association, the Royal College of Midwives, the Royal College of Nursing and the Engineers' Guild. At the invitation of the N.U.T., representatives of these associations established a 'joint emergency committee of the professions' so that contact between the various associations of professional workers should be close and continuous. In a letter to the Clerk of the Durham County Council, the Joint Emergency Committee stated that 'the policy of compulsory membership is deeply repugnant to professional workers. The professions are profoundly attached to the principle of free association which implies also the freedom not to associate if the individual so chooses in the unfettered exercise of his judgement or conscience. The professions find themselves united in opposition to the Durham County Council's policy of compulsory membership ... and request your

Council to give an undertaking that its professional employees should not be subjected to this policy in whatever manner, direct or indirect, it may be applied'. It insisted that the County Council should withdraw the offending regulation by 30 April. This the Local Authority refused to do, and it fell to the N.U.T. to call on its members in Durham to resign from their posts.

How did the teachers respond to this call for militancy, for the sake of what was, after all, an abstract principle which had little effect on their daily work, and bore no relation whatsoever either to their pay or to conditions of teaching in the schools? How far were the teachers of Durham prepared to forgo all chances of professional advancement, probably for the remainder of their careers—for it was obvious that there could be no advancement for a teacher prepared to defy his employers to the extent of withdrawing his labour, unless, indeed, there was a change of political complexion of the Durham County Council—a most unlikely event in an area traditionally ruled by the Labour Party.

The N.U.T. call to its members in Durham to hand in their resignations came on 18 May, and union officials started to collect the notices during the last fortnight in May; the resignations were to take effect as from the beginning of September, the start of the new school year. In response to the union call to its 4,900 members in Durham County, 4,652 placed their resignations in the hands of the N.U.T. official within a matter of two weeks. If allowance is made for some members in independent schools, in schools under the jurisdiction of the Home Office, and teachers on leave of absence because of illness or other causes, and for those due to retire at the end of the summer term, it is quite clear that the response to the call for resignations was virtually 100 per cent.

A survey of the reports of meetings held in Durham at the time, and contact with individual members who were actually involved, confirm the solidarity of the membership, and the utter determination of the teachers to see the struggle through. At a meeting of representatives of all local N.U.T. associations in Durham, held on 19 May, the atmosphere was tense and indignant and the use of the words 'closed shop' was enough to incense the teachers. Each area representative submitted a report on the attitude of members in his local association, including details on the formation of local action committees. The meeting passed the following resolution unanimously: 'Having considered reports of recent action in connection with the closed-shop dispute, this meeting of the County Council Section of the Durham Teachers' Association endorses the decision of the Union Executive to call for notices from its members serving in the County. It further pledges its support of this action, in every possible way, until the issue is brought to a successful conclusion.'[12]

Other meetings held at this time reflect the general trend of determination and militancy. Almost without exception, attendances at meetings doubled or trebled, and at most branch meetings four-fifths of the total membership were present. The Jarrow, Washington, Chester-le-Street, Felling, and Bishop Auckland N.U.T. branches all reported very well-attended meetings pledging support, and the three leading members of a very active County Action Committee managed to address twenty-three local meetings in Durham within a space of six days. But perhaps the best indication of the rank and file attitude was seen in the schools, where it was the task of the individual school collector to distribute the resignation notices to colleagues and to obtain their signatures. One staff common room after another met, discussed, and decided, usually very quickly, to support union policy. The prevailing atmosphere was one of exhilaration and even enthusiasm. More than ever before, the teachers felt themselves to be members of a learned profession, whose sense of justice and decency had been outraged by the high-handed action of the County Councillors, most of whom had had no education beyond an elementary schooling. Whilst many teachers expressed concern for the welfare of the children in case of a strike, there was a deeply-held conviction that it was the employers, not the teachers, who were endangering their welfare. The bond that linked the teachers of Durham was thus an idealistic one: it had fallen to them to uphold the principle of the freedom of the individual against the philosophy of the 'closed shop', a principle which many of them felt to be fundamental to the democratic way of life itself. The 'closed shop' might be acceptable to miners, dockers and factory workers, but no one who taught and was entrusted with the task of passing on the heritage of civilization to the rising generation was going to be tyrannized by the County Council. Such were the sentiments which roused the teachers of Durham who, at the time, were fortunate in having among them a number of able local leaders who were unafraid, capable of making decisions, and above all, of inspiring in their colleagues a sense of solidarity and unity. The teachers had decided that the time for talks and futile negotiations was past and that a 'showdown' was inevitable. No one who entered a Durham school during these last days of May 1952 could fail to be struck by the sense of purpose, the spirit of unity, and the tremendous confidence shown by the members of staff from the small primary school in the country to the big secondary school in the town. Within twenty-four hours of launching the campaign for resignations, nearly a thousand notices had reached the Divisional N.U.T. Secretary, and several local associations quickly obtained a nearly 100 per cent response; for example, the Bishop Auckland Association reported that out of 315 serving members, 290 had sent in the resignation forms. This kind of response was not confined to the towns, but extended to the schools in the remote valleys, covered by the Weardale and Barnard Castle Association.

Faced with the resignation of about 5,000 teachers, the Durham County Council next decided to refer the dispute to the Minister of Labour as an industrial dispute. A compromise resolution drafted by the Council's own Emergency Committee, that applications for sick pay should be made through 'designated persons' instead of organizations, was defeated in full Council meeting. In an angry statement, the County Council accused the teachers of malice, and of siding with the Conservative Party. Replying, the union recalled the attitude of the Labour Minister of Education, and stated bluntly that the County Council had violated both the letter and the spirit of Mr Tomlinson's directive, and that it stood by its strike threat! 'It [the union] is prepared, even for a protracted struggle, and ... should the need arise, arrangements in accordance with union rules will be made to ask members throughout the country to give financial support to their colleagues in Durham.' The Minister of Labour, Sir Walter Monckton, held separate meetings, first with the Durham County Council representatives, and then with representatives of the Joint Emergency Committee of the Professions.

Both parties finally agreed to ask the Minister to set up an independent Board of Arbitration, and agreed in advance to accept and implement the Board's award, which was announced within a short time: 'We have carefully considered the statements and submissions made on behalf of the parties and ... we find and so award that in so far as the present regulations governing the making of applications for extended sick pay require that such applications shall be made through "a trade union or other appropriate organization", they are in conflict with the principle of voluntary membership of a trade union or professional association, and should be withdrawn.' As promised, the Durham County Council accepted the judgement of the Board and withdrew the offending regulation. The struggle was over. The teachers had won.

In the Durham incident the members of the N.U.T. had been aroused to militant action by a threat to their professional status; but there have been other instances where teachers have responded to threats to their economic status in a similar fashion. For example, they behaved much as might have been expected of members of any manual workers' trade union when the Government proposed to increase the teachers' superannuation contribution. The behaviour of members of the N.U.T. and the response of the union to the situation that was created by the Government's decision are examined below.

A Fight with the Government

In July 1952, the Minister of Education informed the union that the Government proposed to increase the amount paid by the teachers towards their pensions from 5 to 6 per cent of their salaries, because the Government Actuary had reported an actuarial deficiency, due to increases in salary, in the Teachers' Superannuation Fund. The N.U.T. opposed the proposed increase on the grounds that the teachers' superannuation scheme was originally conceived as a non-contributory scheme, that the teachers were being subjected to unfair discrimination by the Treasury (since other superannuation funds also showed actuarial deficiencies) and that the Local Authorities had consistently refused to consider amendments of the scheme asked for by the teachers, to include provisions for widows and orphans.

A joint working-party, consisting of representatives of Teachers' Associations and their employees, was set up to consider not only the Minister's proposals but the whole issue of teachers' superannuation; however, it reached no agreement. The local authorities agreed to pay 6 per cent towards teachers' pensions but were not prepared to sanction any additional expenditure in respect of a scheme for widows and orphans. The teachers, in their turn, would not hear of higher contributions without extra benefits; they regarded the possibility of fluctuating rates of contributions as highly undesirable, and destructive of stable conditions of service. Nevertheless, the then Minister of Education, Miss Florence Horsbrugh, proceeded with the Bill against the strenuous opposition of the N.U.T., which manifested itself mainly in continued representation to the Government, and in lobbying of M.P.s by teachers. The teachers succeeded in obtaining support on both sides of the House of Commons, and the Government decided to delay the proposed Bill.

When Sir David Eccles replaced Miss Horsbrugh as Minister of Education in October 1954, he announced his intention of presenting a revised Superannuation Bill, which, however, still increased the contributions payable from 5 to 6 per cent. The N.U.T. immediately called a special private conference at which the Executive proposed the following motion: 'This Conference declares its opposition to the proposal of the Minister of Education to increase the rate of superannuation contributions from teachers. Further, Conference calls upon the Minister to incorporate in any scheme provision for widows and orphans and dependants of the teachers as additional benefits, to which the employers contribute their share of the cost.'

The writer attended this Conference at which feeling was running high, for teachers regarded the extra 1 per cent as a cut in salary, at a time when their pay was hardly keeping pace either with the increasing cost of living or with pay increases obtained by industrial workers. At times, certain speakers on the platform had difficulty in making themselves heard, and the Chairman of the Salaries and Superannuation Committee of the Executive, who attempted to ignore the numerous interruptions from the floor asking what action the Executive were ready to take, met with considerable hostility. It fell to his seconder to steer a resolution through the Conference, but not before it had been strengthened by an amendment from the floor (instructing the Executive to 'employ the full resources of the union to defeat the Minister's proposal') which was carried with acclamation in the face of a somewhat embarrassed Executive. The Conference, held in December 1955, marked the beginning of the struggle, for a few days later, on 1 December, the Minister announced that the Second Reading of the Bill would take place on 6 December.

Knowing of the opposition which Miss Horsbrugh had faced on this issue and which, judging by the Conference, showed no signs of weakening, Sir David had decided to take the bull by the horns, to rush the Second Reading through the House of Commons, and to rely on the respectability of the N.U.T. to accept the will of Parliament. However, no sooner had the date of the Second Reading been announced than a wave of spontaneous indignation and protest swept staff rooms all over the country. Nearly all the union's 681 Local Associations called special protest meetings, and attendances, usually well below 30 per cent at branch meetings, jumped to 75–80 per cent. At national level, a Press Conference was called at Hamilton House, at which the General Secretary, Sir Ronald Gould, outlined the union's case against the Government; space was bought in the national press, M.P.s were flooded with letters, telegrams and personal calls from teachers in their constituencies, and on Monday, the day before the Second Reading, nearly a thousand teachers from London and the Home Counties lobbied M.P.s at the House of Commons.

The Establishment of a Fighting Fund

It was, however, the spontaneous reaction at local level, rather than the organized opposition in London, which emerged as the most significant feature of membership participation. The angry demand for actions varying from the withdrawal of teachers' services from voluntary activities to a general strike, far surpassed in its intensity anything which the Executive of the Union had expected. The rank and file pressed for any or all of the following steps to be taken:

(*a*) withdrawal of teachers' services from the School Meals Service;

(*b*) the cessation of collection of National Savings in Schools;

(*c*) a 'work-to-rule' campaign, involving the withdrawal of teachers from all extraneous duties;

(*d*) strike action.

A few typical examples of what took place at meetings of teachers all over the country will serve to illustrate this feeling of the rank and file. In South Bedfordshire, the Local Association urged an immediate 'work-to-rule' campaign and lobbied meetings of neighbouring teachers for support. The Hertfordshire County Association collected £1,000 (voluntarily contributed at the rate of £1 per head, 40 per cent of the members donating this sum within one month of the issue of an appeal by the officers) towards a Fighting Fund, which originated in the following way. At a meeting of the Council of the Hertfordshire County Teachers' Association, a member got up and said that it was time that the rank and file of the union took the lead. He then took a £1 note out of his wallet and proposed the starting of a £1-a-head fund; this was enthusiastically supported. The following Monday, one Council member proposed a collection in his school staff-room and raised £8 in a day. Later, this fund formed the basis of a National Salary Fighting Fund established by the Executive. In West Bromwich, teachers in all but one of the forty-six schools anticipated the action of the N.U.T.'s Executive and ceased the collection of National Savings forthwith, and the same decision was taken at a delegate meeting at Durham. The largest N.U.T. Local Association, Liverpool, passed a resolution urging national committees of all teachers' organizations 'to prepare for strike action should all other means of opposition prove unsuccessful'. Bristol urged withdrawal from unpaid, voluntary duties, the calling of a one-day national strike, the organization of regional strikes and the immediate raising of a levy; at Ilford, a meeting of over 500 teachers out of a membership of 656 carried with acclamation a motion of no confidence in Ilford's two M.P.s who would not commit themselves to opposing the Bill, and in the Minister of Education.

The picture that emerges from a study of published material, and from contacts with local branches, indicates that the Executive was under considerable pressure from the rank and file to take militant action before the Second Reading took place. The issues of *The Schoolmaster* published during the period of the controversy abound with letters and reports of local meetings held up and down the country, all pressing for militant action of which the following is but one example:

> At a general meeting of the Ashton-under-Lyme, Mossley and Limehurst Association, held on November 30th, strong dissatisfaction was expressed at the Executives' handling of the superannuation dispute. It was felt that the publicity secured by the Minister for his ideas was far superior to that gained by the Union and that members were suffering from a lack of decisive and clear leadership. The following resolution was passed unanimously:
>
> > That this Association feels that the Executive of the Union is not pressing the campaign against the Minister of Education's Superannuation Proposals with sufficient vigour, and calls upon it to give members of the Union more energetic and forceful leadership. We should like to see:
> > (a) Misleading statements in Press publicly and officially corrected;
> > (b) A detailed statement of the action that the Executive is prepared to instruct Union members to take to prevent the Bill becoming law.[13]

On the Saturday prior to the Second Reading, the Executive met in London and passed a motion asking union members to cease the collection of National Savings in schools. At the same time, following the lead given by the Hertfordshire County Teachers' Association, it authorized expenditure of £100,000 on a press and publicity campaign by launching an appeal for contributions to a £100,000 Fighting Fund.

Although the decision to cease collecting National Savings was considered to be entirely inadequate by the more militant spirits in the union, there is no doubt that it achieved two important results: firstly, it hit the headlines of the press and obtained widespread publicity for the union; secondly, it aroused those members who were still inactive and lukewarm, and forced them off the fence. The union's publicity campaign was certainly without parallel in its history: the N.U.T.'s action featured in B.B.C. news bulletins and television newsreels; it hit the headlines of such papers as *The Observer*, *The Sunday Times*, *The Sunday Express* and *Reynolds News* on the Sunday after the Second Reading, and of most of the dailies on the following Monday. Leader and feature writers were busy commenting on the teachers' case, and almost daily references to the dispute appeared in the national and local press. On the air, apart from featuring in the regular news bulletins, the union's stand was discussed in 'Topic for Tonight' on 13 December; on 15 December, the General Secretary spoke in 'At Home and Abroad', and the following day he appeared in a news feature on the I.T.A. bulletin.

It is not surprising that the Executive directive to cease the collection of National Savings in schools met with practically 100 per cent response from the general membership. Although a few voices were raised in protest—mainly from teachers who held official positions in the National Savings Movement—and a handful resigned from the union rather than carry out the directive, in the vast majority of primary and secondary modern schools no savings were taken from the beginning of the Spring Term 1956. In many schools, staff meetings were held at which the N.U.T. collector informed his colleagues of the Savings Campaign, and there was unanimous agreement to support the Executive. In some schools, the Head, or assistant teacher responsible for the collection of money, simply failed to restart the savings machinery at the beginning of the new term. The significance of this almost complete unanimity in carrying out the Executive's directive was not to be underestimated, for teachers had played a large part in building up the National Savings Movement, and School Savings were in a flourishing state.

Demands for Strike Action

At the second meeting of Standing Committee D in the House of Commons on 20 December, the Opposition, which had supported the N.U.T.'s case from the beginning, tabled an amendment that Clauses 1 to 4, dealing with the payment of increased contributions, should be postponed; this was defeated, and the Minister declared his intention of proceeding with the Bill. The rank and file was now thoroughly roused, and the campaign against the Superannuation Bill became identified with a claim for higher salaries. More and more local associations agitated for greater militancy, and there was a perceptible body of opinion within the union in favour of strike action. Those who urged caution and 'respectability' met with less and less sympathy at local meetings, and one of the many correspondents in *The Schoolmaster*, pressing for a teachers' strike, aptly expressed this attitude:

Sir,
    There is a common feeling among the professional classes and the middle classes, that to participate in strikes is somewhat 'déclassé'. This view clearly

has its uses for those against whose measures strikes are directed, and is, of course, not discouraged by them. Yet the origin of this view probably lies in the fact that, for the most part, manual workers only have found strikes to be a necessary weapon in the defence of their living standards, and it has been to the advantage of the middle classes to deplore such action. Moreover, even where possible disadvantage may accrue through continual deprecation of strike action, the professional classes still retain the psychological satisfaction of identifying themselves with the middle and upper classes, and being considered responsible.

For example, teachers may claim that they must put their duty to the school-children above their own economic interests. But if this entailed failing to strike over a salary cut, or anything which is tantamount to it, this could lead to a teaching profession staffed by less capable and less well qualified members, who might be more attracted by more remunerative posts elsewhere. Would then, the children suffer?

We live, unfortunately, in a competitive and economically acquisitive society, and if any wage or salary earning group—irrespective of social status—finds its living standards threatened by economic action on the part of its employers, then the threatened group must work together to protect themselves, and one weapon which has been found most useful in such actions is that of the strike.[14]

A sample taken of nineteen local meetings held in various parts of the country showed that thirteen of the associations were in favour of going beyond the Executive directive, and urged that all voluntary duties, such as the collection of dinner money, and after-school activities, should cease. Six of the associations declared themselves in favour of strike action, and all of them were critical of the Executive because they considered that the National Savings directive did not go far enough. The Fighting Fund was approaching £5,000 by the end of January; many local associations continued to have the best-attended meetings within living memory, and literally hundreds of resolutions poured into N.U.T. headquarters urging strike action. work-to-rule campaigns, and the opening of salary negotiations, Some locals urged immediate action of an unofficial nature, and N.U.T. headquarters issued a policy brief to all locals, which contained the following warning:

To achieve success, discipline, unity and determined action will be necessary from all of us. Ill-conceived and misdirected actions which divide the profession, confuse the public, and hinder or prevent the attainment of our objectives, must be guarded against at all costs. Our full strength will be needed in the difficult months ahead. To dissipate it could damage our cause irretrievably. Other organizations may indulge in wild talk about a variety of actions, and in consequence, personal loyalties may be strained. But if local action is taken contrary to Union advice, chaos will result and we shall fail in our tasks. The Union has taken the lead throughout the salary and superannuation campaigns: it would be folly for its members to be sidetracked by other would-be leaders.

It is highly significant that the leaders of the union, who year after year appealed for support and increased membership participation, should have considered it necessary to issue such a statement, which was a clear indication that the rank and file were anything but apathetic on the superannuation and salary issue.

Whilst the campaign initiated by the rank and file did not achieve a complete reversal of Government policy, it gained the teachers the biggest salary increase since the end of the war, because the Government indicated that it was prepared to postpone the operation of the new bill if a new salary agreement could be reached quickly. The existing Burnham agreement between the teachers and the Local Authorities had another fifteen months to run. In view of the Government's statement, negotiations were completed within a relatively short time, and new salary scales came into force on 1 October 1956, six months before they were due to operate. There was no doubt that the union had won a victory when Sir David Eccles tabled an amendment at the Committee Stage of the Superannuation Bill, postponing the operative date of the Bill from April to October, so that it coincided with the introduction of higher salaries.

Militancy and Professional Status

What has to be resolved is the apparent paradox of a membership which, judging by its participation in elections and its lukewarm interest in everyday union affairs, can hardly be called active, but which suddenly awakens and forces its leaders into a dynamic, concentrated campaign—not against its employers, but against the government of the day—and forces this government, in spite of its majority in Parliament, to postpone the operation of one of its proposed laws. What are the reasons for this awakening of the rank and file? How do they fit in with the general picture of membership participation?

One explanation is that the teachers' discontent, accumulated over the years, boiled over. The immediate post-war era had not been a prosperous one for them. Such salary increases as they received compared unfavourably with those of industrial workers and it is no exaggeration to state that the young teacher with a family could not live on his salary, but had to undertake some outside work to augment it. Nor did conditions of work come up to the expectations which the post-war enthusiasm for education aroused. Admittedly, new school buildings were erected in many areas, but the post-war rise in the birth-rate brought with it large classes, coupled with the extension of many non-teaching activities, giving the teacher more and more work outside the classroom. For the majority of the two-year-trained teachers, seeing their standards of living dwindle in a period of inflation, facing large classes, doing more work than ever before, and smarting under the educational economy measures of the early 1950s, the Superannuation Bill was the last straw. The 1 per cent extra demanded added insult to injury, and drove the profession to shed its respectability and force its leaders into a virile campaign.

In many quarters the N.U.T. is viewed as a 'respectable' organization, strictly non-political, not affiliated to the Trades Union Congress,* and not given to militant action. The Superannuation Campaign showed that this view ought to be modified and that teachers, like other trade unionists, can shed their respectability and display militancy when roused—and roused they certainly were in this dispute with the Government.

In the case of the Durham dispute the N.U.T. was motivated by different factors, and behaved like a professional association. A number of factors combined to ensure that the teachers would win their fight with the Durham County Council. There was the affront to the teachers' dignity, to their concept of professional status, and the implied threat to their professional freedom, which acted as the strongest unifying force. The jealousies and tensions, the manipulations of sectional interests, the internal rivalries, the uneasy compromises which for many years have prevented the union from developing a clear and forceful salary policy—all these were absent in the Durham dispute. This was not an occasion where the interests of head teachers and assistant staff diverged, as they did on a salary issue where special treatment for graduates embittered those without degrees, or where the primary school teacher could complain that favouritism was extended to his colleague in the secondary school. The issue was clear, simple, and understood by everyone who stood in a classroom. It was nothing more or less than an attempt on the part of their employers to coerce the teachers into compulsory unionism. Here was an attack on what was surely the right of every professional man—whatever conditions might prevail in industry— the right to join or not to join a union.

Teachers as a group have always been sensitive about their

* The N.U.T. eventually became affiliated to the T.U.C. on 1 May 1970.—[Ed.]

'professional status'. Indeed, the very fact that the fruits of this status—as enjoyed by doctors and lawyers in the shape of better salaries and independence from local control—have so far eluded them, makes them even more sensitive. One often hears, in teachers' meetings, complaints that all ills in education are due to the single fact that the teachers are not a self-governing profession, that they lack a body akin to the British Medical Council or to the Law Society, and that instead of managing their own affairs, they have to submit to the interference and petty tyranny of people whose only qualification to govern is the ability to poll a small number of votes in an election in which less than a third of the electors bother to vote, and in which the amount of rates payable is considered of far more importance than the process of education. Grumbles at meetings about interference by laymen, by governors of schools or members of education committees, may be exaggerated, but there is more than a grain of truth in such complaints, and most experienced teachers, and, in particular, heads of schools, could list many examples which show that 'professional status' for teachers is still very marginal, and that there is more than one local councillor who believes in making sure that the teachers 'keep their place' and 'don't get above themselves'. As a Durham colleague of the writer put it: 'Today they try to force us into a union, tomorrow they will tell us what to teach and how to teach it.' In Durham, the County Council went too far and succeeded in producing a situation which not only welded the teachers into one force, but gave their struggle the idealistic objective which could be relied upon to rouse the profession. The attack on the teachers by party politicians and the need to defend 'professionalism' acted as the greatest unifying force within the union itself, and not only prevented the disturbance of such unity by the many heterogeneous elements within the union, but actually made possible a close liaison with other associations of professional workers.

Teachers generally prefer to settle their problems in a 'respectable manner', but the superannuation dispute and the more recent conflict with the Government over salaries, show that however much professional status might be desired, teachers, like doctors, are also prepared to fight hard to improve their real income and to use the same methods (including the threat of strike action) as the traditional trade unionist. Militancy might not often come to the surface, but it cannot be concluded that teachers will under all conditions shun the behaviour patterns of the non-professional bodies. Reluctant as teachers might be to strike, their behaviour indicates that under certain conditions they will place the conventions of professional status second to their desire to achieve what they consider to be a fair standard of pay. The narrowing of income differentials between manual and non-manual employees has greatly altered the attitude of teachers towards the policy that they expect the N.U.T. to pursue in defence of their interests. It could well be that aggressive bargaining and a willingness to strike will become less repugnant to professional associations in the future as the differences between classes disappear, and as the conditions of employment of wage and salary earners are evened-up still more. There will, of course, always be factors that are likely to make teachers less prone to resort to militant action than some groups of wage-earners, but they will not arise so much, as in the past, from notions of status and respectability as from the responsibility that teachers feel for the children they educate. Thus the members of the National Union of Teachers are likely to be torn by conflicting desires, but it would be false to assume that teachers will in the future be as much deterred as they have been in the past from resorting to militant action in support of their economic interests, because they belong to a profession.

Notes

1 There are, of course, other similarities, notably in organizational structure, method of working and organization of external pressure groups, which arise from the functional adaptation which the N.U.T. has had to make as its size increased.

2 W. Roy, 'The National Union of Teachers—A Study of the Political Process within an Association of Professional Workers'. (Unpublished Ph.D. thesis, London University, 1963.)

3 Figures for 1960. See Ministry of Education Report, Cmnd. 1439, table 73, p. 298, and N.U.T. Membership Report for 1960.

4 B. C. Roberts, *op. cit.*

5 *Op. cit.*

6 J. Goldstein, *The Government of British Trade Unions* (Allen and Unwin, 1952).

7 Roberts, *op. cit.*

8 Roberts, *op. cit.*

9 See the leading article in *The Schoolmaster*, 23 November 1960.

10 Extract from Councillor E. F. Peart's broadcast in B.B.C. programme 'The World Today', 17 April 1951.

11 Statement issued to Press Bureau at N.U.T. Conference at Llandudno, 26 March 1951.

12 See 'Durham Teachers Will See It Through', *The Schoolmaster*, 30 May 1951.

13 Report of Ashton-under-Lyme, Mossley, and Limehurst Association, held on 30 November 1955.

14 Letter by C. W. Grainger, Nottingham, published in *The Schoolmaster*, 10 December 1955, p. 179.

Some Aspects of the T.U.C. and C.B.I. as Pressure Groups *

Richard Kimber and J. J. Richardson

I. The Trades Union Congress

Even though an organized interest may be aligned with (as in the case of business interests) or even affiliated to (as in the case of organized labour) a particular political party, it is not precluded from close contact with a government controlled by the opposing party. As the T.U.C. has itself pointed out, 'governments treat the T.U.C. as a sort of industrial Parliament',[1] since they need the benefit of trade union advice in formulating policies and indeed hope to secure trade union endorsement of (or at least compliance with) such policies. The fact that the T.U.C. bitterly opposed many of the key policies adopted by the Conservative Government elected in 1970 (in particular the Industrial Relations Act[2] and the wages 'freeze') did not prevent the Congress from continuing to participate in the work of a vast range of advisory committees alongside the Government. It is rarely appreciated just how extensive these formalized contacts are; they extend well beyond the confines of central government departments. The list below indicates in some detail the extent of the T.U.C.'s representation (as reported in June 1972) on official and unofficial bodies concerned with matters of interest and importance to trade unionists.

T.U.C. Representation

Advisory Unit for Service by Youth
Agricultural Marketing Act—
  Consumers' Committee
Army Recruitment, Working
  Party on
British Association for Commercial &
  Industrial Education
British Atlantic Committee

B.B.C. Further Education Advisory
  Council
British Council
British Council for Rehabilitation
British Epilepsy Association
British Film Institute
British Institute of Management
British Standards Institute

British Travel Association

Census of Distribution, Advisory
Committee

Census of Production, Advisory
Committee

Central After Care Council

Central Council for Physical
Recreation, Industrial
Sub-Committee

Central Training Council

Cinematograph Films Council

City & Guilds of London Institute,
Council

Civil Defence: Industrial Advisory
Committee

Coal Consumers' Councils

College of Special Education,
Governors

Committee for Education on
Operational Sciences in Industry

Commonwealth Institute

Community Relations Commission:
Advisory Committee on
Employment

Cotton Board Special Committee

Council of Industrial Design

Covent Garden Market Authority

Covent Garden Traffic Committee

Crime Prevention: Home Office
Standing Committee

Dental Estimates Board

Disabled Persons Employment
Council

Duke of Edinburgh's Award:
National Advisory Committee

Education for Management:
Advisory Council on

Energy Advisory Council

E.F.T.A. Consultative Committee

Executive Committee of European
Confederation of Free Trade
Unions in the Community: Panel
of E.F.T.A.-T.U.C. Representatives

Export Guarantees Advisory Council

Fatstock Guarantee Scheme: Joint
Advisory Panel

Fire Service Departmental Committee

Fleming Memorial Fund for Medical
Research

Food Hygiene Advisory Council

Hansard Society

Hillcroft College Governing Council

Hops Marketing Board

Industrial Estates Corporations

Industrial Health Advisory
Committee

Industrial Injuries Advisory Council

Industrial Safety Advisory Council

Industrial Training Boards Joint
Committee on Training for Work
Study Practitioners

Institute of Manpower Studies

Institute of Patentees and Inventors

Inter-Departmental Committee on
Condition of Tidal Thames

International Apprentice Competition

International Confederation of Free
Trade Unions

International Labour Organization

Iron & Steel Advisory Committee

Iron & Steel Consumers' Council

Joint Committee of T.U.C. and
London School of Economics

Legal Aid and Advice Act Advisory
Committee

Local Employment Acts, Ministry of
Technology Advisory Committee

London Transport Passengers'
Committee

London Youth Clubs: Industrial and
Commercial Committee

Mary Macarthur Holiday Home
Management Committee

Meat and Livestock Commission

Metrication Board

Monopolies Commission

National Advisory Council on
Education for Industry and
Commerce

National Committee for the
Certificate in Office Studies

National Economic Development
Council

National Electronics Council

National Examinations Board in
Supervisory Studies

National Industrial Fuel Efficiency
Service

National Institute for Adult Education

National Joint Advisory Council to
the Secretary for Employment

National Insurance Advisory
Committee

National Joint Committee of Working
Women's Organizations

National Savings Committee

National Youth Employment Council

Nuclear Safety Advisory Committee

Open University Advisory Committee
on Adult and Higher Education

Overseas Labour Consultative
Committee

Pneumoconiosis and Byssinosis
Benefit Board

Potato Marketing Board

Post Office Users National Council

Pre-Retirement Association

Radiological Protection Board:
Advisory Committee

Radiological Protection in Research
and Training: Standing Committee

Remploy Ltd

Retail Prices Index Advisory
Committee

Royal College of Art: Court

Royal Institute of International
Affairs

Royal Society for the Prevention of
Accidents

Ruskin College Governing Body

Schools Council

Social Science Research Council—
Industrial Relations Research
Unit Advisory Committee

Soldiers, Sailors & Airmen's Families
Association

St John Ambulance Association

Technical Education and Training
for Overseas Countries, Council on

Tool & Gauge Advisory Council

Trade Union Committee for the
European Free Trade Area

Transport Consultative Committee

Transport Co-ordinating Council for
London

Trade Union Advisory Committee
to O.E.C.D.

United Kingdom Automation Council

United Kingdom Committee for
U.N.I.C.E.F.

United Kingdom Committee for the
World Health Organization

United Kingdom Council for the
Freedom from Hunger Campaign

United Nations Association

Welbeck College Governors

Women's Employment Advisory
Committee

Women's National Commission

Wool Marketing Board

Workers' Educational Association

Work Measurement Standard Data
Foundation

Workmen's Compensation
Supplementation Board

Source: The A.B.C. of the T.U.C., June 1972.

In considering the importance of the T.U.C. and its key role in the policy process, it should of course be remembered that the Congress by no means speaks for all workers or indeed for all unions as several unions still remain unaffiliated to the T.U.C. Even in 1971, as white-collar unions began to join the Congress after long years of internal debate, the total membership stood at only just over ten million; as the table on page 113 indicates, the membership is drawn from a wide spectrum of British industry.

	Trade Group	No. of Unions	No. of Delegates	Membership	Affiliation Fees £ p
1	Mining and Quarrying	2	61	302,842	22,713·14
2	Railways	3	39	302,790	22,709·25
3	Transport (other than Railways)	9	91	1,761,998	132,149·85
4	Shipbuilding	2	13	127,285	9,546·38
5	Engineering, Founding and Vehicle Building	12	99	1,539,995	115,499·62
6	Technical Engineering and Scientific	5	45	359,949	26,996·17
7	Electricity	1	32	420,588	31,544·10
8	Iron and Steel and Minor Metal Trades	11	37	158,432	11,882·39
9	Building, Woodworking and Furnishing	9	54	375,628	28,172·10
10	Printing and Paper	7	66	403,199	30,239·93
11	Textiles	24	43	149,173	11,187·97
12	Clothing, Leather and Boot and Shoe	7	47	268,866	20,164·95
13	Glass, Ceramics, Chemicals, Food, Drink, Tobacco, Brushmaking and Distribution	11	70	476,269	35,720·17
14	Agriculture	1	19	100,000	7,500·00
15	Public Employees	11	135	1,358,403	94,116·83
16	Civil Servants	14	100	689,213	51,691·00
17	Professional, Clerical and Entertainment	11	50	350,002	26,250·16
18	General Workers	2	63	857,572	64,317·90
		142	1,064	10,002,204	*£742,401·91

* Fees payable in respect of the financial year ended December 31, 1970.
Total membership includes 7,607,289 men and 2,394,915 women members.

Source: T.U.C. Annual Report 1971.

113

The fact that the T.U.C. represents such a diverse membership is of course both a strength and a weakness of the organization as a pressure group. On the one hand it can claim, despite the fact that it represents only approximately half of the total labour force, that it speaks for the most significant fields of employment and that its view is therefore 'authoritative'. There is certainly evidence that governments take this view, as for example the Conservative Government's direct negotiations with the T.U.C. over the development of a prices and incomes policy during 1973. On the other hand the Congress, because of the diversity of interests represented within it, may find it difficult to reach a unanimous standpoint from which to confront the government. At least one large union represented on the General Council, for example, refused to participate in any negotiations with the Conservative Government over the operation of Phase Three of its incomes policy because it disagreed with the Council's general approach to the issue. Also the problem of resolving direct conflicts of interest within the T.U.C. can at times be serious. For example, the formulation of a policy for a fully integrated transport system in Britain presents considerable difficulties for the Congress in that the interests of railwaymen do not coincide with those of other transport workers such as lorry drivers. Any policy which advocated a substantial shift from road to rail could be seen as a direct challenge to the interest of the road haulage members of the T.G.W.U. to the advantage of members of the various railway unions (which themselves often disagree on railway policy!). There is, as Truman observes,[3] a danger that in referring to a particular category of groups like the unions we may imply a cohesion which does not really exist.

II. The Confederation of British Industry

In a similar way, the C.B.I. runs the risk of becoming so diverse that it may prove impossible to maintain cohesion within its ranks. Formed in 1965 as the result of a merger between the F.B.I., B.E.C., and N.A.B.M., it has pursued a policy of extending its membership towards becoming the 'voice of British business'. It may well be a laudable aim to wish to speak for the whole of British business (and it would certainly be convenient from the government's viewpoint), but it should be emphasized that 'business' is not homogeneous. For example the interests of small firms, often employing less than a hundred people, may well conflict with those of large conglomerates such as Imperial Tobacco. In fact the C.B.I. was sharply reminded of this divergence when a breakaway group formed the Society of

Independent Manufacturers (later to become The Smaller Businesses' Association). By 1971 the S.B.A. was claiming a membership of some 3,000 small companies.

Partly in response to this challenge, the C.B.I. has made special efforts to ensure that the interests of the small firm are not forgotten in the formulation of the Confederation's policies. Its by-laws, for example, suggest a minimum representation on the Confederation's committees and Regional Councils. In its first year it set up a Steering Group for Small Firms to ensure that their views were taken into account 'in a more systematic way'.[4] In the following year the Steering Group became a full Standing Committee of the C.B.I. and in 1970 this was increased in status yet again as the Smaller Firms Council. As the Confederation now includes nationalized industries as well as insurance and banking interests in its membership (see table below) the problems of maintaining unity are likely to increase.[5] Braunthal's study of the German experience suggests that the result of trying to represent a very diverse range of interests within one organization may well be a failure to formulate any clear policy which can unite the membership.[6]

C.B.I. Membership

In membership at 31 December 1972 were:

Companies:	Industrial	11,544
	Commercial	315
	Industrial/Commercial	9
	Public Sector Members	19
	Employer Organizations and Trade Associations	195
	Commercial Associations	37

Source: C.B.I. Annual Report 1972.

The C.B.I., like the T.U.C., is of course represented on a wide range of official and unofficial bodies and the list below indicates the extent of this representation (as at December 1971) ranging from the National Economic Development Council to the Keep Britain Tidy Group.

Government Bodies

CABINET OFFICE
National Economic Development Council
N.E.D.C. Committee on Management

Education Training and Development, and Sub-Committee on Marketing
E.D.C. for the Movement of Exports

Richard Kimber and J. J. Richardson

CUSTOMS AND EXCISE
Joint Customs Consultative
Committee

DEPARTMENT OF EDUCATION
AND SCIENCE
Centre for Information on Language
Teaching
National Advisory Council on Art
Education
National Advisory Council on
Education for Industry and
Commerce
National Committee for the Award
of the Certificate in Office Studies
Regional Advisory Councils for
Further Education

DEPARTMENT OF EMPLOYMENT
National Joint Advisory Council and
Committees
N.J.A.C. Committee on Methods of
Payment of Wages
Central Training Council and its
Committees
Retail Price Index Advisory
Committee
Industrial Health Advisory Committee
and its Sub-Committees
Industrial Safety Advisory Council and
its Committees
National Advisory Council on the
Employment of the Disabled
National Youth Employment Council
and its Scottish and Welsh
Advisory Committees

DEPARTMENT OF THE
ENVIRONMENT
Area Transport Users' Consultative
Committees
Central Transport Consultative
Committee
Regional Economic Planning Councils
Central Advisory Water Committee
Technical Committee on Discharge
of Toxic Solid Wastes

Standing Technical Committee on
Synthetic Detergents
Water Pollution Research Laboratory
Central Advisory Committee
Technical Committee on Water
Quality
Technical Committee on Offensive
Odours

DEPARTMENT OF HEALTH AND
SOCIAL SECURITY
Industrial Injuries Advisory Council
National Insurance Advisory
Committee
National Consultative Council on
Recruitment of Nurses and
Midwives
National Radiological Protection
Board Advisory Committee

DEPARTMENT OF TRADE AND
INDUSTRY
Anglo-Finnish Joint Commission for
Technological Collaboration
Census of Distribution Advisory
Committee
Census of Production Advisory
Committee
Standing Advisory Committee on
Patents
Trade Marks Advisory Group
Anglo Soviet Joint Commission
Queen's Award to Industry
Iron & Steel Consumer Council
Area Electricity Consultative Councils
Area Gas Consultative Councils
Energy Advisory Council
Industrial Coal Consumers Council
Simplification of International Trade
Procedures Board

FOREIGN AND COMMONWEALTH
OFFICE
Overseas Labour Consultative
Committee
O.L.C.C. Aid Sub-Committee

HOME OFFICE
Community Relations Commission
Advisory Committee on
Employment
Crime Prevention Committee
Standing Advisory Committee on
Dangerous Substances

MINISTRY OF DEFENCE
Advisory Committee on the
Territorial Army and Volunteer
Reserve

MINISTRY OF POSTS AND
TELECOMMUNICATIONS
Post Office Users' National Council
Post Office Advisory Committees

SCOTTISH OFFICE
Scottish Water Advisory Committee
Scottish Industry Liaison Committee
Scottish Economic Council
Highlands and Islands Development
Board
Scottish Law Commission
Valuation Advisory Council

TREASURY
National Savings Committee

WELSH OFFICE
Welsh Council

GOVERNMENT OF NORTHERN
IRELAND
Northern Ireland Economic Council
Ministry of Development Transport
Committee
Northern Ireland Training Council

INDEPENDENT ORGANIZATIONS
Advisory Council on Calibration and
Measurement
Anglo-Brazilian Joint Committee for
Economic Co-operation
Anglo-Yugoslav Trade Council

Association of British Chambers of
Commerce Language Committee
Australian British Trade Association,
British Council
British Executive Service Overseas
British-Mexican Businessmen's
Committee
British Industrial and Scientific Film
Association Council
British Institute of Management:
Council: Management Consulting
Services (Joint Committee)
British Productivity Council
British Shippers' Council
British Society for International
Understanding
British Standards Institution Executive
Council and Committees
British Trade Council in Germany
British Volunteer Programme
British Work Measurement Data
Foundation
Business and Industry Committee to
the Organization for Economic
Co-operation and Development
Careers Research and Advisory
Centre Advisory Panel
Central Fire Liaison Panel
Ceylon Association in London
C.I.R.E.T. (International Contact on
Business Tendency Surveys):
Co-ordination Committee
City and Guilds of London
Institute, Advisory Committee on
Fuel and Power Subjects,
Advisory Committee on Radiation
Safety Practice
City Panel on Takeovers and Mergers
Committee on Invisible Exports
Coombe Lodge (Further Education
Staff College)
Council for National Academic
Awards Business Studies Board
Council of European Industrial
Federations
Council of Industrial Federations of
E.F.T.A.

117

Council of Industry for Management Education

East Africa and Mauritius Association

Economic Affairs Committee, Canning House

E.F.T.A. Consultative Committee

English Speaking Union Current Affairs Committee

Fire Protection Association

Freight Transport Association

Harlow Occupational Health Service

India, Pakistan & Burma Association

Industrial Education and Research Foundation

International Apprentice Competition: U.K. Committee

International Association for the Exchange of Students in Technical Education

International Chamber of Commerce, British National Committee

International Fiscal Association

International Labour Organization

International Organization of Employers

Keep Britain Tidy Group

Metrication Board and Committees

National Council for Quality and Reliability

National Examinations Board for Supervisory Studies

National Institute of Industrial Psychology

National Marketing Council

National Reference Library of Science and Invention

River Authorities

Parliamentary and Scientific Committee

Public Schools Appointments Bureau

Royal Society for the Prevention of Accidents

Royal College of Art (Court)

Schools Council for the Curriculum and Examinations, and Committees

Sino-British Trade Council

Standing Committee of Statistics Users

Standing Conference on Local Support for Schools Science and Technology

Trade Marks, Patents and Designs Federation

Union of Industries of the European Community (U.N.I.C.E.)

United Kingdom Automation Council

United Kingdom/South Africa Trade Association

United Kingdom Standing Conference on the Second United Nations Development Decade

University Grants Committee

West Africa Committee

West Indies Trade Committee

Source: C.B.I. Annual Report 1971

III. T.U.C./C.B.I. Joint Co-operation

An interesting development concerning both the T.U.C. and the C.B.I. has been the emergence of a desire for joint action on certain policies. Thus in January 1967 the two organizations formed a Joint Committee 'to provide a forum in which representatives of the C.B.I. and T.U.C. can discuss informally matters of common interest'.[7] The monthly meetings of the Committee have been concerned with a wide range of topics including economic policy, prices and incomes policy, industrial relations, industrial training and the

118

position of small firms. The Joint Committee was, however, not intended to replace existing links between the two organizations or indeed prevent the formation of new ones. For example in 1966–7 a joint initiative was taken on a drive for more efficient use of manpower and in 1971 a joint approach to the Department of Health and Social Security on National Insurance medical certificates was initiated. Similarly, in the absence of government legislation, the two organizations entered discussions concerning a joint initiative to encourage better safety arrangements in industry. More recently a C.B.I./T.U.C. Conciliation and Arbitration Service has been set up. Relations between the two bodies have normally been good (apart from a short period in 1969 when the T.U.C. decided to discontinue the Joint Committee)[8]—so much so that the T.U.C. has suggested to its members that where a trade union is finding difficulty in gaining recognition 'the T.U.C. might be able to help by approaching the Confederation of British Industry to put pressure on a firm if it is in membership of the C.B.I.'.[9] It would be wrong therefore to assume that because the C.B.I. and T.U.C. appear to represent conflicting interests within society that they will necessarily oppose each other in all issues. Indeed both organizations have engaged in talks with the government on managing the economy and any lasting economic policies will no doubt depend upon the agreement of all three parties.[10]

Notes

1 Royal Commission on Trade Unions & Employers' Associations, *Selected Written Evidence Submitted to the Royal Commission*, 1968, p. 13.

2 For details of the T.U.C.'s opposition to the passage of the Industrial Relations Bill see *T.U.C. Annual Report*, 1971, pp. 341–77.

3 See our *Introduction*, p. 12.

4 *C.B.I. Annual Report*, 1966, p. 10.

5 They would increase drastically if the proposed 'Confederation of British Business' was actually formed (see *The Times*, 16 November 1972).

6 G. Braunthal, *The Federation of German Industry in Politics*, New York, 1965.

7 *C.B.I. Annual Report*, 1967, p. 34.

8 *C.B.I. Annual Report*, 1969, p. 34.

9 *Trade Union Congress Structure & Development*, T.U.C., September 1970, p. 4.

10 For a short description of the talks see *C.B.I. Annual Report*, 1972, pp. 8–9.

The Re-Emergence of Ideological Politics in Great Britain: The Campaign for Nuclear Disarmament*

Henry J. Steck

In accord with our own peculiar *zeitgeist*, writers of a liberal, empiricist, and reformist disposition have enthusiastically hailed the 'end of ideology'.[1] There is no disputing that old-style ideological politics are quite dead. Evidence accumulates, however, to suggest that we are now witnessing the birth of a new style of ideological politics. In this country, the new moods are expressed in several new socialist journals, in the Peace Movement, and most sharply in the militant segments of the anti-segregation movement. In Gaullist France, there has been a slight rejuvenation of an ideological temper, most noticeably in the *Parti Socialist Unifié* and the intellectuals, publicists, and discussion groups connected with it. The earliest expression of this renaissance occurred in Great Britain where the rapid emergence of a 'ban the Bomb' movement, the Campaign for Nuclear Disarmament (C.N.D.), signalled the revival of ideological politics in the West.

Even now C.N.D. is the largest 'ban the Bomb' movement in the West.[2] Certainly in its heyday its unique demand—that Britain unilaterally renounce the manufacture, use, and possession of the H-Bomb and pursue a policy of 'positive neutralism'—and its characteristic technique—the annual Easter week-end march between the Atomic Weapons Research Establishment at Aldermaston and Trafalgar Square—had a profound influence on British political debate. Altogether, the activities of C.N.D. and its off-shoots have come as a surprise to those Americans who have long admired the British propensity for quietly staying within the political boundaries and playing the game according to the rules.

* Reprinted by permission of the University of Utah, Copyright holder, from the *Western Political Quarterly*, vol. 18, no. 1, March 1965, pp. 87–103. The author wishes to thank the Ford Public Affairs Committee at Cornell University for making possible a trip to London for the purpose of gathering materials for research in this and related subjects. He also wishes to acknowledge the assistance of Mr Harvey Simmons in the preparation of this paper, which was completed in March 1963.

120

In this paper, my concern will be with the British context of the formation of C.N.D. as a mass movement. More specifically, I will deal with (1) the relative absence of organized protest to atomic policies prior to 1957 and the emergence in 1957 of the broadly based opposition to these policies which led to the creation of C.N.D.; and (2) the political and social factors which allowed C.N.D. to grow so rapidly.

Before turning to C.N.D., it is worth recalling several features of the British political scene which are important for an understanding of its growth. First, British political life and the communications media are national in scope: at the same time, they are London-centred. Therefore a political cause worth its salt must make its name in London if it is then to make its name in the country. For a pressure group on-the-make, there is one set of politicians and administrators to influence—they are located in the corridors of Whitehall, the committee rooms of Smith Square, and the lobbies of Westminster. There is, further, one set of journalists whose ears must be caught—they are (figuratively) located on Fleet Street. The informed political public is small, but it is relatively agreed on the issues it thinks important. While it may be difficult to shape public opinion, it is easy to gain its attention: a good demonstration in Trafalgar Square will usually do the trick.

Secondly, an embryonic mass movement can draw upon the habits of political participation nourished by the party system. As both Labour and Conservative are mass parties, individual political commitment and regular participation for non-electoral purposes are familiar to political activist and casual party member alike. Neither shies away from non-party 'causes' as his American counterpart might. Finally, there is an established historical tradition of organized mass dissent. C.N.D. represents no new departure from earlier forms of protest politics in Britain: the Chartists, the Anti-Corn Law League, the suffragettes, the unemployment marches of the thirties, the various popular front movements, even the fascists—all these have made extra-Parliamentary agitation and moral crusades accepted modes of political activity. Marching, mass meetings, public demonstrations, mass lobbying at Westminster are all legitimate techniques of making demands on the political system.

When C.N.D. came into being, then, these factors assured it of both an audience willing to listen to its arguments and a potential following well socialized in the forms of extra-Parliamentary political action. Its initial success was due to the purposeful response of thousands of persons to the pleas of a few leaders. Its success could only have come about in a society where a tradition of dissent

121

could be quickly activated by changes in the intellectual, political, and social climate.

I

Before 1957, there was no significant organized opposition to the Government's nuclear policies. Very solemn statements about the horrors of atomic war were frequently and widely made,[3] but they did nothing to disturb established agreement that the Bomb was necessary to British power. What is surprising is not the wide consensus regarding the Bomb, but the relative absence—in a society with a tradition of protest—of organized protest against Government policy. Even those political groups on the left—the Labour party, the left-wing of the Labour party, and the pacifists—from which some opposition might have originated were quiet.

Little could be expected from the leadership of the Labour party. For despite a residual antipathy to power politics [4] Labour leaders throughout the early and mid-fifties were so committed to the foreign policy of Ernest Bevin as to be politically, ideologically, and psychologically incapable and unwilling to oppose those policies when continued by a Tory Government. In 1955, for example, Labour leaders first supported the Government's decision to manufacture the Bomb and then, in the General Election, successfully defused the controversy surrounding the Government's decision.[5]

The diffidence of the Labour Left is more surprising. From 1946 the Labour Left in Parliament had consistently opposed the cold war policies of Bevin and Eden. Despite this consistent opposition, it failed to make the Bomb either a major public or Parliamentary issue in any sustained way.[6] In 1954, to be sure, there was a minor revolt and a short-lived public campaign; and in 1955 the left rebelled against Labour's acquiescence in the Government's decision to manufacture the Bomb.[7] But in neither instance did the left, in Parliament or out, follow through in any significant manner.[8] Indeed, by 1956 the official leadership hardly hesitated in accepting a mild left-wing resolution 'expressing fears' at the dangers of nuclear tests and 'requesting' the party to 'work toward the abolition of all *atomic* weapons'.[9] Nor, finally, did the major pacifist groups attempt to mount an anti-Bomb campaign aimed at the public—even though a substantial segment of the public did not think Britain should make the Bomb.[10]

Despite their lack of organized protest, however, the Labour Left and the pacifists constituted the infrastructure of a mass movement. The left was served by two weeklies, *Tribune* and *New States-man*, while pacifist views were expressed in the weekly *Peace News*. The left had, further, a Parliamentary base in the loose Bevanite group between 1951 and 1955. The revival of the old Labour Pacifist Fellowship as the Labour Peace Fellowship gave pacifism a fresh base in the Parliamentary Labour party.[11] There were, moreover, several other national pacifist groups whose activities had never ceased. These groups subsequently initiated the first public anti-Bomb demonstrations.[12] Ideologically, the Labour Left had developed a fairly distinctive foreign policy.[13] The pacifists, of course, had little trouble in adapting pacifism to the new situation. Finally, there existed an élite of left-wing dissent: a network of notables— political and non-political, Labourites and non-Labourites, M.P.s and non-M.P.s—who had worked (and were working) together in the multiplicity of permanent and temporary groups which always exist on the British left. Well known to each other, they shared not only similar political attitudes, but also a common experience in techniques of persuasion and protest activities. They were known to left-wing activists throughout the country. By 1957, then, all the elements of organization existed. The left needed only to be awakened from its sleep.

II

Early in 1957, the Government announced its decision to test the H-Bomb. Thereafter, the situation changed rapidly. For the first time, serious doubts about Government policies were expressed by non-left-wing elements.[14] Despite these worthy pronouncements, heaviest opposition was concentrated on the non-Parliamentary left. Among non-pacifists, the opposition was led by *Tribune*. The *New Statesman*, by contrast, initially strayed little from the policy of the Labour party, warning in April against foregoing 'all tests unilaterally and unconditionally'.[15] But by autumn the *New Statesman* was firmly in the unilateralist camp, hinting at a neutralist position[16] and opening its pages to J. B. Priestley and Bertrand Russell.[17] By then, however, *Tribune* was leading the opposition: its masthead flaunted the slogan, 'The Paper That Leads the Anti-H-Bomb Campaign.'

As early as February, *Tribune* had already pointed to the 'one way only for defence', 'a bold and active policy of securing peace by negotiation'.[18] Throughout the year it stridently maintained its pressure.[19] In September it urged that 'Britain should give up the

123

H-Bomb . . . unilateral disarmament is no riskier than disarmament on terms. In fact, it has probably become the only kind of disarmament with any chance of success.'[20]

While lending aid to the emerging pacifist campaigns, *Tribune* sought to confine the anti-Bomb fight within the existing political framework, i.e., within the Labour party. The 'H-Bomb maniacs' could be stopped, it insisted, 'only if the Labour Movement shakes itself from its lethargy'.[21] It thus called on the Labour leadership to organize

> a nation-wide campaign, starting with an official Trafalgar Square demonstration. . . . A vote of censure on the Government should be moved by the Labour Opposition in Parliament. Every church organization in the country should be approached officially by the Labour Party. . . . every by-election should be used to shout aloud the fact. . . . Every speech by the Party's leaders, every political broadcast should hammer home the same theme. The conscience of the nation must be stirred. Only Labour can do it.[22]

Within the Parliamentary Labour party, the response to these pleas came not from the official leadership, which initially was adamant on behalf of Britain's Bomb.[23] It came from left-wing and centre Labour opinion. This combination was sufficiently strong to stir the leadership into qualifying its policy on testing by accepting a compromise which urged renewed British initiative for international negotiation and proposed a limited unilateral suspension of British tests.[24] In September, a handful of Labour M.P.s, many of whom had already spoken from other platforms, turned from limited Parliamentary action to organize an 'H-Bomb Campaign Committee'.[25] Considerations of intra-party politics forced left-wing M.P.s to restrict their activities.[26] They were, in any case, reacting to events, not directing them. Some weeks earlier more than a hundred resolutions, submitted by Constituency Labour parties for the Conference agenda, contained demands ranging from moderate opposition to nuclear testing to more extreme demands for the unilateral renunciation of nuclear weapons. Significantly, many echoed *Tribune* in calling on the N.E.C. to 'mobilize' the movement by intensifying pressure in the House and by organizing a mass, national campaign.[27]

Clearly, the rank and file were rallying ideologically to the banners of *Tribune* and, to a lesser extent, the *New Statesman*.[28] These two journals gave direction to widespread discontent with both the Government's and the Labour party's policies. Persons with no commitment to existing pacifist organizations turned not to the Parliamentarians with their narrowly based H-Bomb Campaign Committee, but to these journals. Three lonely souls in South

Croydon, for example, appealed in the correspondence column of the *New Statesman* to Priestley, Russell, and others 'to form an organization whose principal object is for Britain to abandon the H-Bomb'.[29] 'Critic' (*New Statesman*) referred to 'a steady stream of letters asking us to hurry up with an anti-suicide organization. They must address themselves', he said, 'for the moment to the Council for the Abolition of Nuclear Weapons Tests'.[30]

While left-wing opinion was coalescing against the Government's nuclear policies, pacifist protest was rapidly organizing. The spearhead of organized opposition was the National Council for the Abolition of Nuclear Weapons Tests (N.C.A.N.W.T.).[31] 'Formed by some pacifists in the offices of the National Peace Council,'[32] N.C.A.N.W.T. preceded the formation of the Labour H-Bomb Campaign Committee.[33] Despite its pacifist origins, however, N.C.A.N.W.T. spoke for more than the pacifist community. Geographically and politically it was a national organization. Thus, its original demands were confined to urging the unilateral suspension of tests, a limited policy which diverse opinions could agree upon; thus, non-pacifists and non-unilateralists spoke from its platforms. By December, regional and local councils were active.[34] As none of its leaders were M.P.s, its policies and activities were free from the constraints of party politics and the ambitions of party politicians. Untouched by years of disillusion and compromise, pacifist leaders and activists could more fervently preach the moral case against the Bomb. The moralistic content of this case had great appeal to young people, among whom a pronounced distrust of conventional politics existed. N.C.A.N.W.T., and later C.N.D., could claim to be above party politics. C.N.D. was formed directly from N.C.A.N.W.T. The latter left its impression on the former in terms of leadership, technique, policy, emotional appeal and ambience.[35]

At the same time that the National Council was organized, another group, the Emergency Committee for Direct Action Against Nuclear War (known as the Direct Action Committee [D.A.C.]) was formed to 'challenge' the Christmas Island tests directly.[36] If, in its outlook, membership, and methods, N.C.A.N.W.T. remained within the sphere of legitimate political action, D.A.C. turned away from conventional structures of party and pressure group politics and from accepted norms of political action.[37] D.A.C. was, however, only the latest offspring of an old tradition.[38] It would be incorrect to associate D.A.C. primarily with pacifism: behind it lay the methods and philosophies not only of individual protest, pacifism, and non-violent passive resistance, but also of civil disobedience, of direct political and industrial action, of anarchism, and of syndicalism.[39] The technique of the sit-down, for example, was first used against the Bomb in 1952 when '11 pacifists in Operation Gandhi sat down outside the War Office and were fined 30s. apiece'. It was employed periodically thereafter.[40]

By late 1957, then, the personnel, policies, and techniques were ready. Growing opposition to the Bomb, political developments elsewhere, and rank-and-file pressure all indicated the need for a new organization to consolidate the diverse anti-testing groups and to mobilize mass support behind a programme of nuclear disarmament.[41] This step was taken early in 1958 when representatives from the Labour Left and the pacifists [42] met and decided to inaugurate a campaign for nuclear disarmament. N.C.A.N.T.W. closed down, 'handing over its staff, files, offices, and funds' to C.N.D.[43] An inaugural public meeting was held in February, and in the following months similar meetings were held throughout the country. At Easter, the first Aldermaston march, organized by D.A.C. and taken over by C.N.D., was held. Demonstrations, meetings, and pamphleteering continued at an intensive pace. By late spring, C.N.D. was a successfully established mass organization.

III

The decision to test the H-Bomb was the occasion, not the cause, for the emergence of C.N.D. For the causes, one must look beyond that decision to the convergence of a number of political and social developments.

The first of these was the impact on public opinion of the Government's defence policies, especially those associated with the then Minister of Defence, Duncan Sandys.[44] Briefly, the Sandys policy, which, as Lawrence W. Martin emphasizes, 'created the impression of being a new departure', was based explicitly upon the doctrine of deterring any level of aggression by threatening massive nuclear retaliation.[45] This blunt dependence on a first-strike strategy came at a time when Dulles was moving away from his policy of massive retaliation, at a time when the Soviet Union was acquiring its own nuclear retaliatory power, and at a time when Britain was increasingly unable to bear the economic burden of a sophisticated and expensive military technology. Sandys' policies were, therefore, bound to cause widespread consternation.[46]

But the shifting arguments employed after 1957 to defend this policy only exacerbated critics and gave rise to a certain lack of confidence in the intellectual integrity of the Government. To nuclear disarmers, the Sandys 'defence' policy seemed a flimsy web of inaccurate conclusions drawn from dubious premises.[47] With the growth of Soviet thermonuclear power, for example, it was evident that should the deterrent fail—and Britain's contribution was really too slight to affect the credibility of the Western deterrent—Britain would be consumed in the ensuing holocaust. The last argument became a direct not a remote probability when, also in 1957, Britain agreed to the construction on British soil of American missile bases. British strength thus rested, as one impartial observer has put it, 'not in capacity to wage war, but in willingness to face national annihilation'.[48] For the nuclear disarmer, Britain was reduced to the status of an off-shore launching pad for the Pentagon.

The Government further claimed that an independent deterrent was necessary in the event that an increasingly vulnerable America might not 'go on looking at things in quite the same way'.[49] And though it soon abandoned this claim,[50] it was clear to critics after the abandonment in 1960 of the Blue Streak missile that Britain was destined to tag along behind the United States. When both the Government and the Labour leadership insisted that the deterrent enlarged Britain's diplomatic influence and reduced her dependence on the United States, their opponents could point to Britain's shamefaced retreat at Suez or to Eisenhower's reluctance to go to the summit even in the face of British prodding as evidence that possession of nuclear weapons added little to British influence on American policy. The Government had also argued that an independent nuclear deterrent was the most economic deployment of resources. But after Blue Streak, it was clear—despite the Government's reliance on the problematic, American-made Skybolt missile—that the expense of developing and maintaining a complicated nuclear weapons system was far too costly for Britain

Possession of an increasingly incredible deterrent seemed neither to enhance Britain's military position nor to preserve her slipping diplomatic stature. Those critics who were unilateralists now protested that the Government, not they, was playing with the safety of the country. The only purpose of Britain's Bomb was, as they saw it, to ensure that, should war occur, Britain would commit national suicide while contributing to the revengeful destruction of the Soviet Union—all, they would add bitterly, in the name of Western civilization. Despite the apocalyptic quality of much of the polemics, the critical analysis of the nuclear disarmers was far from wrong. This was especially true as the Government's policies came less to reflect reasoned strategic-military considerations than a mixture of psychological fears and political rationalizations.[51] What is crucial for an understanding both of C.N.D.'s rapid growth and of the guarded willingness of the informed public to listen to it, is that the intellectual attack against the policy came not only from the nuclear disarmers or a small group of expert critics. 'A sense of disquiet', wrote Alastair Buchan of the Institute for Strategic Studies, 'stretches all the way from the Aldermaston marchers at one end of the spectrum, to the military and civilian planners behind the scenes at Whitehall. ... On the Right as well as the Left, in Whitehall as well as in Fleet Street—the argument for and against the British deterrent ... can be considered within the rather more dispassionate framework of strategic and economic planning.'[52]

C.N.D. neither 'falsified' nor 'simplified' the alternatives open to Great Britain. The alternatives the Sandys doctrine presented were clear: the easy slogan—'red or dead'—acquired for the British a relevance lacking in the United States. For while Americans could reply that not all would be dead, the British—as the 1957 Defence White Paper admitted—could not. They would all be quite dead.[53] This prospect, combined with a growing concern over the effect of nuclear fallout, created an intellectual and emotional atmosphere receptive to the cool arguments and heated slogans of C.N.D. Wayland Young concluded that 'together with the extremist Direct Action Committee, the C.N.D. has nearly broken down the wall of silence with which, out of timidity and doubt, the right and centre press, the B.B.C. and I.T.V., originally met criticism of the Government's defence policy'.[54]

A second set of factors which accounts for the success of C.N.D. was the abandonment of the Labour Left by Aneurin Bevan in 1957 and the political situation within the Labour party after 1958. Of the two, Bevan's action is perhaps more important for the origins of C.N.D. Even before his resignation from the Labour Government in 1951, Bevan was the acknowledged leader of the Labour Left. During the years in which he challenged the policies and leadership of the party, he exerted over his Parliamentary followers and the rank and file a personal authority rare in British politics. What power or influence the left had depended on Bevan's singular political talents. Following Gaitskell's election to the leadership, Bevan began slowly and erratically to accommodate himself to the new leadership. With his appointment late in 1956 to the shadow Foreign Secretaryship, the left was probably confident that their opinions would acquire an influence they had never had.

These hopes were, however, decisively smashed, and smashed by Bevan himself. At the 1957 Party Conference, he rejected for the Executive a resolution calling for the unilateral renunciation of nuclear weapons. In itself, his position was really no surprise—he had never opposed the manufacture or use of the H-Bomb.[55] What was surprising was his vehemence. In a scene unmatched since Bevin drove Lansbury from the leadership, Bevan insisted the unilateral disarmament would send a British Foreign Secretary 'naked into the conference chamber' and he dismissed unilateralism with contempt as 'an emotional spasm'.[56] The delegates were stunned, angry, and bitter. But Bevan's dismissal of them was final.[57] Paradoxically, however, Bevan's action liberated the left, which for many years had been, as the *New Statesman* recognized, 'an army without much discipline or political coherence'. Now freed from its own 'cult of personality', the left moved rapidly to achieve both discipline and political coherence. Following the Brighton Conference, the decision to set up an independent, anti-Bomb organization was reached.[58]

But if Bevan's defection released enormous amounts of ideological energy, C.N.D., not the Labour party, was the beneficiary. It was to be expected that the Labour party would not adopt a policy entirely acceptable to the nuclear disarmers. But, more importantly, it also failed to provide an organizational outlet for the energies of party members who were C.N.D. supporters. At the national level, the Labour party made only a feeble effort to counteract the appeal of C.N.D.; in April 1958, it conducted an abortive campaign whose purpose, as even Labour leaders tacitly confessed, was to thwart the effect C.N.D. was already having.[59] At the local level, the Labour party failed to provide a viable and attractive outlet for young people.[60] C.N.D. and the Youth Campaign had little competition. Though the Labour party attacked C.N.D. as a splinter group, it never proscribed C.N.D. membership, and party militants were never forced to choose between C.N.D. and the Labour party.

As the party became the primary institutional target for C.N.D., the party hierarchy found itself unable to cope with C.N.D.'s emotional and intellectual appeal.[61] Because of the propensity of Labour leaders to compromise—at least verbally—Labour's policies underwent change not only in 1957, but also in 1958, in 1959, and in 1960. The unilateralists were thus certain they would eventually succeed on their own terms. In 1960, they very nearly did. Following a complex intra-party struggle on several issues, the Party Conference approved a policy of unilateral nuclear disarmament.[62] Though this decision was reversed the following year, the long agony of the Labour party was both cause and effect of C.N.D.'s successes.

A third factor contributing to the rapid success of C.N.D. was the end of the lethargy which characterized British politics for many years. The social, cultural, and political background of this change cannot, unfortunately, be dealt with here.[63] But the changes in the climate of opinion and feeling—intangible though they may appear— are of major political importance. If many had been 'depoliticized' by the austere years, the events of 1956–7 produced an intensive repoliticization. Two specifically political events contributed to these changes: the crises of Suez and Hungary and the appearance of the New Left to which they gave rise.

The Suez adventure was the first major act of foreign policy since the war undertaken by a Government without at least the tacit agreement of the Opposition party.[64] In Parliament, Gaitskell and Bevan led the Labour party in an attack against Eden Government so intense, so impassioned, and so violent that at one point the sitting of the House was suspended by Mr Speaker. Outside Parliament, the Labour Movement as a whole conducted a vigorous 'Law—Not War' campaign. For a week several hundred demonstrations were held in all parts of Britain, and these were climaxed by two large meetings in Trafalgar Square and Albert Hall. For the first time in years, the Labour party had resorted to extra-Parliamentary, though not unconstitutional, forms of opposition. The campaign against the Government gave the militant rank and file a new taste for mass action. The trauma of Suez destroyed the 'sham fight' at Westminster, and the myth that Labour had stopped the Government gave politics a meaning it had for so long lacked. Here is a lyrical picture of the response of Labour's rank and file:

> Such an upsurge of enthusiasm . . . had not been seen since 1945. From factories, from offices, from colleges, from groups of neighbours who had made their streets into strongpoints of peace, deputations swarmed to lobby their MPs. Everywhere—at factory gates, pitheads, docksides, shopping centres—meetings were held, petitions signed, telegrams dispatched. Trade unions . . . expressed the anger of the working class. The protest spilled out into the streets. . . . [The demonstration in Trafalgar Square] was the greatest demonstration in our history concerned with any issue that was not one of domestic policy.[65]

Peter Worsley describes the broader effects as follows: 'For the young . . . Suez was a devastating experience in disillusion . . . the peculiar intensity of the reaction . . . arose from the conjunction of the Old Left reacting to Old Imperialism, and the new young liberal generation reacting to the betrayal of all they had been taught of a reformed Britain, the dutiful servant of the United Nations and of the Free World.'[66]

Once the dust had settled, the militants were in no mood to seal envelopes for county council elections. There is no doubt that the moods of Suez and the emotional force behind the founding of

C.N.D. are related. There was, further, a direct connection between the techniques of opposition used during Suez and those later employed by C.N.D. The relation is clearly reflected in frequent, left-wing demands for a campaign against the Bomb 'along the lines of the Suez Campaign'.[67]

As the Suez experience rejuvenated the Old Left and awakened the hitherto apolitical youth, the de-Stalinization campaigns and the events in Hungary led to the emigration from the British Communist party of a qualitatively significant number of intellectuals and political activists.[68] Hungary was, one of them wrote, 'the cockcrow' which 'lifted the spell of impotence'.[69] The consequences of these events for the anti-Bomb campaign were varied and far-reaching. On the one hand, they caused an influx to the non-Labour left (and C.N.D. must be placed in this category) of a vast reservoir of political intelligence, energy, and expertise. Intellectually and emotionally, on the other, it freed many leftists from a certain enthraldom with the Soviet Union, and thus made possible a coherent and sometimes sophisticated statement of the noncommunist, but anti-Nato, anti-'Anglo-American', anti-cold war position.[70]

The conjunction of the turmoil within the Communist party during 1956 and the revival of political militancy in the universities and elsewhere during Suez resulted in the birth of the New Left.[71] Primarily an intellectual movement composed of young academics, students and professionals, the New Left, both in its theorizing and its overt politics, has been independent of both the Labour party and the Communist party. The political viewpoint of the New Left was expressed initially, but not exclusively, through two journals, the *New Reasoner* and the *Universities and Left Review*, and subsequently through the *New Left Review*, created by the merger of the former two. The New Left also was articulated in New Left Clubs throughout the country.

Ideologically, the New Left represented a long-needed attempt at a revival of socialist theorizing. It sought definitions of socialism which would break with the sterile categories of Stalinist thinking on the Communist left and with the ultra-moderate tones of 'Labourism' on the Labour right. In its international outlook, and this provided an important intellectual link with C.N.D., the New Left saw the cold war as the source of both the conservative attitudes and centralized power structures prevalent in the West and of the widespread political apathy these engendered. In terms of policies, the New Left moved more rapidly than C.N.D. toward a position of 'positive neutralism'. New Left thinkers were the ideological vanguard of C.N.D. policies.

For the New Left, C.N.D. was 'the most remarkable single political phenomenon of the decade'[72] and the success of C.N.D. represented an important revolutionary (in the special sense used by various New Left writers) potential.[73] C.N.D. was recognized as one of the essential bases of the New Left and, in turn, the New Left was a powerful sustaining force within the unilateralist movement. There was clearly a symbiotic relationship between New Left thinking, journals, and clubs and C.N.D.[74] The interpenetration of the two, especially at the university level was common. In some areas, New Left clubs and the Young C.N.D. were probably different organizational titles for essentially the same groups of activists. In Croydon, for example, the New Left Club 'evolved from the spontaneous demands of those people within Croydon Y.C.N.D. and the Croydon Young Socialists'. Elsewhere, New Left clubs arose directly from defections from the Communist party. While it is difficult to generalize about the relationship between the New Left and C.N.D., it is probably correct to say that C.N.D. groups preceded New Left clubs and that the latter arose out of the desire 'for some independent socialist body, in which topics of a *wider scope* could be discussed and acted upon'.[75] The importance of the New Left lay precisely in this 'wider scope', though this must be understood in ideological terms. Its major weaknesses lay in its lack of a non-university base—or even a university base considerably broader than the London-Oxford axis—the resistance to it on the part of the established Labour Left, a certain 'sectarian' tendency, and persistent organizational troubles.[76]

Nonetheless, the importance of the New Left to C.N.D. cannot be underestimated. Its clientele were in many instances the most highly politicized and active of C.N.D. supporters, and whereas not all who marched were of the New Left, the latter were thinking in unilateralist and neutralist terms from the start.[77] The New Left provided both organizational expertise and ideological leadership. As their intellectual position was more coherent, more articulate, more developed, and broader than the demands of C.N.D., New Left intellectuals—especially those in universities—exerted an influence beyond their numbers. Its strategic position in the university community at a time when students' political awareness and moral protest was at an extremely high pitch (if only among a minority), made the New Left a significant force in shaping C.N.D. policy and sustaining C.N.D. activity.[78]

The preceding discussion is not, of course, exhaustive. At least two other factors require brief mention. First, the situation in the trade union movement began to change between 1955 and 1957. On the one hand, there was a discernible rise in industrial militancy, and the left hoped that this quickened feeling could be directed into political channels. On the other, the accession of the left-wing trade union leader, Frank Cousins, to the General Secretaryship of the Transport and General Workers' Union—hitherto the fortress of right-wing trade union political attitudes—raised the possibility that, for the first time, a durable left-wing coalition could be built upon the trade union bloc vote at the Labour Party Conference.[79]

Secondly, C.N.D. was able to acquire a degree of freedom, and even respectability from the position taken toward it by the Communist party. From the start the Communist party withheld organizational support from C.N.D. and opposed its unilateralist policies.[80] The chief reason for the Communist party's standoffish attitude—aside from C.N.D.'s noncommunist origins—appears to have been the diplomatic emphasis of the Soviet Union on the need for international, i.e., multilateral, agreements regarding nuclear weapons.[81] While the Communist party recognized that C.N.D. was a valuable part of the 'peace movement',[82] it preferred to support the policies approved by the previous Labour Party Conference, and, according to its view, being insufficiently carried out by the Labour party and the T.U.C. George Matthews argued, 'The Communist Party believes that the essential urgency at present is to organize public opinion, to unify all the powerful activities for peace which are taking place around a common policy already agreed on almost unanimously by the T.U.C., the Communist Party, and the trade union and co-operative conferences. This is why we feel to put the emphasis on unilateral renunciation of the bomb is tactically incorrect.'[83] Unilateralism was regarded by the Communist party as a diversion from the main business of the peace movement. At the same time, the Communists displayed a pronounced distrust of the 'anti-political-party' tendencies in C.N.D., and called for 'a special effort' to associate with and influence the Labour movement.[84] The Communist party also urged the coordination of all peace activities on the basis of a common policy—preferably that of its front organization, the British Peace Committee.[85]

Whatever the reasons for its stand, the Communist party, until May 1960, continued to hold that unilateralism was a divisive force obscuring the need for international agreement on disarmament. There is evidence to suggest, however, that this line was unpopular with Communist rank-and-file members and that some unofficial, informal cooperation with C.N.D. took place at the local and trade union level.[86] For C.N.D., the effects of the attitude of the Communist party were several: first, it was freed from the taint of Communist participation; secondly, its energies were not taxed by the internal consequences which might have arisen from Communist endorsement and participation. C.N.D. was thus able to defend its uniqueness and its honesty against its right-wing detractors.[87]

IV

Whatever the persuasiveness of its case, the rapid growth of C.N.D. was only partially due to the national debate over defence policy. In typically British style, it emerged within an established tradition of extra-Parliamentary protest. But the appearance of organized agitation against the Bomb during 1957 was due to a unique concatenation of political and social circumstances. Until Suez the political land was dry and still. The bland acceptance of the welfare state by the Conservative party, the wide areas of agreement between the two parties, the intellectual and political sluggishness of the ultra-respectable Labour leadership, the ultimate sterility of the Bevanite struggle—all these robbed the political scene of anything more than surface meaning. The 'Establishment' combined with Tory prosperity, it seemed, deprived the politically active of the 'good, brave causes' Osborne's Jimmy Porter spoke of and consigned all dispute to the quiet reasonableness of a B.B.C. round table. For the intensely political, the arrival of C.N.D. was the first stage in a broader struggle to alter the structures of power both domestic and international. C.N.D. must be seen as part of the broad revolt against the 'Establishment'.[88]

C.N.D. appeared to be an alliance between a generation nostalgic for the thirties and a new generation which had known only the politics of austerity. For the latter, C.N.D. was more than a reaction to the even rhythms of party politics or the social strains of the welfare state society. It was also an intense reaction to Britain's diminishing role as a world power. In 1954, Leon Epstein accurately anticipated this development. 'Perhaps in time', he wrote, 'neutralism would have a future in Britain. Its blandishments could become attractive to a new generation reared entirely in the consciousness of the nation's secondary power status.'[89] But far from accepting Britain's world position complacently, the new generation acted as though Britain could still determine the course of world affairs. This assumption in their argument was contingent upon another, namely, that a change in Britain's foreign policy must be accompanied by political and social change at home.

Even at the start, C.N.D. represented a movement of social and

134

political protest. Its demands looked beyond short-term decisions on foreign policy to a redefinition of British politics. Its simple cry— 'Ban The Bomb'—was moral and political in content, absolutist in tone, and, in consequence, productive of action. Differing in style and meaning from the prevailing Labour-Tory consensus, C.N.D.'s demands were immediately ideological in nature. For the young hopefuls on the road to Aldermaston, banning the Bomb was the 'road to action'.[90]

Notes

1 Daniel Bell, *The End of Ideology: On the Exhaustion of Political Ideas in the Fifties* (rev. ed.; New York: Collier Books, 1961). Seymour Martin Lipset, *Political Man* (New York: Doubleday, 1960). In England, the mood is expressed in the pages of *Encounter* and in the 'revisionist' writings of C. A. R. Crosland, *The Conservative Enemy* (London: Jonathan Cape, 1962). Bryan Magee, *The New Radicalism* (London: Secker and Warburg, 1962). For a contrary view, see Stephen W. Rousseas and James Farganis, 'American Politics and the End of Ideology' (unpublished, 1962).

2 See the critical and, in some respects, misleading account of C.N.D. by H. A. DeWeerd of the Rand Corporation, 'British Unilateralism: A Critical View', *Yale Review*, 51 (September 1962), 574–88. See also David Marquand, 'England, The Bomb, The Marchers', *Commentary*, 29 (May 1960), 380–6.

3 Some of the most eloquent came from Churchill: see 520 *H.C. Deb* 30–1 (November 3, 1953); 526 H.C. *Deb* 43–4 (April 5, 1954); 537 *H.C. Deb* 1893–1905 (March 1, 1955).

4 Thus Clement Attlee could propose a motion recognizing in the H-Bomb 'a grave threat to civilization' and urging an immediate diplomatic initiative for 'the reduction and control of armaments'. 526 *H.C. Deb* 36 (April 5, 1954); 535 *H.C. Deb* 608 (December 6, 1954); and 538 *H.C. Deb* 951 (March 14, 1955). See also the debate on the genetic effects of testing, 538 *H.C. Deb* 1881 (March 22, 1955). Even the semi-official Labour paper broke with party orthodoxy on the occasion of the first American nuclear test to conduct a front-page campaign to 'Stop that Bomb', *Daily Herald*, April 1, 1954.

5 D. E. Butler, *The British General Election of 1955* (London: Macmillan, 1955), pp. 31, 74, and 90–1.

6 Of those left-wing M.P.'s who protested the Government's decision to manufacture the Bomb in 1955, only Sir Richard Acland carried his protest farther: he vacated his seat to fight a by-election as an independent on the issue of the H-Bomb. The General Election intervened and Sir Richard ran a poor third as an independent in his constituency.

7 In April 1954, sixty-five Labour M.P.s defied the official leadership to vote for a back-bench amendment to the Atomic Energy Authority Act. Many of these were non-Bevanites. See 526 *H.C. Deb* 1795–1840 (April 29, 1954). For the life and times of the short-lived Hydrogen Bomb Campaign Committee, made up of M.P.s and non-M.P.s, see *The Times* (London) April 8, 1954, May 1, 1954, and January 1, 1955. For the debate preceding the rebellion against Labour's amendment approving the decision to manufacture the Bomb, see 537 *H.C. Deb* 1893–2011 (March 1, 1955), and cc. 2066–2190 (March 2, 1955).

8 Rank-and-file leftists did carry on the argument. *Report of the Annual Conference of the Labour Party, 1955*, pp. 139–41.

9 *Report of the Annual Conference of the Labour Party, 1956*, pp. 142–50. Italics added. But see the plea for 'unilateral disarmament' by Emrys Hughes, p. 146.

10 The figure in a Gallup Poll was 32 per cent. Leon Epstein, 'Britain and the H-Bomb, 1955–1958', *Review of Politics*, 21 (July 1959), 512.

11 *The Times* (London), August 9, 1953.

12 The most prominent of these were the Peace Pledge Union and the National Peace Council, itself a federation of associated bodies.

13 R. H. S. Crossman, Michael Foot, and Ian Mikardo, *Keep Left* (London: *New Statesman* pamphlet, 1947); Aneurin Bevan, *In Place of Fear* (London: Heinemann, 1952); *Keeping Left* (London: *New Statesman* pamphlet, 1950); *One Way Only* (London: *Tribune* pamphlet, 1951); *It Need Not Happen* (London: *Tribune* pamphlet, 1954).

14 For the resolution of the British Council of Churches, see *The Times* (London), April 3, 1957. See the report of the General Assembly of Unitarians and Free Christian Churches, *ibid.*, April 25, 1957. For the remarks of the Bishop of Manchester, *ibid.*, May 21, 1957, and for the debates of the General Assembly of Churches of Scotland, *ibid.*, May 28, 1957.

15 April 6, 1957, p. 425.

16 November 2, 1957, p. 541. 'The Rocket Race', August 31, 1957, p. 237.

17 J. B. Priestley, 'Britain and the Nuclear Bomb', November 2, 1957, p. 454. Bertrand Russell, 'Open Letter to Eisenhower and Khrushchev', November 23, 1957, p. 683.

18 February 2, 1957.

19 See the editorials and articles throughout *Tribune* for the following dates: March 22, March 29, April 5, April 12, May 24, August 30, and Bertrand Russell's article, August 2, 1957.

20 September 27, 1957. See also *Tribune* for September 20, 1957.

21 September 27, 1957.

22 March 29, 1957. This theme was repeated in *Tribune* for April 5 and September 20, 1957.

23 See the radio broadcast of George Brown, reported in *The Times* (London), April 1, 1957.

24 *The Times* (London), April 3 and 4, 1957. For text, see the *Annual Conference Report of the Labour Party, 1957*, p. 66.

25 *Tribune*, September 13, 1957.

26 Early in 1958, for example, the moribund left-wing socialist group, Victory for Socialism, was revived as an intra-party 'ginger group'. With the anticipated general election in mind as well as the memories of the long Bevanite struggle, the leadership lost no time in quickly and ruthlessly clipping V.F.S.'s wings. A Parliamentary group such as the H-Bomb Campaign Committee could not have gone far in the unilateralist direction without provoking the leadership into retaliatory action. V.F.S., in fact, disclaimed any formal connection with the first Aldermaston March. See the letter by Ian Mikardo, M.P., in the *Observer*, March 23, 1958. The H-Bomb Campaign Committee did, however, 'sponsor' the March, *Manchester Guardian*, March 4, 1958.

27 *Labour Party Conference Agenda, 1957*, pp. 24–41.

28 See the extended correspondence in the *New Statesman* from November 9 to December 21, 1957.

29 *Ibid.*, December 7, 1957, p. 776. See a similar appeal in the correspondence column of *Tribune*, April 5, 1957.

30 *New Statesman*, December 31, 1947, p. 846.

31 *Youth Against the Bomb*, May 1962, p. 4.

32 Nicholas Walter, 'Damned Fools in Utopia', *New Left Review*, No. 13–14 (January–April 1962), pp. 119–28.

33 Advertisements in *Tribune*, April 26, 1957, and *New Statesman*, April 26, 1957, p. 556.

34 *New Statesman*, 'Correspondence', December 21, 1957, p. 855, and 'Correspondence', February 18, 1958, p. 73.

35 Not all pacifists fully supported C.N.D.; see the letter by Stuart Morris, *New Statesman*, October 4, 1958, p. 450. See also *Peace News*, September 26, 1958. For C.N.D.'s attitude toward militant pacifism, see R. Calder's letter in *New Statesman*, September 27, 1958.

36 *Tribune*, April 12, 1957.

37 These differences ultimately led to an organizational split when the successor to D.A.C., the Committee of 100, broke away from C.N.D. See the correspondence between Lord Russell, the Rev. Michael Scott, and Canon L. J. Collins, *The Times* (London), September 29 and October 25, 1960.

38 Walter, *op. cit.*, traces its antecedents to World War I: it derived 'from the Non-Violent Resistance Group which was formed under the name "Operation Gandhi" by some members of the Non-Violent Commission of the Peace Pledge Union, which soon after its formation absorbed the No More War Movement, which derived from the No-Conscription Fellowship, the organization of extremist conscientious objectors during the First World War' (p. 120). See also Alan Lovell, 'Where Next for the Campaign?', *Universities and Left Review*, No. 6 (Spring 1959), pp. 5–6.

39 Walter, *op. cit.*, pp. 121–3.

40 *Ibid.*, p. 121.

41 'Campaign for Nuclear Disarmament' (Campaign for Nuclear Disarmament, 1962, mimeo.), p. 1.

42 These were: Canon L. John Collins; Bertrand Russell; J. B. Priestley; Michael Foot, editor of *Tribune;* Professors J. Rotblat and C. H. L. Waddington; Kingsley Martin, editor of *New Statesman*; and the chairman and the secretary of N.C.A.N.W.T., Arthur Goss and Sheila Jones. *Loc. cit.*

43 *Loc. cit.*

44 The writing on British defence and foreign policy is voluminous. In the following discussion I have tried to indicate only certain aspects of it as they relate to the general appeals of C.N.D. Some of the publications of C.N.D. are listed in footnote 47, *infra*. For a fuller discussion of British policy, the reader is referred to the annual *Defence White Papers* and the following sampling: P. M. S. Blackett, *Studies of War* (Edinburgh: Oliver and Boyd, 1962); Denis Healey, *The Race Against the H-Bomb* (London: Fabian Society, 1960); F. S. Northedge, *British Foreign Policy* (New York: Praeger, 1962); Robert E. Osgood, *Nato: The Entangling Alliance* (Chicago: University of Chicago Press, 1962), pp. 238–52; Bertrand Russell, *Common Sense and Nuclear Warfare* (London: Allen and Unwin, 1959); John Strachey, *The Pursuit of Peace* (London: Fabian Society, 1960); C. M. Woodhouse, *British Foreign Policy Since the Second World War* (London: Hutchinson, 1961); Wayland Young, *Strategy for Survival* (Baltimore: Penguin Books, 1959); A Young Fabian Publication, *Nato or Neutrality* (London: Fabian Society, 1961); and Symposium on British Defence Policy in *Political Quarterly*, 21 (January–March, 1960).

45 Lawrence W. Martin, 'The Market for Strategic Ideas in Britain', *A.P.S.R.*, 56 (March 1962), 26. *Statement on Defence, 1957* (London: H.M.S.O., 1957), Cmnd. 124, p. 3, and *Statement on Defence, 1958* (London: H.M.S.O., 1958), Cmnd. 363, p. 2.

46 Alastair Buchan, 'Britain Debates the "Balance of Terror"', *Reporter*, April 3, 1958, pp. 8–11.

47 The numerous and various arguments of C.N.D. may be found in the following publications published or sponsored by C.N.D.: Frank Allaun, *Stop the H-Bomb Race* (London: Union of Democratic Control, 1958); *Nuclear Disarmament and the Labour Movement* (1959); *Campaign for Nuclear Disarmament* (1960); *The Economic Case for Nuclear Disarmament* (1960?); Konni Zilliacus, *Anatomy of a Sacred Cow* (1960); Stuart Hall, *Nato and the Alliances* (London Regional Council Discussion Pamphlet (1960?); Frank Beswick *et al.*, *Let Britain Lead* (1960); *Old Lamps for Old: A Comment on the Labour Party's New Defence Policy* (1960); John Rex, *Britain Without the Bomb* (New Left Pamphlet, 1960); *The Big Breakthrough* (1961); Adam Roberts, *The Truth about Polaris* (1961?); Raymond Fletcher, *Military Thinking and Unilateralism*; Herbert Butterfield, *Human Nature and the*

Dominion of Fear (Christian C.N.D. Pamphlet, No. 3); Mervyn Jones, *Freed from Fear* (1961). The reader is also referred to the writings of Bertrand Russell and Stephen King-Hall.

48 Michael Howard, 'Skybolt: Where the British Erred', *Washington Post*, December 28, 1962.

49 Sandys quoted in Osgood, *op. cit.*, p. 241.

50 Alastair Buchan, 'Britain and the Nuclear Deterrent', *Political Quarterly*, 31 (January–March 1960), p. 40.

51 This was true, Osgood seems to say, as early as 1958: *op. cit.*, p. 243. See also Denis Healey, 'Britain and N.A.T.O.', in *N.A.T.O. and American Security*, ed. Klaus Knorr (Princeton: Princeton University Press, 1959), p. 221. The Government's difficulty was that many of the assumptions in its arguments, e.g., regarding American intentions, could not be spoken about too loudly in public while many of its military arguments made sense only in political terms. In military terms, they seemed illogical, and C.N.D. speakers had no trouble in regaling the audiences merely by reading excerpts from *Defence White Papers* and *Parliamentary Debates*.

52 Buchan, 'Britain and the Nuclear Deterrent', p. 40.

53 *Statement on Defence*, 1957 (London: H.M.S.O., 1957), Cmnd. 124, p. 2. The *White Paper* confessed that there existed 'no means of providing protection for the people of this country against the consequences of an attack with nuclear weapons.'

54 Young, *op. cit.*, p. 41. By 1961, C.N.D. intellectuals formally met military leaders in confidential meetings. *Sanity*, February 1961.

55 In the 1955 Defence Debate he had abstained, not, as most of the abstainers had, for pacifist or ethical reasons, but because Attlee would give no assurance that nuclear weapons would not be used first against any level or form of aggression.

56 *Report of the Annual Conference of the Labour Party, 1957*, p. 181.

57 Hugh Massingham, 'Bevan—Where are the Loves of Yesteryear?', *New Republic*, November 4, 1957, pp. 7–8. Some months later, Bevan was to cry out, 'There you are! There are the moralists! There are the pure saints ... these comrades [who] like to polarize the movement.' *The Times* (London), April 28, 1958. 'The End of Bevanism', *New Statesman*, October 12, 1957, p. 448.

58 Personal interview with C.N.D. personages. See also 'Campaign for Nuclear Disarmament', *op. cit.*

59 See Bevan's remarks reported in *The Times* (London), April 15, 1958. See also *Report of the Annual Conference of the Labour Party, 1958*, p. 41. See also A. J. P. Taylor, 'Campaign Report', *New Statesman*, June 21, 1958, p. 800.

60 The reasons for this failure are too complex to explain here: roughly, Labour leaders and officials have always feared that an organization for young Labourites is bound to become a hotbed of Communists and Trotskyites.

139

They have thus consistently restricted the freedom and controlled the activities of the party's many youth groups. After the 1959 election, it had another go at it. The result was the same; the Young Socialist Conference of 1961 ended up 'Banning the Bomb' and calling on 'Gaitskell to Go'. Even so, it could not compete with C.N.D. or with the New Left clubs.

61 See the defensive tone of the official pamphlet, *Scrap All the H-Bombs*, by John Strachey (Labour Party, 1958). See also *Report of the Annual Conference of the Labour Party, 1958*, pp. 186–222.

62 *Report of the Annual Conference of the Labour Party, 1960*, pp. 170–202.

63 Norman Birnbaum, 'Great Britain: The Reactive Revolt', in Morton A. Kaplan (ed.), *The Revolution in World Politics* (New York: Wiley, 1962), pp. 29–68.

64 Leon Epstein, 'Partisan Foreign Policy: Britain in the Suez Crisis', *World Politics*, 12 (January 1960), pp. 201–24.

65 Michael Foot and Mervyn Jones, *Guilty Men, 1957* (London: Victor Gollancz, 1957), pp. 238–9.

66 E. P. Thompson (ed.), *Out of Apathy* (London: Stevens and Sons, 1960). Also see 'U.L.R. Clubs', *Universities and Left Review*, No. 2 (Summer 1957), p. 79.

67 *Labour Party Conference Agenda* (London: Labour Party, 1957), p. 27 and passim. *Tribune*, September 25, 1957.

68 Neal Wood, *Communism and British Intellectuals* (New York: Columbia University Press, 1959), pp. 195–213.

69 Peter Worsley, *Out of Apathy, op. cit.*, p. 189.

70 See for example: 'Hungary, H-Bomb and Germany', *Universities and Left Review*, No. 2 (Summer 1957), pp. 3–4. E. P. Thompson, 'Nato, Neutralism and Survival', *Universities and Left Review*, No. 4 (Summer 1958), pp. 49–51. Peter Sedgwick, 'Nato, the Bomb, and Socialism', *Universities and Left Review*, No. 7 (Autumn 1959), pp. 7–13. John Rex and Peter Worsley, 'Campaign for a Foreign Policy', *New Left Review*, No. 4 (August 1960). Stuart Hall, *Break-Through* (Combined Universities Campaign for Nuclear Disarmament, 1958).

71 Editorial, *Universities and Left Review*, No. 7 (Autumn 1959), pp. 1–2. A good summary of what the New Left is can be found in the essay 'Britain: The New Reasoners', by G. L. Arnold in Leopold Labedz (ed.), *Revisionism* (New York: Praeger, 1962), pp. 299–312.

72 *Out of Apathy, op. cit.*, p. xix.

73 *Ibid.*, pp. 3–15.

74 See the 'Editorial', *Universities and Left Review*, No. 7 (Autumn 1959), pp. 1–2. It argues, with reference to the unilateralist movement, that the New Left has helped to develop 'some of its socialist implications'. But 'if the *New Left Review* has any political roots, they will be there. Without C.N.D.

supporters, Anti-Ugly protests, African demonstrators, Free Cinema and the Society for the Abolition of the Death Penalty, we would be nowhere.' Again, 'the real growing points of socialism are going to be found, increasingly, in groups and movements which . . . share . . . something of the same spirit which moved people from Aldermaston to London . . . some of the outrage of Trafalgar Square, Suez Day'.

75 'Left Club News', *New Left Review*, No. 4 (July–August 1950), pp. 68–70. Italics added.

76 On the troubles of the New Left, see 'Notes for Readers', *New Left Review*, No. 12 (November–December 1961), inside cover.

77 See footnote 70, *supra*.

78 See *Out of Apathy, op. cit.*, p. 239. Opinion in the universities is easy to generalize about and the generalizations hard to prove. See David Marquand, 'Oxford Angst', *New Statesman*, March 15, 1958, pp. 329–30, and 'The Secret People of Oxford', *New Statesman*, July 13, 1947, pp. 42–3. For the results of various university polls on the nuclear question see *The Times* (London), March 3, 11, 16, May 3, and June 5, 1958.

79 In 1959 the most right-wing of the six major trade unions, the National Union of General and Municipal Workers, voted for a policy of unilateral nuclear disarmament—much to the astonishment and dismay of its leaders. Those gentlemen wasted no time, however, in convening a special 'recall' conference which obediently overturned the earlier vote. The whole incident revealed the degree to which the unilateralist heresy had penetrated the union movement.

80 The most complete statement is to be found in George Matthews, 'Fight for Peace' (based on a report to the Communist Party Executive Committee, July 12, 1958), *World News*, July 19, 1958, pp. 449–51. The *Manchester Guardian* reported that 'obvious communists were few—if any' on the first Aldermaston March in its April 5, 1958, issue.

81 George Matthews, 'Unilateralism and the Fight for Peace', *World News*, March 15, 1958, pp. 163–5. *Daily Worker* (London), February 28, 1958. The assumption was that unilateralism and multilateralism were mutually exclusive.

82 *Daily Worker* (London), April 5, 1958.

83 'Don't Tilt at Windmills, Mr Strachey', *World News*, April 15, 1958. See also *Daily Worker* (London), April 11 and 19, 1958.

84 Matthews, 'Fight for Peace'. Cf. also William Wainwright, 'Summit Stock-Taking', *World News*, April 19, 1958, pp. 211–12, and 'Gathering Force', *World News*, April 19, 1958.

85 Matthews, 'Fight for Peace', and *Daily Worker* (London), July 8, 1959.

86 On both points see the 'pre-Congress' correspondence in *World News*, February 18, 1961, pp. 87–8, and March 4, 1961, pp. 116–19. See also the letter by an ex-staff member of the *Daily Worker* in *Tribune*, May 12, 1957.

On the other hand, there is no doubt that Communist militants also worked against unilateralism, thus producing a *de facto* alliance between the C.P. and the right-wing leadership. See 'The Communists and the Bomb', *Tribune*, September 12, 1958.

87 See the claim made by John Gollan, general secretary of the Communist party, quoted by DeWeerd, *op. cit.*, p. 578. The role of the Communist party after 1960 is very unclear, and beyond the scope of this article.

88 See footnote 74 *supra*.

89 Leon Epstein, *Britain—Uneasy Ally* (Chicago: U. of Chicago Press, 1954) p. 113.

90 Bell, *op. cit.*, p. 393.

Capital Punishment and British Politics: the Role of Pressure Groups *

James B. Christoph

One of the most striking developments in the study of British government in the past decade has been the 'discovery' of pressure groups. Contrary to the earlier assumption that strong political parties, Parliamentary supremacy and traditional British propriety had obviated the need for and weakened the power of pressure groups, much evidence has come to light showing that outside associations are both numerous and powerful elements in the British political process.[1] In their haste to revise previous judgments, some observers have gone so far as to attribute to pressure groups the dominant role in public policy-making in this system. An examination of the capital punishment controversy reveals the limitations of any such attempt to force the myriad materials of politics into a Procrustean bed.

Pressure groups played an important but necessarily limited role in the capital punishment controversy in the period 1945–57. Most of the groups that figured in these events did not come into being during the period, nor did they withdraw from the political scene once the 1957 decision was reached; and it is safe to predict that so long as public attitudes toward the death penalty continue to be aroused periodically, organized groups on the several sides of the issue will remain active. Despite the fairly heavy concentration of organized activity on their part, abolitionists did not comprise the sole groups interested in the controversy. Official groups such as the Home Office, party associations such as the National Union of Conservative Women, and certain fundamentalist religious organizations, although never welded together into a formal retentionist pressure group, nevertheless acted in a manner quite similar to one. Throughout most of the period the group struggle was between a passionate and organized minority on the one side and a less organized, less dedicated, but more numerous coalition of official groups,

* Reprinted with permission from *Capital Punishment and British Politics*, Allen and Unwin, London, 1962, pp. 185–90.

143

heavily reinforced by majority opinion and control of Parliamentary institutions, on the other.

The several abolitionist organizations that figured in the controversy belong more in the category of 'attitude' than of 'sectional' groups. The chief difference between a sectional spokesman group and an attitude group, according to Allen Potter, lies in the fact that 'it is the political task of the former to try to reflect the particular interests of its section, while it is the political task of the latter to try to persuade people, regardless of their sectional affiliations, to subscribe to its point of view'.[2] Groups such as the Howard League[3] and the National Campaign[4] are generally small in size, poor in finances, and unable to reap for their memberships any but intangible satisfactions. They are pressure groups based on shared attitudes and the advocacy of changes in public policy rather than interest groups held together by the desire to obtain benefits for their section of the community. This type of group rarely cuts a significant figure on the stage of politics; most of the time it fails to achieve the successes that come to the powerful sectional bodies such as trade unions, trade associations, professional societies and veterans' groups. The fact that usually to succeed it must appeal far beyond its normal membership base is itself indicative of the relative weakness of the attitude group when compared with those sectional groups that can boast of large and stable memberships, efficient bureaucracies and continuous access to high places.

The very nature of their purpose imposed upon the abolitionist groups special requirements. For example, they wanted a single important change—the elimination of the death penalty for murder —and would settle for nothing else. Thus although on occasion some of their supporters in Parliament were forced to accept compromises and half-measures, the abolitionist pressure groups refused consistently to have anything to do with the middle ground. Unlike many sectional groups, they were unable to deliver to their membership yearly dividends and occasional pieces of their programme. Indeed, their dedication to a single, indivisible goal was an element of strength, for most abolitionists were not to be dissuaded from their efforts by the promise of a negotiated peace. Furthermore, this single-mindedness was responsible for the abolitionist field being divided between two pressure groups: the older, multiple-purpose, research-oriented Howard League and the newer, single-issue, propagandist National Council[5] and its successor, the National Campaign. Because they shared a common purpose, the two types of groups were able to supplement rather than compete with each other, so that in practice they were able to divide the labour, the

Howard League providing much of the research, contacts with government and the world of criminology, and a reputation for integrity, and the Council and Campaign the larger membership, finances and propaganda. This particular symbiosis was made necessary by the fact that the Howard League was not equipped for or desirous of engaging in large-scale campaigns for abolition, especially since it felt that to do so would jeopardize its standing with the Home Office and prison officials and rebound against its other penal reform activities.

Abolitionist groups initially were put at a disadvantage because they were unable to make use of two important elements of power in the British political system: parties and administration. Students of recent trends in that system are agreed that the simultaneous rise of centralized party government and the administrative state have shifted the loci of political power strongly toward these institutions, and that the most successful pressure groups are those that have continuous access to party leaders and key figures in the ministries. It was in these realms that the abolitionists were the weakest. In the first phase of the struggle in the late 1940s, they were unable to convince the leadership of either major party of the desirability of abolition, and they were forced to fall back upon the lesser weapons of backbenchers and the myth of non-partisanship. Most of their efforts to achieve their aims by exerting pressure upon administrative officials were also unavailing, partly because the basic change that they wanted required not administrative but Parliamentary action and partly because the ministry responsible for administering capital punishment policy, the Home Office, was also the ministry responsible for police and prison services in Britain and thus more likely to react to the 'inside' retentionist pressures of organizations of these officials than to the 'outside' pressures of the abolitionists. Ironically, although it was engaged in continuous consultation with the Home Office and the Prison Commissioners, the Howard League was unable to use its many administrative contacts to advantage on this issue.

In order to overcome these weaknesses, the abolitionist pressure groups turned to the dual tasks of converting Parliamentary and public opinion. The outside organizations played a secondary role in the conduct of strategy in the House of Commons, operating chiefly as servicing units for the Parliamentary leadership and as instruments for the creation of sympathetic public attitudes. This meant that they had to launch and carry out campaigns. Here again the established pressure group in this field, the Howard League, was inadequate to the need, and an awareness of this special problem by

145

'lay' abolitionists such as Gollancz and Koestler led to the creation of the National Campaign and its manifold attention-getting tactics. Unshackled by the limited budgets, sensitivity to administrative opinion, and primness of its predecessors, the National Campaign proved that a group of relative newcomers could be better organizers of mass opinion than 'professional' abolitionists of several decades' standing.

It is a sign of the comparative weakness of attitude groups that, in contrast to most sectional pressure groups, they must often resort to burdensome and unpredictable mass campaigns. The power contrast does not end here, either. If the abolitionist experience is in any way representative of that of attitude groups in general, these groups are less potent than sectional groups because they do not really have an identifiable clientele or possess much control over their subject matter. When they are dealing with questions such as the murder rate, attitude groups must grapple with human behaviour over which their own small membership can have little control. The Howard League and the National Campaign might hope that if their goal were achieved, i.e., if the death penalty were abolished, the incidence of murder would drop markedly. But until that time arrived these groups were at the mercy of events that were clearly beyond their control. Almost by accident several murder cases broke favourably for the abolitionist cause in the mid 1950s, and the pressure groups were able to use them to great advantage; but it is equally possible that in the future other murder cases will offer equally rich opportunities for persons and groups favouring the stiffening of the use of hanging. When compared to the possibilities for control over their domains possessed by, for example, trade union and organized business groups, the domestic base of attitude group power seems slight indeed.

A further difficulty for attitude groups such as the abolitionists grows out of their generally small size, lack of economic power, and sporadic success in gaining the attention of the public. It is their inability to threaten official groups with political or economic consequences for any refusal to accede to their demands. Because the capital punishment question lay beyond the established programmes of the political parties, it scarcely carried weight in electoral terms, and groups such as the abolitionists were unable to raise the prospect of penalizing retentionist M.P.s at the polls. (More important than the polls, in fact, were the M.P.s' constituency associations, whose memories for matters such as these were much sharper than the electors'.) Nor could the abolitionist groups threaten to or actually withhold essential services from the Government and the community, as is occasionally possible in the case of unions and employers' confederations.[6] They had few services to render in the first place. The prospect of the Howard League refusing its cooperation and bringing a Government to its knees over the death penalty issue is ludicrous to contemplate.

It is difficult to escape the conclusion that compared to most interest groups operating in Britain today the abolitionist organizations had little to work with except ideas. These ideas were hoary with age and not even 'packaged' or communicated in a strikingly new manner. But they possessed a potency that grew as the outside climate changed from unfavourable to uncertain. As intermediaries between the ideas and the process of government the various pressure groups performed essentially four main functions.

First, they kept the death penalty issue alive. In the past century and a half the issue has had full-scale Parliamentary consideration on no more than a half-dozen occasions, with large gaps in between. Even in the years examined here, there was no automatic guarantee that the issue would not disappear from view once again for many decades. It was a basic task of the abolitionist groups, along with interested M.P.s, to maintain the requisite organization, research activity, and propagandistic effort to insure that Parliament and the public were not allowed to forget. For an attitude group to lose a wide audience for its ideas would be fatal.

The second function performed by these groups was in a sense a negative one. This was to prevent the cause of abolition from getting the crackpot label. All too often reformist groups put themselves beyond the pale of the political process by becoming identified with harmless or questionable fringe elements in society. Respectability sometimes is attached to numbers, but also (when numbers are not available) to association with prominent and respected sectors of the community. In their search for the power of respectability abolitionist organizations employed several techniques. They emphasized the empirical nature of their case and went out of their way to dissociate themselves from highly emotional and sensational appeals, which they feared would earn them the label of 'mere sentimentalists' in Parliament. They made fairly conspicuous use of the resources of the Howard League, an organization known for its responsible approach to penal reform. They took special pains to include in their membership persons of avowed conservative views, such as a number of Tory humanitarians, peers and social leaders. In the public image of the abolitionists the 'friends of Princess Margaret' partially offset 'Mr Silverman and his friends'. Indeed, by the beginning of 1956 the cause of abolition had become an acceptable outlet for the reforming energies of Britons of all classes, not merely those of a few middle-class ladies.

The pressure groups performed a third function, that of mobilizing favourable public opinion and providing outside support for the small band of abolitionists in Parliament. To this group of back-benchers such support was politically and psychologically necessary in their arduous uphill struggle. As intermediaries between the mass public and the forces in Parliament, the pressure groups served in the dual capacity of registering to Parliament what outside support there was and of conveying to sympathizers in the public the specific actions they could take to strengthen the hand of the political leadership.

A fourth role was forced on the abolitionist pressure groups by the general inability of political parties in a two-party system to adopt and press unpopular ideas. It has been observed that the impetus in such a system is toward compromise and the integration of viewpoints in such a way that, had they no other outlet, strongly-felt ideas would be in constant danger of disappearing or being hopelessly blunted. As Professor Eckstein has said, 'In attempting to win mass support, necessarily from a large variety of groups, [political parties] do not so much "aggregate" opinions . . . as reduce them to their lowest and vaguest denominators, sometimes distorting the perspectives and goals they seek to mobilize out of all recognition.'[7] By entering terrain on which the parties feared to tread, the abolitionist groups were able to present to Parliament ideas and choices that its Members might have avoided facing in the normal course of party government. The capital punishment controversy confirms the view that a viable political system requires the complementary activities of parties and pressure groups.

Despite what has just been said, it would be a mistake to put too high the overall effect of pressure group behaviour on the outcome of the political events chronicled here. Ideas and events were more crucial than the actions of groups, and happenings inside Parliament generally overshadowed those on the outside. To cite just one example, it will be recalled that in spite of the general uneasiness about his reputation and the desire of outside groups to replace him with a moderate, Sydney Silverman was able to maintain his leadership of the abolitionist group in the Commons throughout the struggle. The lines of influence were many and not susceptible to scaling. A paradigm of the forces at work in these decisions would have to include the four-cornered relationship between (1) the structure of government, (2) pressure group behaviour, (3) the weight of public opinion, and (4) the events of history, including the formulation of the classic cases for and against capital punishment and the murder cases that called them into play in this period. In other words, this case study is testimony to the validity of multiple causation in politics and a warning against the temptation to view the political process in Britain as altogether easy and coherent.

[*Editor's note:* the death penalty was abolished (with the exception of certain specified cases in Northern Ireland) in 1965.]

Notes

1 Especially in: S. H. Beer, 'Pressure Groups and Parties in Britain', *American Political Science Review*, 50, March 1956; H. Eckstein, *Pressure Group Politics: The Case of the British Medical Association*, London, 1960; S. E. Finer, *Anonymous Empire*, London, 1958; J. D. Stewart, *British Pressure Groups: Their Role in Relation to the House of Commons*, Oxford, 1958.

2 'Attitude Groups', *Political Quarterly*, 29, January–March 1958, p. 72.

3 Full title: The Howard League for Penal Reform.

4 Full title: The National Campaign for the Abolition of Capital Punishment.

5 Full title: The National Council for the Abolition of the Death Penalty.

6 See S. E. Finer, *op. cit.*, Chapter IX, and Arnold Rogow and Peter Shore, *The Labour Government and British Industry*, Oxford, 1955.

7 H. Eckstein, *op. cit.*, p. 162. For a discussion of the aggregate function of interest groups, see Gabriel A. Almond and James S. Coleman, eds., *The Politics of the Developing Areas*, Princeton, 1960, pp. 38–45.

How the Abortion Lobby Worked *

Keith Hindell and Madeleine Simms

On April 27 1967 the Abortion Act came into force. The Act states that a doctor may terminate a pregnancy if he and another doctor consider

'1.—(1) ...
(a) that the continuance of the pregnancy would involve risk to the life of the pregnant woman or of injury to the physical or mental health of the pregnant woman or any existing children of her family greater than if the pregnancy were terminated; or
(b) that there is a substantial risk that if the child were born it would suffer from such physical or mental abnormalities as to be seriously handicapped.
'(2) In determining whether the continuance of a pregnancy would involve such risk of injury to health as is mentioned in paragraph (a), account may be taken of the pregnant woman's actual or reasonably foreseeable environment. ...'

This Act represents a substantial change. Until now the basic law on abortion has been the Offences against the Person Act 1861, s. 58, which made abortion an offence carrying a maximum penalty of 'penal servitude for life'. This total rejection of abortion was first breached by the Infant Life Preservation Act 1929 which made it legal for a doctor to terminate a pregnancy in order to save a woman's life. The law was subsequently widened through interpretation in the courts but still remained fundamentally hostile to the idea of abortion.

Now for the first time British statute law specifically makes it legal to remove a foetus from the womb on grounds other than to save the life of the mother. As the paragraphs quoted above show, the Act allows doctors a great deal of discretion although not the total discretion which they enjoy with virtually all other operations. Argument will, of course, continue as to when abortions are both

* Reprinted with permission from *The Political Quarterly*, vol. 39, no. 3, 1968.

ethical and legal and when they are not, certainly among the members of the medical profession, perhaps even in the courts. But by shifting the balance from illegal to legal, medical termination of pregnancy will also cross the line from unethical to ethical, and from generally not done to commonly acceptable. It is safe to predict that in a few years' time abortion by surgical, vacuum, and perhaps pharmaceutical means will become normal medical practice and not the secret and expensive business it has largely been hitherto.

The Bill, which grew into the Abortion Act, was sponsored by David Steel, Liberal M.P. for Roxburgh, Selkirk and Peebles. It was the eighth Abortion Bill to be presented in Parliament. Previous Bills had been presented by Joseph Reeves 1952, Lord Amulree 1954, Kenneth Robinson 1961, Renée Short 1965, Lord Silkin 1965 and again in 1966, Simon Wingfield Digby 1965. Apart from David Steel, Lord Silkin was the only one to make any progress with an Abortion Bill. He piloted one Bill through the Lords to an unopposed Third Reading, only to have it overtaken by the 1966 General Election, and a second Bill all the way through Committee. Subsequently, David Steel and Lord Silkin guided the final Bill through the Commons and Lords respectively after a very long and involved parliamentary struggle. The law was finally changed in 1967 because of many factors—medical, social, legal, political and personal; but a key factor was the activity of the Abortion Law Reform Association —the Abortion Lobby.

The Founding of A.L.R.A.

The Abortion Law Reform Association came into existence in 1936, against a background of falling population, economic uncertainty, high maternal mortality resulting from criminal abortion, and threatening war. The devastating losses of the First World War were still vividly in the public mind, and there was much concern about how, in this situation, Britain would be able to maintain her role in the world, and continue to carry out her imperial responsibilities. The problem of the declining population was a recurrent theme in the Britain of the thirties, agitating the public mind much as the problem of over-population does today. Coupled with this were fears about the dilution of quality. The healthiest, most vigorous, and most able of the younger generation had been slaughtered in the trenches; the professional classes had mastered the art of birth control; the feckless and the unfit, it seemed to

151

many, were the ones who remained to breed the next generation of Britons.

Early in 1936 Dr Joan Malleson, a surgeon and birth controller with an interest in sexual reform, invited a number of people to a private discussion about the high maternal mortality rate to see whether there were any views about how this might be combated. As she was to inform the Birkett Committee on Abortion the following year, 'in England nearly 20 per cent, and in Scotland 30 per cent of the total maternal deaths, were due to causes which were aggravated by child bearing'. She estimated that 90,000 women resorted to criminal abortion each year. 'This is good enough reason to consider facilities which might transfer some of these desperate mothers from the hands of the criminal abortionist into proper medical care.'

Out of this private meeting arose the Abortion Law Reform Association, founded on February 17, 1936, by three women: Janet Chance, who became the first chairman; Stella Browne, the first vice-chairman; Alice Jenkins, the first secretary. They were to remain associated with the cause until their deaths two and three decades later. In its early years, the Association was financed largely out of the pocket of Mrs Janet Chance, the wife of a wealthy stockbroker who was interested in eugenics. He served for many years as treasurer of the Eugenics Society. She herself ran a pioneer advice centre on sexual problems, and had, in 1931, published a highly controversial book entitled *The Cost of English Morals*, in which she exposed the harmful results of conventional English morality, denounced the 'spinster-minded of both sexes', and demanded for women the same right of sexual enjoyment that men had always taken for granted. Stella Browne, a somewhat eccentric blue-stocking of Canadian origin, had been the first to advocate abortion law reform in public as long before as 1915. Among the more notorious of her translations into English was Van de Velde's *Ideal Marriage*, another controversial book of the period. Alice Jenkins, an experienced administrator, had previously been active in the Labour Party and in various suffragist organizations. All three had graduated into abortion law reform through the birth control movement, were used to pioneering, and were not easily deflected by apathy, ridicule or hostility.

In their first year they recruited 35 members. By 1939 this number had risen to nearly 400, mostly recruited from women's Labour groups, and the women's branches of the co-operative movement. Working women now aspired to the privileges that the moneyed classes had enjoyed for years.

The Development of A.L.R.A.

Between 1936 and 1939 the Association was very active. Speakers were sent round the country to address mostly Labour or Equal Citizenship groups. Letters and articles were provided for newspapers—though rarely published, the subject being still taboo. Evidence was given to the Government's Birkett Committee, and a number of conferences were held. Meanwhile, the British Medical Association had already set up its own committee of inquiry. It came to remarkably liberal conclusions. Efforts were made to prevent the publication of its report, but these did not succeed. Published in June 1936, the report recommended that abortion be legalized (i) where the patient's physical or mental health required it; (ii) in cases of rape below the age of consent; (iii) where the baby might be born abnormal. The B.M.A. even reached out to a tentative view about the social grounds for abortion: 'While the Committee has no doubt that the legislation of abortion for social and economic reasons would go far to solve the problem of the secret operation, it realizes that this is a matter for consideration by the community as a whole, and not by the medical profession alone.'

Two years later, a member of this same committee, Mr Aleck Bourne, was involved in one of the most publicized criminal trials of the decade, which decisively liberalized the law on abortion. From that time on, it seemed likely that a court would regard abortion as permissible to save not only the mother's life, but also her mental or physical health. Mr Bourne was a member of A.L.R.A.'s Medico-Legal Committee. The fourteen-year-old girl who had been raped, whose pregnancy he had terminated, had been sent to him by Dr Joan Malleson, a progenitor of A.L.R.A.

In May 1937, spurred by the women's organizations and the maternal mortality campaigners, the Government had set up the Birkett Committee. It included one working-class woman, Dorothy Thurtle, the wife of one of A.L.R.A.'s vice-presidents, Ernest Thurtle, M.P., and the daughter of George Lansbury. She issued a notable Minority Report recommending sweeping reforms which were not acceptable to Mrs Stanley Baldwin and the high-born ladies and fashionable physicians who filled out the other committee places. They were content to recommend that the law be amended to make it 'unmistakably clear that a medical practitioner is acting legally, when in good faith he procures an abortion of a pregnant woman in circumstances which satisfy him that continuance of the pregnancy is likely to endanger her life or seriously to impair her

153

health'. They pointed out that the judge's ruling in the *Bourne* case would not necessarily be binding upon judges of the High Court. 'We are inclined to believe that the absence of any binding decision introduces a further element of uncertainty which it is desirable to remove.' But this would have provided little advance. Janet Chance commented: 'The Committee sat for many weeks, collected a great deal of valuable information, and issued a feeble report.' Mrs. Thurtle's Minority Report gained wide publicity and the movement for reform gathered pace. The war intervened, the reports and recommendations were filed away in pigeon holes, and the cause, like so many others, fell into abeyance.

After the war the Association revived slowly and started all over again, lecturing, writing and educating. In the fifties, political action became possible for the first time. Professor Glanville Williams, A.L.R.A.'s President and legal mentor, drafted a model Bill which served as a basis for future abortion law reform efforts. Mr Joseph Reeves, a Labour M.P., presented a Private Member's Bill in 1952 which had only a few minutes' debate and never came to a vote. Lord Amulree presented a Bill in the Lords in 1954 but withdrew it before any debate. From then on, however, political action became central to A.L.R.A.'s activities. In 1960, Mr Kenneth Robinson, the present Minister of Health, drew a place in the Private Members' Ballot, and the next year presented the second abortive Bill in the House of Commons. A.L.R.A. had attempted systematically to gather support in the House of Commons, and had intensified its publicity in the country. But the scale of its operations was necessarily limited by the small number of its active supporters and the increasing age of its executives.

By 1962, Janet Chance and Stella Browne were dead, Alice Jenkins was ill and Dorothy Thurtle was about to retire. The Association coasted quietly, waiting for a younger generation. They came with Thalidomide.

Thalidomide and After

Thalidomide produced a profound sense of shock and horror throughout the country. As the appalling details of the deformities inflicted by this drug seeped into the Press, many of the younger generation felt grateful that their own children had escaped unscathed, and some felt a sense of shame at the idea that any contemporary who had swallowed this drug might be forced by society to carry such a pregnancy to term. When Lady Summerskill asked

154

a question in the House of Lords on this subject, Viscount Dilhorne blandly replied that abortion on grounds of foetal deformity would not be tolerated. The *Daily Telegraph* castigated Lady Summerskill for daring to ask such a question. 'Lady Summerskill, who presumably subscribes to the Hippocratic Oath, seriously proposes in Parliament that abortion be legalized ... merely because the pregnant woman has taken the so-called 'tranquillizing' drug Thalidomide, and it is by consequence possible that her child may be born grievously deformed. ... It does not justify Lady Summerskill's revolting conclusion' adumbrated the leader-writer. But when National Opinion Polls asked the question to the public, they were solidly behind Lady Summerskill. 72·9 per cent of the public favoured abortion where a child might be born deformed.

This was the emotive starting point of the new campaign. Its flames were fanned by the tragic details of the Liège Trial, which were reported in detail in the British press that year. A Belgian mother had killed her deformed baby. She was acquitted of murder by the jury. The Roman Catholic hierarchy denounced the verdict. Britain, as well as Belgium, heaved a sigh of relief.

The New Generation of Reformers

In 1963 a small group, most of whom were in their early thirties, stimulated into action by Thalidomide and irritated by the ineffectiveness of the Association, pushed themselves forward. In the space of five months four senior members of the Executive Committee stood down, including the Chairman, Vice-Chairman and Secretary. By March 1964 a new generation of reformers had taken charge. For their new Chairman they elected Mrs Vera Houghton, one of the old Committee. She was an experienced administrator, having been Executive Secretary of the International Planned Parenthood Federation for ten years. As the wife of Douglas Houghton, M.P. (soon to be a Labour Minister charged with co-ordinating social policy), she was also well connected in high places. Other members of this group were Mrs Diane Munday, Vice-Chairman, Mrs Madeleine Simms, Press Officer, and Alastair Service, Accounts Secretary, but soon to be Lobby Organizer. They revitalized the Association, and, with the help of many others, including Mr Christopher Chataway, mobilized sufficient forces inside and outside Parliament to change the law, and then maintained the pressure until the parliamentary process was finally concluded. For the next three and a half years, under Vera Houghton's firm and skilful guidance, they devoted most of their energy to the cause. They were in constant touch with each other, coping with work which very quickly snowballed when first Lord Silkin's and then David Steel's Abortion Bills reached Parliament.

While the transference of power was still going on the new leaders of A.L.R.A. initiated activity in several directions. They made abortion a subject of public debate by bombarding the newspapers and specialist journals with articles and letters. Diane Munday worked on the women's organizations, encouraging the reaffirmation of support for reform. Unaware that there had already been an A.L.R.A. *Newsletter* in the 1930s, Madeleine Simms started a quarterly with this same name which kept the membership informed about the medical, psychiatric and social arguments, and which fanned its sympathy for reform with stark newspaper cuttings showing the dire results of unqualified abortion. Three medical members of the Association carried the discussion into the medical organizations. One of them, Dr Malcolm Potts, travelled in Scandinavia and Eastern Europe gathering scholarly evidence on the results of abortion law reform in countries where it had actually been tried. The most original activity of the revived A.L.R.A. was that it organized a series of opinion surveys which established that the public and the doctors supported reform. But first of all the Association built up its own membership.

A.L.R.A.'s Members

In the early 1960s A.L.R.A. had less than two hundred members, but with the advent of Thalidomide and the rejuvenation of the Executive Committee membership grew steadily. By 1966 individual membership had passed the thousand mark. After the law was eventually reformed A.L.R.A. was able to question its members about their beliefs, occupations and personal characteristics. Nearly two-thirds of them turned out to be women, two-thirds had had higher education and one-fifth were doctors or para-medical. One in three of the women members had required an abortion at some stage in her life, and one in four had obtained one, mostly legally, mostly privately. Although most of the members had been brought up in the conventional religious denominations, the rate of lapse from religious observance was striking. 74 per cent were now atheists or agnostics. Half the members had been born into Anglican homes but only 10 per cent were still Anglicans in 1968. 13 per cent of A.L.R.A.'s members had been brought up as Nonconformists, and

13 per cent as Jews. Their figures had fallen to 8 per cent and 5 per cent respectively. 51 per cent were Labour supporters, 21 per cent Conservatives, and 13 per cent Liberals; quite different from the spread of party loyalty in the country as a whole. Membership overlapped heavily with that of the Family Planning Association (39 per cent), the National Trust (31 per cent) and the Fabian Society (21 per cent), but members showed little interest in the other reform groups. Only 39 per cent were satisfied with the 1967 Abortion Act; 57 per cent hoped for further reform.

Local Groups

As part of the membership campaign and the effort to increase public awareness of the need for reform, the Association formed local groups in Birmingham 1962, North West London and Bristol 1963, Manchester 1964, and South East London 1965. The local groups supplied speakers to other organizations and sparked off local interest by getting reports and letters into the local Press. At a later stage the groups were to play an influential part writing to M.P.s, but until 1966 the most striking part of their work was research.

Partly because of the criminal law, abortion had been taboo as a subject for ordinary conversation or investigation for over a hundred years. Consequently there were many aspects of it to which a group with small resources could make a contribution. The Birmingham Group of A.L.R.A., led by a biologist at Aston University, Dr Martin Cole, investigated abortifacient drugs. They visited 40 shops in London and Birmingham (20 chemists, 17 rubber shops, and 3 herbalists) asking for products 'to bring on a delayed period' and 'terminate a pregnancy'. 'The impression was gained', they said in their report, 'that this sort of request was so common as to occasion no distinctive reaction'. They were sold 'Doctor Brotton's Golden X and Anaemia Pills,' 'Menoroids', and other choicely named preparations. After expert chemical analysis the Group reported that most of these preparations had no abortifacient functions and that some of them were highly dangerous. Limited as the survey had been it highlighted the fact that an antique law had the effect of encouraging large numbers of women to resort to such drugs instead of consulting their doctors.

The North West London Group, which drew most of its members from Hampstead, produced an even better piece of ammunition for the cause with their survey of London doctors. They sent out a questionnaire about abortion and law reform to all the doctors (over 2,000) on the London Medical List of the National Health Service. In January 1965 they published an analysis of the 751 replies which had been received. The most valuable result was that 69 per cent of those replying approved of A.L.R.A.'s aims as stated on the questionnaire. Two other results which made good publicity were that 84 per cent of these London doctors thought that abortion was a safe operation and 75 per cent thought it ought to be available on the National Health Service.

Despite the fact that the survey was not carried out by an independent, professional organization, its conclusion made an impact. In any case on the subject of abortion, almost all figures were (and still are) subject to dispute. The impressive point was that this was the first systematic attempt to sound out medical opinion on this subject. Certainly this survey looked authentic enough to be taken up by national as well as local newspapers. Thus simple statements, such as that doctors thought abortion was safe and desired a change in the law, became established in print as 'facts'.

Demonstrating Public Support

The Association was itself very surprised by the results. When the survey was first proposed there had been a good deal of opposition on the national executive to its being carried out. It had long been assumed by many in A.L.R.A. and oft-repeated by opponents of reform that the medical profession as a whole was strongly opposed to liberalizing the grounds for abortion. This survey of London doctors broke down one of the psychological barriers which in the past had prevented the Association taking bolder action. Suddenly the cause was no longer hopeless. It might even be popular.

With the survey of London doctors A.L.R.A. had stumbled onto a match-winning tactic. Alastair Service, who was chiefly responsible for the survey, realized that A.L.R.A. could now demonstrate support from other sections of the public. The new generation of A.L.R.A. activists rose to the top of the organization at just the right time to go with the tide of public opinion. The horrors of Thalidomide during 1961 and 1962 had softened up the public's attitude to abortion. In July 1962 a National Opinion Poll had asked, 'Would you be in favour of a change in the law allowing doctors to terminate pregnancy where there is a good reason to believe that the baby would be born badly deformed?' 72 per cent of the public said 'Yes' and only 23 per cent said 'No'.

158

At the same time there was all sorts of other evidence that the society's attitude to sexual behaviour, particularly to the frank discussion of the subject, was changing fast. The Consumers' Association, responding to the requests of a large membership, published their Supplement on Contraceptives at the end of 1963. After the unnecessary death of a girl undergraduate, a thousand Oxford students sent a petition to the Prime Minister demanding the legalization of abortion and the Oxford Union Society passed a motion condemning the existing abortion laws by a 3/1 majority. An article in the *Observer* by Katharine Whitehorn about the Roman Catholic anti-birth control lobby evoked a vast response from readers. All were straws in the wind of change.

In March 1965 National Opinion Polls returned to the subject of abortion. The results were very important to the cause of reform. N.O.P. asked a representative cross-section of electors if they thought abortion should be legal. Two-thirds said they thought it should be legal in some cases and only a quarter thought it should be illegal in all cases. National Opinion Polls concluded that the opposition to abortion was strongest amongst old people, those living in Scotland and the North of England, working-class people and Roman Catholics. However, even among Catholics the majority were still in favour of abortion being legal in some circumstances.

Encouraged by these results and the results of its own earlier survey of doctors, A.L.R.A. commissioned a survey of women's attitudes and experiences. After a cautious pilot in case the replies should be unfavourable, sealed questionnaires were given to 3,500 women in the course of N.O.P.'s normal fortnightly surveys. 2,100 women replied. When the replies were analysed National Opinion Polls concluded that three-quarters of all women in Britain thought that abortion should be easier to obtain. Most of the grounds for abortion outlined in A.L.R.A.'s platform, such as abortion on grounds of rape or incest and abortion if the mother's health was likely to suffer, received overwhelming support. But if a baby was likely to be born deformed, a crushing 91 per cent of women thought abortion should be permissible. A third of the women even supported the extreme view that the woman alone should decide whether or not she should have an abortion.

Ninety-one of the women replying (4 per cent) were prepared to admit that they themselves had once had an abortion. On the basis of this sample N.O.P. estimated that in the previous twenty years there had been at least 40,000 abortions annually, 31,000 of which had been illegal. Moreover, the survey also indicated that twice as many abortions were attempted as were completed. Alto-

159

gether a minimum of 600,000 women in Britain had had an abortion since the war and, of these, 125,000 had had more than one.

These results and estimates were published in July 1966, a week before the second reading of David Steel's Abortion Bill. The conclusions were plain for every M.P. to read. Thousands of women needed an abortion every year and most of them were prepared to ignore the criminal law in order to get one. The great majority of women never needed abortions but nevertheless favoured a change in the law so that all women could get skilled and legal abortions in almost all circumstances.

During the passage of the Bill, A.L.R.A. continued to demonstrate support by publishing two further polls. The South East London group surveyed the clergymen in their area, and N.O.P. were commissioned once again to sound out the opinion of all 21,000 General Practitioners in the country. The results were that both doctors and Protestant clergymen seemed to be solidly behind the Abortion Bill. The opponents of abortion law reform acknowledged the effectiveness of these opinion polls by commissioning a poll themselves. At the very last minute, in October 1967, Social Surveys (Gallup) polled the public on what they thought of the two crucial amendments which had been made to the Bill by the Lords in committee. According to this poll the public seemed to support the idea that all abortions should be approved by a consultant and disliked the idea that a woman's family circumstances should be grounds for an abortion. But there were an abnormally high percentage of 'Don't knows'. Anyway, this ammunition came too late. Both amendments were reversed by the Bill's supporters at the final stage in the Lords.

In the later stages of the abortion campaign some leading members of A.L.R.A. were doubtful about the real worth of the local groups because few of them were viable for more than brief periods, and in Birmingham, at least, seemed to provoke local opposition. Whatever the balance-sheet on that account, it was the local groups which came up with the best idea of the whole campaign—the idea of 'proving' you had majorities on your side.

A.L.R.A. Funds

One place in which the sudden upsurge in A.L.R.A.'s activities shows itself precisely is the accounts. In the 1950s and early 1960s expenditure fluctuated between £50 and £600 a year. But in the first year after the new generation took over, expenditure doubled to £1,300. By 1966 expenditure exceeded £4,000, and for the final period covering the parliamentary passage of David Steel's Bill, A.L.R.A.'s expenditure rose again, this time to nearly £6,000 in the year 1966–7.

The funds for the rapid increase in activity and expenditure came from two main sources. Subscription and donation income increased nearly sixfold, partly through the upsurge in membership, but also because a number of well-off sympathizers were persuaded to make sizeable donations. Rather more important than this source was largesse from America. The Hopkins Donation Fund of Santa Barbara, California, which aimed to assist 'poorly supported and pioneering causes', gave A.L.R.A. a grant of $2,000 in 1961, and six further grants in subsequent years. By 1967, the Hopkins Fund had given A.L.R.A. $24,500 (over £8,500)—more than half A.L.R.A.'s total income. But for the Hopkins money A.L.R.A.'s activities would have been severely curtailed and it is unlikely that the opinion polls could have been commissioned.

Thorough Lobbying

Until the 1960s A.L.R.A.'s activities were mainly educational rather than directly political. Although it managed to get two Bills sponsored in 1952 and 1954 neither made much progress. It was not until 1961 that the Association began to gather in many supporters among Members of Parliament. This became much more professional and systematic after the 1964 election. The new Parliament with a new vintage of younger Members looked promising. From 1965 A.L.R.A. sounded out support among M.P.s and kept careful records of their views. Two Abortion Bills were presented in the Commons in 1965 by Mrs Renée Short and Mr Simon Wingfield Digby. Neither had much chance of getting through, but both gave the association plenty of experience in the age-old practice of waiting around in the Lobby of the House of Commons and pouncing on M.P.s to find out their views. Vera Houghton and Alastair Service carried the brunt of this lobbying but they were helped by other committee members and by the efforts of the general membership. Early in 1966 A.L.R.A. had three organized lobbying sessions: what are known in the trade of politics as mass lobbies. A.L.R.A.'s 'mass' consisted of about 30 members who would come to the lobby sometime during an afternoon and evening. These members contacted both their own M.P.s and others whose views were unknown.

In June 1965, when Mrs Short introduced her Bill for abortion law reform under the ten-minute rule, A.L.R.A. knew of 150 sup-

161

porters. By February 1966, when Simon Wingfield Digby had a Second Reading debate for his Bill, A.L.R.A. had found a total of 340 supporters for some measure of law reform. The election five weeks later swept a number of these supporters out of the House. Influenced by the progress of Lord Silkin's liberal measure in the House of Lords, the new Abortion Bill introduced by David Steel was more radical than Wingfield Digby's. The old lists of supporters therefore had to be completely rebuilt. But by the time the parliamentary battle was properly joined in the Second Reading on July 22, A.L.R.A. reckoned nearly 400 supporters. 223 M.P.s voted for the Second Reading and only 29 against. A.L.R.A. had done its staff work well. It was only after the shock of this majority had sunk in that the opponents of abortion law reform began to stir themselves and it was not until January 1967 that a counter-organization, the Society for the Protection of the Unborn Child (S.P.U.C.), was actually formed.

The main core of opposition was of course the Catholic Church, but this organization, though infinitely bigger and stronger than A.L.R.A., had not yet concentrated its efforts on abortion. It was to play an important part later. Together with S.P.U.C. it inspired a dogged and cohesive parliamentary opposition, which capital punishment and homosexual law reform never had to face, and which continued to threaten the life of the Bill until the very last moment of the session in October 1967. But that is another exciting story.

Conclusion

The Abortion Law Reform Association can be categorized as a small pressure group with a single clear-cut purpose. It should be compared with organizations such as the National Campaign for the Abolition of Capital Punishment and the Divorce Law Reform Union. Its active members were largely middle class, articulate, left of centre, and female. The one-sixth of them who had had abortions themselves might be described as having a private sectional interest in reform—some perhaps even had a desire to justify their own decisions retrospectively. But for the great majority, disinterested, emotional and intellectual considerations were the only motivations.

For years A.L.R.A. was widely regarded as a morally subversive, crank organization. Government ignored A.L.R.A.'s views even when one of its own committees established the case for reform by admitting that a huge number of illegal abortions were performed every year. In the end, of course, it was Mr Wilson's administration, with pressure from the new intake of younger M.P.s, which provided unlimited parliamentary time so that the law could be changed. When this journal ten years ago devoted a whole issue to pressure groups A.L.R.A. was merely listed. Despite many rebuffs the Association continued in being and bided its time until public opinion and the political situation at last became favourable. To that extent A.L.R.A. is certainly a model for other pressure groups.

The abortion lobby did not secure everything it hoped for. It did not achieve an unequivocal statement in law that bad social conditions were in themselves a justification for abortion, or that a girl pregnant under the age of consent, or as the result of rape or incest, had undeniable grounds for abortion. But the vague terms of the clauses quoted at the beginning of this article seem to embrace all these circumstances, and sympathetic doctors will probably act upon this assumption. Despite the fact that many A.L.R.A. members are dissatisfied with its shortcomings, the Abortion Act does fulfil the core of A.L.R.A.'s demands and must rank as a major change in the criminal law.

The abortion lobby became successful when it was able to demonstrate to Parliament that despite religious opposition, public opinion had finally caught up with the views it had been expressing for thirty years. The lobby did not create this opinion, for many factors were at work, but it did influence public opinion, hasten it, and organize it when the time was ripe. If A.L.R.A. had not worked steadily for many years in a hostile climate, and campaigned intensively during the last four years, reform would not have come as early or as radically as it did.

The National Parks Campaign[1]*

Richard Kimber, J. J. Richardson and S. K. Brookes

This study is concerned with the efforts in 1971-2 of the British amenity and environmental movement to secure an independent planning administration for each National Park area. It sheds light on the strategy adopted by the environmental movement in its relations with both Government and Parliament, and on the problems (in terms of the level of popular sympathy and the opposition of powerful interests) with which it was faced. In particular it discusses the use of the public campaign as a means of influencing policy decisions.

As a case study in pressure group politics, it illustrates the value of many of the general propositions and descriptive statements made by group theorists, regarding the nature of activity and constraints under which some groups have to operate. In dealing, however, with groups which have hitherto received little attention from political scientists, it indicates that there are some points of emphasis on which it is necessary to take issue.

An important controversy has centred on the administration of the National Parks for almost thirty years, and to understand the significance of the events of 1971-2 a brief background summary is essential.

National Parks and Local Authority Power

Statutory form was given to the National Park idea by the National Parks and Access to the Countryside Act 1949.[2] The Act departed in a number of ways from the recommendations of the Dower[3] and Hobhouse[4] Reports which had been previously commissioned by the Government in its search for an adequate Parks formula. The Reports had urged strong financially independent administrations for the Park areas, relatively free of local authority control, with overall direction by an equally strong National Parks Commission. In response to pressure from the county councils (who were unwilling to concede any diminution of their power) the Labour Government put forward a compromise solution.

The National Parks Commission (N.P.C.), created by the Government, was denied any direct involvement in the administration and management of the Parks and was given merely advisory and supervisory functions. In single-county Parks the county council retained control with the provision of a council committee or sub-committee with delegated responsibility for the Park. One-third of its members, however, were to be appointed on the recommendation of the Secretary of State to look after national as opposed to purely local interests. In multi-county Parks, however, the Act provided for the creation of Joint Planning Boards, to which planning powers would be delegated and which would have power to appoint their own Chief Officer and planning and administrative staff. Again one-third of the members would be appointed by the Secretary of State, the remaining two-thirds being elected representatives of the local authorities over whose boundary the Park extended.[5]

An escape clause was embodied in the Act and allowed the Minister to revoke the provisions regarding the creation of Joint Planning Boards, if by 'reason of any special circumstances it was expedient to do so, for the efficient administration of the Park'.[6] Despite reassurances given in Parliament that this provision would only be used in special circumstances, its application became the rule rather than the exception in the creation of administrative arrangements for the Parks.

In the designation and establishment of the multi-county Parks, the Government and the National Parks Commission encountered strong opposition (and in some cases obstruction)[7] from the affected county councils, and on behalf of its members, the County Councils Association (C.C.A.) pressed successive ministers not to implement the Act. As the first designated, the Peak District National Park benefited from the novelty of the new Statute, and acquired the administrative structure actually envisaged by the Act. Subsequently the Board appointed its own Planning Officer and recruited the planning and administrative staff required to promote the purposes of the Park. Of even greater significance was the power invested in the Board to precept without limit on the constituent local authorities,[8] for a rate to meet the development and administrative expenses that it incurred. This financial independence set the Peak Park Planning Board apart from all other National Park authorities and provided the basis for its nationally acclaimed vitality and success. For the Lake District National Park, a rather hybrid Special Planning Board was constituted with severely limited

165

precepting powers, which eventually decided not to appoint its own Planning Officer but to use the services of the three County Planning Officers of Lancashire, Cumberland and Westmoreland. The Order designating the Snowdonia National Park structure produced fierce opposition from the affected Welsh County Councils.[9] Harold Macmillan, the Minister of Housing and Local Government, acceded to their demands and under the administrative structure eventually agreed (following the alternative arrangements set out in the 1949 Act) a Park Planning Committee was created for each constituent county council, to be responsible for that portion of the Park in its area. A virtually powerless Joint Advisory Committee was established, to which, on the initiative of the council or at the insistence of the National Parks Commission, matters of importance could be referred. Thereafter, as a result of continuing pressure from the county councils, this particular administrative pattern was adopted for the Yorkshire Dales, Exmoor, and Brecon Beacons multi-county Parks.

These varying administrative arrangements have been reflected in the degree to which individual Parks have fulfilled the purposes for which they were originally established. In particular national and international tribute has been paid to the Peak Park Planning Board for the quality and extent of its work. The Council of Europe has twice awarded the Park its Diploma 'in recognition of the high quality of conservation measures taken therein'. It is viewed by all voluntary organizations concerned with amenity and the environment as a model administrative structure on which basis all National Park Authorities should be reconstituted.

Although the county council committees responsible for the administration of the majority of Parks have similar membership (in terms of the percentage of appointed and elected members) and nominally can exercise the same functions as Joint Planning Boards, the difference lies in the prevailing attitudes of Board members towards the National Park and their acceptance that special considerations, and policy decisions, must therefore be applied. A more crucial difference, however, lies in the sense of collective responsibility for the Park that exists amongst the Board's full time planners and administrative staff, and the opportunities available for them to initiate schemes and proposals which are consistent with prescribed National Park purposes. In those Parks where a greater degree of local authority control has been exercised, local considerations regarding employment, general prosperity and financial stringency have usually had priority over the more amorphous and national considerations inherent in the National Park idea.[10]

In the period following the designation of the first National Park, several organizations consistently urged the Government to adhere to the spirit of the National Parks Act. Notwithstanding the drift of Government policy, the National Parks Commission, in its annual reports, and in its recommendations with regard to the establishment of specific Parks, continually reaffirmed the principle of Joint Board administration.[11] Similar encouragement came from the voluntary organizations such as the Council for the Protection of Rural England (C.P.R.E.), the Ramblers' Association and the Standing Committee on National Parks (S.C.N.P., see below) which had been at the forefront of those originally campaigning for the establishment of the National Parks.

The Ramblers' Association, which has always nurtured a radical and campaigning spirit, drew many of its original members from the early Labour movement, and was famous for its organized mass trespasses, over private land, to establish the principle of access for the purpose of public enjoyment. Although its grass roots membership is now somewhat less radical, its national and regional executives still campaign vigorously, and are now concerned with all matters relating to amenity and the environment. Together with numerous other organizations, the Ramblers' Association is represented on the S.C.N.P.

The S.C.N.P. was formed in 1936, its membership comprising representatives of those organizations which had given evidence to the Addison Committee on National Parks in 1931. The sole purpose of the S.C.N.P. is to press for the realization of the National Park idea. Its representative membership has now grown to include several groups not essentially concerned with the environment, but this is balanced by the more militant organizations such as the Ramblers' Association and by the active quality of its leadership.[12] Its finance and secretariat are provided by the C.P.R.E., and the Council for the Protection of Rural Wales (C.P.R.W.). Since the passage of the 1949 Act, the S.C.N.P. has maintained a watching brief on the National Parks. In addition to its general concern with the principles and administrative form of the National Parks, it undertakes case work in defence of the Parks, negotiates with local authorities, and gives evidence to Public Inquiries when particular areas are threatened.

Despite the constant pressure from these organizations, the Labour Government's Countryside Act of 1968 did nothing to change the machinery for planning and management in the National Parks. In effect it indirectly jeopardized the Parks by its reconstruction of the National Parks Commission as the Countryside Commission.[13]

167

Notwithstanding Government assurances to the contrary, the Commission's broader powers and responsibilities constituted a diversion of time and energy away from the National Parks, and its new membership reflected this change in emphasis (see below p. 177). In recent years the National Parks have been threatened more directly by increased public mobility, afforestation, the construction of power stations and reservoirs, and by mining companies eager to exploit the low grade mineral deposits in the upland regions. In some cases mineral mining and pump storage schemes etc. have been encouraged by the local authorities responsible for the Parks in the hope of improving local prosperity. For those concerned with the 'necessary wilderness' these developments constitute the ultimate criticisms of local authority control. In their eyes the prospect for the National Parks appeared decidedly grim.

However, the opportunity for a concentrated effort to secure modifications in National Park administration, came with the commitment of both major political parties to a fundamental reorganization of local government.

National Parks and Local Government Reform

The Redcliffe-Maud Commission on Local Government, which reported in June 1969, devoted a mere two paragraphs of its Report to the problems of the National Parks.[14] Nevertheless it suggested that each Park should be administered by a special authority, employing its own administrative staff and meeting its expenditure by means of precept on the main local authorities within the Park.[15] The Labour Government, in its White Paper on the Reform of Local Government in England, accepted these recommendations.[16] However, the satisfaction of the amenity societies was to be short-lived. Despite representations by the S.C.N.P. to the new Government,[17] following the Conservative Election Victory in June 1970, the subsequent White Paper[18] noted that in the Government's view very little change was required in the statutory provisions governing planning functions in the National Parks. Further memoranda from the S.C.N.P.[19] emphasizing the national nature of National Parks and the inadequacy of local authority control were to no avail and the Government's non-interventionist view was embodied in the Local Government Bill presented to Parliament in November 1971.[20] It should be noted that the Government's local government proposals were generally favourable to the existing county authorities, and it was therefore not surprising that this policy was also pursued in relation to National Parks.

This inflexible attitude on the part of the new Government was the major stimulus behind the developing campaign for administrative reform in the National Parks. The participants in this campaign included not only the established bodies with traditional interest in the Parks, but also some of the newer environmental organizations, together with some behind-the-scenes support from the Government's own agency responsible for National Park affairs (the Countryside Commission).

Muzzling the Watchdog

The Countryside Commission had fully endorsed the recommendations of the Redcliffe-Maud Report, and was somewhat disturbed by the new Government's failure to incorporate these arrangements in their proposals for Local Government Reform. The Commission therefore asked one of its leading members, Jack Longland, to prepare a report on the 'Administration of National Parks in relation to Local Government reorganization'. This Report was submitted to the Secretaries of State for the Environment and for Wales in June 1971, and recommended that there should be a Special Planning Board for each National Park. In Longland's opinion the Board should have powers to appoint its own Chief Officer and administrative staff and should be able to precept on the local authorities. Additional expenditure, he urged, should be met by an Exchequer grant.[21] The Longland Report was received with little enthusiasm at the Department of the Environment, and the Countryside Commission quickly ascertained that its proposed solution was almost certain to be rejected by the Government. In the light of this information it was clear that the Government's disposition was towards the County Councils and the representations which had been made by the County Councils Association (C.C.A.). Accordingly the Commission, in the hope of obtaining some concessions, approached the C.C.A. to secure a compromise agreement satisfactory to the Secretary of State.[22] Throughout the summer of 1971 there was a great deal of consultation between the D.O.E., the C.C.A. and the Commission, but the amenity societies were not represented at these discussions. In late October the Countryside Commission and the C.C.A. issued a joint statement—*National Parks and Local Government Reform*—outlining the compromise that they had managed to reach. Under this agreement the National Park committee would remain a committee of the new county councils. In the case of multi-county parks the Joint Advisory Committees would be abolished and a new joint county council committee would be set up after negotiations between the councils concerned. The new committees would have full planning powers (with the exception of the preparation of development plans) and would be under a statutory obligation to prepare a National Park Plan in consultation with the county councils. To co-ordinate the planning and management functions of the National Park committee, a full-time National Park Officer would be appointed to the staff of the county council.[23]

During the Second Reading of the Local Government Bill, the Secretary of State for the Environment, Peter Walker, indicated his intention to use this agreement as the basis for Government amendments to the Bill.[24] However, in the view of the S.C.N.P. the Countryside Commission's action had been the result of superior direction from the D.O.E., and the agreement therefore could not be regarded as freely negotiated.[25] In an attempt to meet this criticism, Mr Walker, during the Parliamentary debate, produced a letter from the Chairman of the Commission denying the charges. This stated that 'at no time did [the Secretary of State] or any member of the Government request or suggest that [the Commission] should have discussions with the County Councils Association.'[26] This statement of course avoided the question of whether permanent officials of the D.O.E. informed permanent or appointed members of the Commission that the Secretary of State would prefer a unanimously agreed solution. It would have been very embarrassing for the Government to proceed with administrative arrangements which were totally rejected by its own National Parks agency, as indeed the Minister had a statutory obligation to consult the Commission. It is not unreasonable to assume that his Department took steps to avoid such a situation.

With the Government's position firmly established by the Commission's *volte-face*, any further fundamental change in the administrative structure of the National Parks was dependent either on Parliamentary pressure, or on the development of a public outcry, or both.

The Campaign in the Country

The established amenity organizations, although expressing their concern for the Parks in their own journals, and at meetings of the Committee for Environmental Conservation (CoEnCo), were slow to canvass general public support for the principle of independent Park administration. This is particularly surprising in view of the fact that CoEnCo comprises representatives of over fourteen amenity organizations (including the Ramblers' Association and the C.P.R.E.) and is designed to provide an organization at national level to speak to the Government on matters of general principle affecting the environment. The reason for the delay in the important period between the publication of the White Paper and the publication of the Bill, was possibly due to overconfidence in the Countryside Commission's ability to defend the Parks, but may also have been due to the difficulty of co-ordinating the vast range of rather independent groups forming the 'environmental movement'. The initiative for a specific national *campaign* to highlight the problems of the National Park areas came from Eric Robinson, Chairman of the West Midlands Liberal Party and Chairman of the small but active Wolverhampton Civic Society.[27] Robinson's interest stemmed initially from his concern over mining threats to the Parks. At the Liberal Party Assembly in September 1971, he had successfully proposed an amendment to a resolution on rural landscape, which had committed the Party to 'press for increased independence in the administration of the National Parks'. In November 1971 (just as the Local Government Bill was being published) he began to contact amenity societies and Park Authorities suggesting a meeting which would discuss a co-ordinated campaign both in Parliament and the country at large to further this aim. At this stage Robinson had little idea of a campaign 'strategy' and was to some degree unaware of the other organizations' activity promoting the National Park cause. His initiative meant that from the beginning, the campaign had the support of the caucus of conservationist Liberal Peers, in particular Lord Henley, who was to play a major part in the campaign.

Support for Robinson's suggestion came from the Ramblers' Association, The Youth Hostels Association, Friends of the Earth, Friends of the Lake District, The Conservation Society, the Forestry Action Group, The Commons Society[28] and the Standing Committee on National Parks. These organizations, together with the Wolverhampton Civic Society, subsequently formed the *ad hoc* committee under the auspices of which the 'National Parks Campaign' was run. On the other hand the National Trust noted that its general policy was not to become involved in attempts to mobilize public opinion, or in campaigns in Parliament, and it therefore felt that it should leave the campaign to the other amenity societies.[29] In a similar vein the Clerk of the Lake District Park Planning Board replied that, although sympathetic, the Board as a local authority

171

should not involve itself with amenity pressure groups, but should act within its own sphere of influence, i.e., the Government and the Countryside Commission.[30] The Peak Park Planning Board, somewhat characteristically, had no such reservations and informed Robinson that its Chairman and Chief Planning Officer would attend the meeting.[31]

In order to protect the delicate position of the local authority representatives, minutes were not taken at the meeting, which was held in Wolverhampton in December 1971. Unanimous agreement regarding objectives was immediately achieved, but there was slight reluctance from some members to embark on a costly public campaign. Most of the ideas for campaign strategy and tactics were put forward by the Ramblers' Association and by the Standing Committee on National Parks. It was agreed that the efforts to obtain public support would culminate in a National Parks Day (on 24 February, 1972) when simultaneous meetings would be held throughout the country to reiterate the call for administrative reform. It was hoped that National Parks Day would coincide with the consideration of the relevant Sections of the Local Government Bill by the House of Commons Standing Committee; and that the volume of public opinion would induce both M.P.s and Ministers to support the amendments which were already being drawn up by the S.C.N.P.

The Wolverhampton meeting, organized by Eric Robinson, was considered by the Ramblers' Association and the S.C.N.P. as a useful initiative providing a convenient umbrella under which to work. In their view, however, had the National Parks campaign not developed out of the meeting, they themselves would have undertaken a similar operation. Also, because of their superior resources (for example the Ramblers' network of local and regional bodies) and their undoubted experience in these matters, the responsibility for the conduct of the campaign inevitably fell on these two organizations. Even so, the early initiative by Robinson had in part been prompted by the apparent inability of the established organizations to react quickly to a crisis.

A National Parks Campaign leaflet was drawn up by Chris Hall, Secretary of the Ramblers' Association, and was designed by a member of the Ramblers' Executive Committee. In January 1972, 10,000 copies were distributed through the members of the *ad hoc* committee to their constituent, affiliated and branch organizations. Emphasis was laid on obtaining support from the urban areas, and copies of the leaflet were sent to the 900 or so civic and amenity societies registered with the Civic Trust. Printing costs were initially met by the Ramblers' Association, which was reimbursed out of the varying contributions made by members of the *ad hoc* committee.

The leaflet called on all societies to make representations to local M.P.s and to organize a local meeting for National Parks Day. Coverage of the campaign, and advance publicity for National Parks Day, was easily obtained in the Press. In addition to sympathetic copy, and the willing publication of letters from amenity societies, leading newspapers gave editorial support to the principle of independent Park administration.[32] Against the barrage of campaign publicity the County Councils Association fought back with a statement by its Secretary, that 'it was vital that a democratic system should apply wherever possible' in the administration of the Parks. The new Parks Committees, he argued, should be financially responsible to local authorities and must be committees of the county councils concerned.[33] In its evidence to the National Park Policy Review Committee published at this time, the County Councils Association castigated the ill-informed criticism of the efforts made since 1949 by National Park authorities.[34] T. M. Haydn Rees, Secretary of the Welsh Counties Committee of the C.C.A., continued this counterblast with a public attack on the 'jaundiced views of various conservation organizations' who postulated 'biased and misinformed arguments'. He argued that the administration of National Parks should be within local government if the correct balance between conflicting considerations was to be achieved.[35]

With National Parks Day close at hand, the Government itself attempted to undermine the strategy of the amenity societies. In a Lords debate (on National Park administration) initiated by Lord Henley, Lord Sandford, Under Secretary of State, replied that the 'Government intended to put an end . . . to the fragmented responsibility in the administration of the Parks', and would provide for a single statutory body to be concerned with their planning and management.[36] From his additional remarks both in and outside the Lords, it was clear that these new bodies would be committees of the county councils, and that the Government's proposed amendments to the Local Government Bill would closely follow the compromise agreed by the Countryside Commission and the C.C.A.[37] These statements were, however, seen by the amenity societies as an effort to give the public the impression that the Government was acting reasonably and had made considerable concessions to its critics. A spokesman for the D.O.E. did much to support this interpretation, by stating that the Government's intention was to remove the new committees from any direct association with the county authorities so that they would not have to reconcile conflicting interests.[38] Significantly, several reporters did contact the

173

campaign organizations for their comments on the apparent 'victory' that they had achieved. This move was considered by members of the *ad hoc* Committee to be an insidious manipulation of public opinion, and they were quick to deny that the Government's decision represented any real change of heart. Chris Hall accused the Government of 'spreading a thick smokescreen of confusing words around its proposals for the Parks', and pointed out that the new committees would still be deprived of the initiative and drive that only independence could bring.[39] Despite this criticism of the proposed *control* over National Parks, a major concession had been made; Lord Sandford had promised that a 'lion's share' of the administrative costs of each Park would be met by the Exchequer (although specific proposals for this would not become available until the Government promoted legislation on Local Government Finance). This in itself provided scope for the excercise of further initiative by the new Committees and was enough to convince many in Parliament that adequate provision had been made for the Parks. Though welcome as a concession, it had the effect of weakening the position of the amenity societies in terms of Parliamentary support.

On the eve of National Parks Day, the Countryside Commission, without endorsing the campaign platform, characterized the various public meetings as a 'heartening expression of support for the National Parks'. Unfortunately for the campaign organizers, 24 February coincided with a national power strike, and the venue of several meetings had to be changed at the last minute or meetings had to held by candlelight. Even accounting for such disruption, however, the public's response to the *ad hoc* Committee's appeal was disappointing from the campaigners' point of view. The majority of members of urban civic societies did not feel strongly enough on the National Parks question to participate actively in the campaign. Campaign organizers also felt that the efforts of the rural amenity and preservation groups were equally disappointing. Even some of the national organizations from which the membership of the *ad hoc* Committee was drawn showed little initiative with regard to the sponsorship of meetings. Most of the events were organized by the regional branches of the Ramblers' Association (thereby confirming the expectation of the Ramblers' H.Q.)[40] while individual efforts were made by the Conservation Society, the Dartmoor Preservation Association, Friends of the Lake District, and the Sheffield and Peak District Branch of the C.P.R.E. An impressive list of speakers was drawn up for the regional meetings and at the main London rally the Chairman was Lord Henley, and on the platform were Lord Kennet (Chairman, C.P.R.E.), F. A. Bishop (Director

General, National Trust) and Carol Johnson, M.P.[41] The total attendance (at all meetings) was however, estimated at only 2,500. National Parks Day did little to enhance the campaign. As an indication of the ground-swell of opinion, designed to convince Government and Parliament of the political as well as functional desirability of independent Park administration, it can hardly be considered effective. The campaign merely mobilized that section of the public which in the circumstances one would expect to respond (i.e. it preached to the converted) and there was no apparent effect on the public in general. In addition the press coverage did not live up to the Committee's expectations; most of the points had been covered in the build up to National Parks Day and the meetings produced little which was new or newsworthy. The major achievement of National Parks Day had therefore been to reveal the basic weakness in the campaign—its lack of broadly-based popular support. This had not been previously apparent because of the extensive press coverage which had been achieved. As far as can be gauged it had provided nothing with which to encourage M.P.s or, more importantly, to convince Ministers that further concessions were required. The National Parks Campaign was in fact an example of what Professor Finer has termed a 'fire brigade' campaign, i.e. a campaign designed to influence action being taken, or about to be taken, in Parliament.[42] It should, however, be noted that the specific National Parks Campaign, prompted by Robinson's Wolverhampton meeting, was preceded by a long 'background' campaign designed to create a specific public demand for better treatment for the Parks.[43] It is therefore sometimes difficult to make a clear-cut distinction between 'fire brigade' and 'background' campaigns in that the former may develop from the latter.

Although Eckstein has stated that the public campaign is characteristic of pressure group activity in Parliamentary-dominated systems,[44] it is still a strategy currently favoured by many environmental groups despite the shift of power to the Executive. Recent campaigns of this kind have culminated (like that of National Parks) in Population Day and National Packaging Day. Eckstein goes on to suggest that, 'the public campaign has largely been replaced by informal and unostentatious contact between officials'.[45] However, for those groups with limited access to the decision-making process at the administrative level, the public campaign is perhaps the only major weapon at their disposal.[46] Its utilization is not really a function of Executive-Parliamentary relationships but of Executive-groups relationships, and the responsiveness (or otherwise) of the bureaucracy. As we have noted, the Government's unresponsiveness

175

was the key factor in the developments leading to National Park Day.

After 24 February, no further efforts were made to arouse popular opinion. The campaign did not disintegrate, however; it was transferred to the Parliamentary arena, where its responsibility was again in the hands of the S.C.N.P. and the Ramblers' Association. Before examining the Parliamentary stage of the campaign we must look more closely at the unsuccessful efforts to convince the Government through the normal administrative channels.

The S.C.N.P. and the Government

The S.C.N.P. has never acquired a 'consultative' status with the relevant Government Departments.[47] Periodically it secures permission to send deputations, and its views on various matters are given an audience. In 1964, following written representations to the Prime Minister, the S.C.N.P. was invited to develop its ideas on the National Parks, and on rural land-use in general, to help the Government in its formation of rural planning policy. The resulting S.C.N.P. memorandum, however, urged a radical departure from conventional land-use priorities and, therefore, received little attention. For the most part the Standing Committee's memoranda and representations are unsolicited and apparently carry little weight. Departments do not accredit the S.C.N.P. with the specialist skills or competence which they require in the formation or implementation of policy, and do not consider that the Committee has any special right to participate in the decision-making process. Perhaps of even greater importance is the S.C.N.P.'s lack of any veto power which it can use in the event of government intransigence. We might note in contrast to this the position of the County Councils Association, enjoying permanent consultative status, accredited with specialist knowledge and administrative skill, and aware that the withdrawal of its members' co-operation could create a whole range of difficulties for the Government of the day (especially during a period of Local Government Reform).[48] At all times throughout the campaign, the S.C.N.P. was operating at a distinct disadvantage compared with the well established local authority Associations.

Traditionally, however, there have been closer ties between the Standing Committee and the Government-appointed Countryside Commission, and its forerunner, the National Parks Commission. For many years, the National Parks Commission consisted of members closely associated with the S.C.N.P. In 1966, however, when it was reconstituted as the Countryside Commission, and its responsibilities extended, almost the entire membership was replaced. This severed the connection with the S.C.N.P. and prompted it to appeal for a closer association with the Commission.[49]

The amenity societies were nevertheless encouraged by the appointment of John Cripps, an Executive Committee Member of the C.P.R.E., to the Chairmanship of the Commission in 1969. This feeling was reinforced by the Commission's endorsement of the Redcliffe-Maud proposals and their adoption in the Labour Government's White Paper. These early encouraging signs were transformed into more optimism by the Commission's specific request that provisions required to implement the Longland recommendations be incorporated in the Local Government, and Local Government Finance Bills.[50] Bitter disappointment was inevitable, therefore, when the S.C.N.P. became aware of the compromise agreement reached between the Commission and the County Councils Association. At no time during these negotiations had the S.C.N.P. been informed by the Commission of its intentions and as a result it felt somewhat betrayed.[51] The S.C.N.P. immediately requested a discussion with John Cripps, and at a meeting at the C.P.R.E. headquarters were informed that, as the Government had found Longland's Report totally unacceptable, the Commission had set out to salvage what it could.[52]

Soon after this meeting, the C.C.A. and the Countryside Commission were asked to submit their views to a meeting to be chaired by the Secretary of State. Prior to this meeting, the Commission informally urged the Standing Committee to take the strongest possible line both inside and outside the forthcoming discussions in order to help them in their efforts to preserve the existing Planning Boards. During the course of the meeting with the Secretary of State, the Chairman of the S.C.N.P. read a short paper outlining the Committee's case and criticizing the intransigence of the local authorities and the indifference of successive Governments. The paper concluded: 'I am normally a peaceful man and the S.C.N.P., of which I am a member, has hitherto worked loyally within the system, but I must warn all concerned that if any such destructive decision (similar to that proposed by the C.C.A. and the Commission) were taken, it is the vast majority of the townspeople of England and Wales whose interests will be at risk, and the Countryside movement that we represent is largely supported by them. We shall therefore see to it that they know what is being taken from them and we shall take all political action open to us to avert the proposed changes'.[53] The Secretary of State thereupon suggested that the

177

S.C.N.P. was threatening the Government, although it was explained that they were merely outlining their next legitimate (and logical) course of action. In fact, later on, the Standing Committee was not circulated with a copy of the Consultation Paper which discussed the provisions (on the basis of the C.C.A./Commission Joint Statement) to be included in the Local Government Bill.[54] Its tenuous links with the D.O.E. were in effect severed and all future attempts to influence policy were to be directed at the Parliamentary rather than the Departmental level.

In retrospect, it is clear that the representations by the S.C.N.P. had been heavily outweighed by those of the County Councils Association. We have already noted the status generally accredited to the Association by Ministers and permanent Civil Servants, but on National Park questions the Association operates at an even greater advantage. The Department has always been unwilling to disrupt the pattern of local government and county council powers established by the Town and Country Planning Act of 1947. The *ad hoc* Planning Board constitutes a major threat to this established system and it has long been felt that if at all possible it should be avoided. Naturally these views coincide with those of the County Councils Association. The Association in fact paid little attention to the question of National Park administration in relation to the Local Government Bill, as it was quietly concerned with securing modifications to more important aspects of the Government's proposals. Only when the Longland Report came to its notice did the Association express its concern.[55] Whilst being unsympathetic towards the demands of the amenity movement, the Government was able to present its policy on the National Parks as a concession to the county councils, thereby possibly hoping to reduce the intensity of their opposition on other issues.

There had thus been little room for the S.C.N.P. to manœuvre at the administrative level. Any real concessions could only be achieved by a successful presentation of its case to a different forum. As we have pointed out, however, the campaign in the country was largely unsuccessful, and did little to reinforce the efforts in Parliament. To this final stage of the campaign we must now turn.

The Campaign in Parliament

The campaign in Parliament, despite wide press coverage, was not particularly intense, and must be seen in the context of the greater significance (to M.P.s) of many other aspects of the Local Government Bill. It was, however, pursued throughout the passage of the Bill in both the Lords and Commons. The decision to mount a full Parliamentary campaign had been taken by the S.C.N.P. in November. The Committee was fortunate enough to have Carol Johnson, M.P. (Lab., Lewisham S.) as a member, and he acted as adviser on procedure.[56] It also had a connection, through the Ramblers' Association, with Arthur Blenkinsop, M.P. (Lab., South Shields), who agreed to table amendments to the relevant Clause.[57] Blenkinsop's task in the Parliamentary Standing Committee was difficult. Few Members had interest in the National Parks issue, and those that had were either constrained by Party discipline on the Conservative side or by local government sympathies on both sides of the House. In an attempt to raise support, the S.C.N.P. prepared a critical analysis of the Government's proposals, together with amendments to the relevant Schedule and Clauses.[58] The amendments subsequently tabled by Blenkinsop differed slightly, but not in substance from those suggested by the S.C.N.P.[59]

In mid-February 1972, following arrangements made by Carol Johnson, the Chairman of the S.C.N.P. led a deputation to the House of Commons to present its case to members of the Parliamentary Standing Committee. In the Midlands, Eric Robinson made personal representations to local M.P.s, and was supported in these efforts by friends in the Civic Society movement. In view of the pressures imposed by the Local Government Bill, Arthur Blenkinsop's activities were limited to sounding out the Government's position, and to establishing how far it was prepared to move towards that of the campaign.

On 29 February 1972, the Parliamentary Standing Committee gave its consideration to the National Park clauses of the Bill. Moving his amendments, Blenkinsop called on the Government to rectify the situation existing in National Parks, and to take an opportunity which possibly might not arise again for forty or fifty years.[60] Patrick Cormack (Cons., Cannock) and Fergus Montgomery (Cons., Brierley Hill)[61] both of whom had been contacted by Robinson, expressed sympathy with Blenkinsop's amendments and Dennis Howell (Small Heath), the Labour Front Bench Spokesman, made a forceful speech on their behalf.[62] The Welsh Labour M.P.s, Goronwy Roberts (Caernarvon) and Barry Jones (East Flint) were eloquent in their defence of the county councils. Their arguments ranged from appeals for the application of the good Conservative principles of pragmatism[63] to reminders that the National Parks were for ordinary people and not for the 'trendy neurotics' who considered the Parks their weekend playground.[64]

179

With the Government promising to table its own amendments (if at all possible) at the Report Stage, Arthur Blenkinsop sought leave to withdraw his own amendments, thereby enabling the issue to be raised at a future date. Blenkinsop had realized that there was no hope of a Parliamentary victory. If he had pressed his amendments to a division, the National Parks campaign would have died on the floor of the Committee. By not doing so the campaigners had avoided revealing outright their essentially weak strategic position and so were able to maintain their pressure for concessions.

To the satisfaction of the Campaign's supporters in the House, the Government tabled its amendments for consideration on Report.[65] These adhered to the Countryside Commission/C.C.A. compromise, in reconstituting the existing Special/Joint Boards and establishing a single County Council Committee (for all other National Parks) with duties to appoint a full-time Officer and to formulate a National Park Plan. Introducing them in the House as the 'National Parks Charter', Graham Page (Minister for Local Government and Development at the Department of the Environment) looked forward to a great future for the Parks, and gave further reassurances that they would be supported financially by the Government. Blenkinsop tabled only one amendment at this stage, which would have given the Government power to establish special Planning Boards in single-county Parks. This was called but was not formally moved and Blenkinsop confined his efforts to seeking reassurances on the status of the National Park Officer and on the financial provisions.[66] Neither the Government nor the County Councils Association had expected any real difficulties in the Commons. Some M.P.s claim that the Government never took the National Parks campaign seriously: the National Parks Clauses were given a low priority by the Government and they had been drafted rather late in the proceedings. The County Councils Association, too, was confident of its strength, especially amongst Conservative M.P.s. In order to counter the efforts of Arthur Blenkinsop, the C.C.A. had merely briefed Goronwy Roberts to ensure that it secured support from both parties in the Standing Committee.

The Association was much more concerned with possible developments in the Lords, where party discipline was weaker and where the considerable cross-bench concern for the environment might favour the S.C.N.P. view. The County Councils Association, however, also had considerable support in the Lords, as it was to show during the passage of the Local Government Bill. But on questions relating to the administration of National Parks, it did not, in the event, become necessary to mobilize this. Chris Hall prepared a long and detailed memorandum for the members of the Upper House which outlined the muddled history of the administration of the National Parks,[67] and indicated the deficiencies of the Government's amendments tabled in the Commons.[68] It put forward the amendments which the S.C.N.P. had originally drafted, with the alternative which, failing the adoption of the major modification, would enable the Secretary of State to establish a special Planning Board for single-county Parks at any future date. Lord Henley, who possibly had reservations about 'rocking the Commission's boat', was briefed by Chris Hall, and agreed to fight the amendments through to a vote. When, however, he received copies of the brief, he sent an accompanying letter to Lords Kennet, Foot and Molson, suggesting that there was no point in pressing the issue to a division. In Lord Henley's opinion, the Campaign had done enough in obtaining the amendments already tabled by the Government. A defeat in the Lords Committee would discredit the Campaign while a success would only serve to annoy the Government, and would be reversed in the Commons when the Lords' amendments were considered. From all points, an intransigent line was undesirable. This was perhaps a pragmatic and politically sophisticated assessment of the situation and reflected Henley's political character and preferred method of operation. Henley in no way 'sold the pass' on the National Parks issue to the Government. His strategy, like that of Blenkinsop, left the Campaign with the option of reopening the case at some future date.[69] This strategy was accepted by Lords Molson and Foot, but Lord Kennet was unsympathetic.

During the Committee Stage, Lord Henley rose to speak on whether the clause 'stand part of the Bill' and characterized the Government amendments not as the 'National Parks Charter' but as the 'Sandford Package'.[70] The Countryside Commission, in his view, had agreed to a compromise which was not in the best interests of the National Parks; the only hope for the future was that the new county councils would improve on the performance of the old ones.[71] Such resignation did not, however, satisfy Lord Kennet who pointedly asked Lord Henley when he would explain the effects of the amendments he had tabled. Henley's reply was that he had already expressed the view that it would not be sensible to divide on the issue, and he was therefore proposing simply to move his amendments formally so that they would appear in Hansard as a testament to the National Parks Campaign. He did, nevertheless, acknowledge that the Committee could press the issue to a division if it so wished.[72]

In the ensuing debate, contributions in support of the Campaign from Lords Foot and Molson were forcibly countered by those with county sympathies (Lords Middleton, Ridley, Lytton and Amery). After the Government's position had been reaffirmed by Lord Sandford, Lord Henley followed the procedure that he had earlier outlined and in the event no objections were raised on this point and there was no division.[73] Lord Henley's leadership of the Campaign in the Lords has been subject to some criticism. It has been argued that Lord Kennet (had he accepted the role) would have been a more forceful and aggressive Whip. Whether such tactics would have been possible or whether they would have been of benefit to the National Parks Campaign is, however, questionable. As we have noted, the credibility of the Campaign was an important factor which Henley, like Blenkinsop, always had in mind. To annoy the Government and characterize the National Parks movement as obstructionist would merely have compounded the difficulties faced by the S.C.N.P. in their relations with the Government. Furthermore, Blenkinsop continually recognized that he might require help on other aspects of the Local Government Bill from Members who were his opponents on the National Parks issue. Considerations of this nature might have been even more appropriate to Lord Kennet (as Opposition spokesman) than to Lord Henley and would surely have tempered any more aggressive general strategy. Henley must therefore emerge with due credit for his performance in a situation which was never favourable to the Campaign.

The Lords debate effectively marked the end of the National Parks Campaign. Its organizers considered it to have been half successful, in as much as it secured the retention of the existing Park Boards and obtained increased staffing and financial assistance for the Park Authorities. This at least should improve their future performance.

Conclusion

Notwithstanding the claims of the Campaign organizers, viewed from an objective position, the Local Government Bill's settlement of the National Parks issue constituted a real victory for the *status quo* and its main advocates, the County Councils Association. Whilst it is unlikely that the various groups campaigning for the National Parks could have achieved more than they did, their chances of success were reduced by several factors. To some extent they had been caught unprepared by the Conservative Government's rejection of the Independent Board system, thus illustrating Finer's suggestion that 'advance intelligence' or its absence is an important factor in group success.[74] They had initially been lulled into optimism by the unexpected conclusions of the Redcliffe-Maud Report and the Labour Government's White Paper, and at a later stage by the total sympathy with their position, expressed in the Longland Report. In this latter respect there was some justification for qualified optimism as the Minister has a statutory duty to seek the advice of the Countryside Commission on matters relating to the Parks. On the face of it, it may not have seemed unreasonable to assume that the Commission's views carry weight with Ministers and Civil Servants. However, for over twenty years the National Parks Commission and its successor have urged the creation of administratively independent Parks with very little success. It was therefore unrealistic to attach too much significance to the Commission's influence and its recommendations. The mere fact that a government has appointed a statutory body to oversee and advise on a particular policy area, is in no way a guarantee of a high priority for that policy area in the government's planning. It is perhaps an indication of the naïvety of some amenity groups that they had hitherto regarded the Countryside Commission as a watchdog of their interests. At best it has proved to be cast in the traditional mould of British institutional watchdogs—bereft of any teeth. At worst its very existence may have done some positive harm to the amenity movement in that it created a false sense of security in the early stages of discussions, yet in the event it proved politically weak and felt compromised *because* it was a statutory body. If the case of National Parks is at all typical, then the Countryside Commission must be considered more as an extension of the machinery of government than as an appendage of the amenity movement. In fact there is some evidence that the Government itself does not rate the Commission as being particularly important in policy-making for it has decided to move the Commission's headquarters out of London altogether. This decision was taken despite the Commission's insistence that it needed frequent access to departments in Whitehall if it was to operate effectively.

Partly as a result of its experiences during the National Parks Campaign, together with the Commission's defeat over its relocation, the Ramblers' Association has openly attacked the Commission for being 'so passive that it is inviting its own destruction'.[75] In a Lords debate on the future of the Commission, initiated by Lord Henley, Lord Kennet (who was involved in the Commission's formation in 1968) pointed out that it was never intended that it should become an offshoot of the D.O.E. and that it should be perfectly free to oppose the Government.[76] In replying for the Government, Lord Sandford revealed that agreement had been reached with the Commission for getting its relationships with the Department 'on a satisfactory footing within the present statutory framework'. 'The agreement', he argued, 'fully recognizes the fact that the Commission has an independent voice of its own which it is entirely at liberty to use.'[77] In the face of such unambiguous assurances, one of the tasks facing the amenity movement will be to pressurize the Commission into using the power which the Government claims it already possesses. In fact, shortly after Lord Sandford's statement, the Countryside Commission publicly expressed its 'deep dismay' at the Government's refusal to designate the Cambrian mountains as a National Park without even holding a Public Inquiry.

Equally clearly, in the light of the success of the county councils in persuading successive governments to depart from their intentions of the 1949 Act, the representations of the County Councils Association were always likely to be given overriding consideration by the Department and Ministers. A conscious acknowledgement of this situation might have produced a less aggressive and therefore more productive approach to the Ministry (whilst maintaining their demands) and might have reduced the sense of disillusion with the Government and the Commission later on. In retrospect, the fate of the National Parks had been sealed by the C.C.A.-Countryside Commission compromise. The Campaign's main effect, as many realized, was to ensure that the Government at least implemented these compromise proposals. As published in October 1971 the compromise agreement was open to flexible interpretation by the Government. An 'unfavourable' interpretation might conceivably have led to the dismantling of the existing Boards (with some justification in the case of the Lake District Planning Board, whose Park under the new boundary arrangements would fall within a single County). Throughout, however, the Government had adhered to its stated position without attempting to modify the concessions secured by the Commission. It had had (by virtue of its heavy drafting commitments) the advantage of presenting its amendments when the National Parks Campaign had reached its climax in the country and had thereby been able to gauge the real strength of the campaign, as opposed to the earlier impression created by the mass media. To the extent that the culmination of the Campaign in National Parks Day was an obvious 'flop', the Government's hand was strengthened. Even so, had it not been for the public and Parliamentary campaign mounted by the amenity groups, the likelihood is that the National Parks would have been in an even weaker position than they are today. Even after the end of the campaign, the S.C.N.P. continued to be active in pressing the Commission to ensure that the agreement (particularly that part concerning the National Park Officers) was actually implemented by the C.C.A.

The National Parks Campaign is fairly characteristic of the 'promotional' efforts of the environmental movement in Britain. The fight to retain areas unspoiled by commercial and industrial development is often seen as a defence of an idea which many see as impracticable in a modern industrial society. Similarly the calls for a demographically and economically stable society have little immediate significance for the majority of people. Concerns of this nature are in most cases not recognized by Governments as being sufficiently legitimate or as carrying enough political weight to warrant changes in public policy. In addition they cut across too many conventional priorities and entrenched interests whose advocates normally play a major part in policy-making. In consequence, therefore, the opportunities for environmental organizations to participate in decision-making at the administrative level have, so far, been severely circumscribed. They have been forced to appeal to Parliament and public opinion to persuade the Government of the day that policy changes are necessary and in fact they have achieved some degree of success in this respect. The mass media are currently (and fashionably) sympathetic to the cause of environmental organizations and help to generate public sympathy on a variety of issues. A 'background campaign' has been mounted which has at least made the environment a significant political issue. As Roy Gregory has suggested,[78] the environmentalists have managed to create a 'halo effect' for environmental issues. They have done this largely through public campaigning and it is an asset which may be used to advantage. For example, following a similar public campaign, the Civic Trust and C.P.R.E. were successful not only in modifying the Government's policy on heavy commercial vehicles, but also in securing formal consultation rights with the D.O.E. They may thus be able to counter the traditional influence of the road haulage and motor manufacturing associations. In effect they have used the technique of public campaigning to secure access to the administrative channels normally used by those sectional interests. Having used public campaigns to some effect, the likelihood is that environmental groups will be faced with similar counter-campaigns mounted by their opponents. They will then need to improve their 'technical efficiency' (for example better 'advance intelligence') if they are to affect government policy significantly.

Richard Kimber, J. J. Richardson and S. K. Brookes

Notes

1 The authors would like to thank the Social Science Research Council for its financial support of their research. In addition they would also like to thank the following for their co-operation in the preparation of this article—Lt-Col. and Mrs Gerald Haythornthwaite (respectively, Chairman of the Standing Committee on National Parks and Secretary of the Peak District Branch of the Council for the Protection of Rural England); Chris Hall, Secretary of the Ramblers' Association; Mr Robinson, Assistant Secretary of the County Councils Association; Fergus Montgomery, M.P.; Arthur Blenkinsop, M.P., and Eric Robinson of the Wolverhampton Civic Society. The views expressed in this article are solely the responsibility of the authors.

2 The purposes of the National Parks, as presented by the 1949 Act, are (a) to preserve and enhance natural beauty in the designated areas, (b) to provide facilities for the enjoyment of persons resorting to the parks.

3 *National Parks in England and Wales*, Cmnd. 6628, 1945. (The Dower Report.)

4 *Report of the National Parks Committee*, Cmnd. 7121, 1947. (The Hobhouse Report.)

5 National Parks & Access to the Countryside Act, 1949, Section 8.

6 *Loc. cit.*

7 See *Report on the Administration of National Parks*. Recommendations on the reform of Local Government in England & Wales submitted by the Countryside Commission to the Secretary of State for Wales and the Secretary of State for the Environment (hereafter cited as the *Longland Report*), p. 12.

8 For an explanation of the power to precept see R. M. Jackson—*The Machinery of Local Government*, 2nd ed., Macmillan, 1967, p. 175.

9 See *Longland Report*, pp. 11–12.

10 See *Longland Report*, Appendix B. *Comparison of Actions Taken by National Park Authorities*, 1954–70. It should be noted, however, that Longland's conclusions regarding the relative success of the Peak Park Planning Board are challenged by the County Councils Association.

11 See Section 3 of the *Longland Report* for references to the position of the National Parks Commission.

12 The present membership of the S.C.N.P. is—C.P.R.E., C.P.R.W., A.A., British Mountaineering Council, Camping Club of G.B. and N. Ireland, Commons Society, Countrywide Holidays Assoc., Cyclists' Touring Club, Fell and Rock Climbing Club, Friends of the Earth, Geographical Assoc., Holiday Fellowship, National Trust, Pedestrians' Assoc., Ramblers' Assoc., R.A.C., Royal Society for the Protection of Birds, Society for the Promotion of Nature Reserves, Workers' Travel Assoc., Y.H.A.

13 See Stanley Johnson, *The Politics of the Environment*, Tom Stacey, 1973, p. 41,

for an outline of the Government's intentions with regard to the reconstitution of the National Parks Commission. See also Government Circular 44/68.

14 *Report of the Royal Commission on Local Government* 1966–9, Cmnd. 4040, vol. I (hereafter referred to as Redcliffe-Maud). The membership of the Commission included Sir Jack Longland.

15 Redcliffe-Maud, vol. I, paras. 356–7.

16 Cmnd. 4276, February 1970.

17 Standing Committee on National Parks memorandum *The Administration of National Parks in England and Wales*.

18 *Local Government in England and Wales*, Cmnd. 4584, Feb. 1971. See also the Consultative document *Reform of Local Government in Wales* (published at the same time).

19 *Local Government Bill—National Parks*, statement published by S.C.N.P., October 1971 and *Further Statement* published in the same month.

20 See Schedule 17 and Clause 179 of the Local Government Bill.

21 See *Longland Report*, pp. 46–7.

22 *Fifth Report of the Countryside Commission*, 1971–2, p. 4.

23 Joint Statement by the County Councils Association and the Countryside Commission, 27 October 1971. The Commission inserted two reservations into the agreement, (a) that the Peak and Lake District Planning Boards would be reconstituted and (b) that the National Park Plans should be local plans within the Development Plan system, the preparation of which should be the responsibility of the National Park Committee.

24 *Hansard*, 16 November 1971, Col. 247.

25 Letter to *The Times*, 8 November 1971, from Lt-Col. Haythornthwaite, Chairman of S.C.N.P.

26 *Hansard*, 16 November 1971, Cols. 246–7. This letter was again referred to by Lord Sandford, Under Secretary of State for the Environment, during a debate on National Parks in February 1972.

27 Eric Robinson is now a member of the Liberal Party's Environmental Panel, and Chairman of the recently formed transport reform group called Transport 2000 until November 1973.

28 Its full title is The Commons, Open Spaces and Footpaths Preservation Society.

29 Letter from the Secretary of the National Trust to Robinson, 12 November 1971. Later, however, the Trust became conscious of its conspicuous absence as a sponsor of the Campaign and the Chairman wrote to *The Times* explaining its concern for the National Parks and its caution with regard to public campaigning. See *The Times*, 19 January 1972.

30 Letter from the Clerk of the Lake District Park Planning Board to Robinson, 11 November 1971. In the event, however, the Board was represented at the meeting.

31 Letter from Peak Park Planning Board to Robinson. Not surprisingly the County Councils responsible for the administration of Parks were unsympathetic to Robinson's proposals and declined the offer of representation, e.g., see letter from the Clerk of Northumberland C.C. to Robinson, 12 November 1971, which challenged the assumption that Joint Planning Boards were the most appropriate form of Park administration and that the level of expenditure was the best measure of an Authority's achievements.

32 See for example an editorial in the *Sunday Times*, 5 December 1971, and an editorial in *The Times*, 19 January 1972.

33 *The Guardian*, 24 January 1972.

34 County Councils Association, *National Parks*, memorandum to the National Park Policy Review Committee, page 1. See also *The Daily Telegraph*, 24 January 1972.

 The National Park Policy Review Committee was set up in mid 1971 under the Chairmanship of Lord Sandford. The terms of reference were 'To review how far the National Parks have fulfilled the purposes for which they were established—to consider the implications of the changes that have occurred, and may be expected, in social and economic conditions, and make recommendations for future policies.' It should be noted that the form of administration for the Parks was specifically excluded from the terms of reference.

35 *The Times*, 4 February 1972.

36 House of Lords, *Debates*, 15 February 1972, Cols. 139–40.

37 For the text of a later speech by Lord Sandford see *The Surveyor*, 25 February 1972, p. 11.

38 *The Guardian*, 17 February 1972.

39 *The Surveyor*, 25 February 1972, p. 3.

40 A Ramblers' Association circular on National Parks Day (E. 1815) stated 'as usual the R.A. will have to bear the brunt, through its better level of organization, in getting the campaign off the ground'. The Association's efforts were in fact quite considerable. In addition to a constant flow of circulars, advice and information sheets, the headquarters prepared speaker's notes for the organizers of National Parks Day meetings, helped to co-ordinate these meetings and maintained press contacts throughout the Campaign.

41 See list of National Parks Day meetings in Ramblers' Association circular E.1929.

42 S. E. Finer, *Anonymous Empire*, Pall Mall, 1966, p. 93.

43 *Ibid.*, p. 84.

44 H. Eckstein, *Pressure Group Politics*, Allen & Unwin, 1960, pp. 22.

45 *Loc. cit.* For further discussion of this point see p. 13.

46 As Eckstein acknowledges, a group '. . . which has no close clientele relationship with the executive department may be driven willy nilly to seek their aims through other channels'. *Ibid.*, p. 21.

47 Eckstein's 'Negotiation—Consultation' continuum which he uses to characterize government/group relationship does not quite accommodate the situation of the S.C.N.P. It has only a 'quasi-consultative' position which, as we shall indicate, seems subject to departmental whim. See Eckstein, p. 23.

48 The importance of local authority co-operation, especially during a period of reform, was acknowledged in an early White Paper, *Area and Status of Local Authorities in England and Wales*, Cmnd. 9831, 1956. (See R. M. Jackson, p. 314.)

49 Deputation to the Ministry of Housing and Local Government, 20 November 1969, by representatives of S.C.N.P.

50 Letter to Secretaries of State for Wales and Environment accompanying the Longland Report.

51 The C.P.R.E. *Annual Report* for 1971 reported that 'The Countryside Commission's change of front had saddened and perplexed its friends in the amenity and open-air movement ... we feel bound to express extreme disappointment at the unheroic posture ... adopted [by the Commission]' p. 17.

52 It is, however, believed by some leading amenity campaigners that one senior member of the Commission's Staff was favourably disposed towards the 'compromise' and considered it to be the best form of administration for the National Parks.

53 Speech by Lt-Col. Haythornthwaite at the meeting held under the Chairmanship of the Secretary of State for the Environment, 29 October 1971.

54 Note by D.O.E. and the Welsh Office, *The Local Government Bill and National Parks Administration*, January 1971.

55 The County Councils Association position is stated in their memorandum to the Government, *The Administration of National Parks*, 6 September 1971.

56 Carol Johnson is a member of the Chairman's Panel, a member of the Council of the National Trust and Chairman of the Commons Society.

57 Arthur Blenkinsop has a long history of support for the National Parks. For example he once tried to introduce a Private Member's Bill which would have established Independent Boards for all the Parks. He has been active as a Vice-President of the Ramblers' Association, member of the Commons Society and Chairman of the Council of the Town and Country Planning Association.

58 Draft letter from S.C.N.P. to selected Members of the House of Commons and House of Lords. The S.C.N.P.'s proposals would have (a) ensured the reconstitution of existing special and joint Planning Boards, (b) ensured the creation of Planning Boards for all single- and multi-county Parks, and (c) increased the percentage of appointed members of each Board from 33 per cent to 50 per cent.

59 House of Commons, *Order Paper*, 29 February 1972, Standing Committee D.

60 Standing Committee D, Debates, Local Government Bill, 35th sitting, 29 February 1972, Cols. 2001–9.

61 Cormack said in the debate that he had received more correspondence on the National Parks Campaign than on any other aspect of the Local Government Bill. *Ibid.*, col. 2011.

62 *Ibid.*, cols. 2041–8.

63 *Ibid.*, col. 2032.

64 *Ibid.*, col. 2041.

65 House of Commons, *Order Paper*, Notice of Amendments, 22 May 1972.

66 *Hansard*, 19 July 1972, cols. 768–9.

67 *National Parks and the Local Government Bill*, Brief for Members of the House of Lords.

68 *Ibid.*, pp. 7–11.

69 The S.C.N.P., after the passage of the Local Government Bill, shifted its attention to the work of the Sandford Committee and to ensuring that the Government honoured the agreement which had been reached earlier.

70 House of Lords, *Debates*, 19 September 1972, col. 952.

71 *Ibid.*, col. 955.

72 *Ibid.*, col. 957.

73 *Ibid.*, cols. 977–80.

74 Finer, pp. 56–7.

75 See report in *The Guardian*, 29 May 1973.

76 House of Lords, *Debates*, 15 May, 1973, col. 792.

77 *Ibid.*, col. 800.

78 Roy Gregory, 'Conservation, Planning and Politics; Some Aspects of the Contemporary British Scene', *International Journal of Environmental Studies*, vol. 4, 1972, p. 37.

Part III

PRESSURE GROUPS AND THE POLITICAL SYSTEM

Introduction

The previous section comprised a selection of studies of specific interests. In this section we move to matters of more general concern. One of the widest interests in society is of course that of the consumer, yet for this very reason the consumer has been in a strategically weak situation. In the first article in this section, Leonard Tivey reviews the various candidates for the role of consumer pressure group in Britain and examines the possibility of a consumers' alliance. From a theoretical point of view, the weaknesses of the consumer's position are that—as Downs and Olson argue—the information costs involved in exerting influence seem to be too great, and there is no rational incentive for an individual to achieve objectives he shares with others. For these reasons they argue that producer groups will receive favoured treatment compared to the consumer; it should certainly be clear from Part II that producer groups in Britain are well-organized and are closely and continuously consulted by the Government. Yet, as Nadel points out (in *The Politics of the Consumer*, Bobbs-Merrill, 1971, p. 240), the problem with the ingenious analyses of Downs and Olson is that consumer legislation *is* passed, even if—so far—it is somewhat limited.

Although in the introductory section we emphasized the ubiquity of pressure groups, most studies have been of groups at the national level. Studies of local government have tended to overlook the wealth of pressure group activity at the local level. We have therefore included two items on local groups. John Dearlove examines the relationship between interest groups and councillors, and in particular the response of the latter to the former, by means of a survey of councillors in a London borough. Richard Bryant discusses the setting, goals, strategies, and achievements of community action.

Underlying each of these articles is the notion of political participation which (if community action of the kind discussed by Bryant is anything to go by) is increasing in Britain. In order to determine whether groups really are agents of political participation, S. E. Finer considers the four main theories which define the desirable relationship of groups to the government. After examining the likelihood of groups being able to play the roles assigned to them in these theories, he concludes that it is the theory which attributes to groups little more than a certain veto power that seems to fit the facts more closely than the others. Finer also considers the subjective aspects of participation and the claim that low levels of participation are due to environmental factors, and that if these were suitably modified the levels of participation might rise.

The last two articles in the book summarize and evaluate the role of pressure groups in the political system. R. T. McKenzie's article compares the respective roles of parties and pressure groups and assesses the effect of groups on government, while J. D. Stewart's conclusion to his study of pressure groups and their relation to the House of Commons asks whether groups have too much or too little influence. He concludes that, while there are dangers which must be guarded against, it would be wrong to argue for a wholesale condemnation of the part pressure groups play in our system, for it is often a valuable one. One of the problematical aspects of the relationship of groups to Parliament, which is receiving attention from politicians as this book is being compiled, is that of the undeclared outside interests which Members may have. The proposal for a register of Members' interests is once again being considered, having last been rejected by a Select Committee in 1969—partly on practical grounds and partly because it would have to be somewhat inquisitional. The Liberal Party keeps such a register, as do the Scottish Labour Party and a number of local authorities. Most commentators are agreed that, while there are practical difficulties, it is the responsibility of M.P.s to make their interests known. After the Poulson and Watergate affairs, not to mention the seemingly endless stream of newspaper reports of corruption in local authorities, the case for such a register is overwhelming if the public is expected to retain any respect for, or trust in, its representatives.

The Politics of the Consumer *

Leonard Tivey

In the political systems of modern industrial society it is usual to
distinguish a number of competing interests, some well organized
and others not. The development of voluntary economic planning
in Britain in the 1960s has revived concern with an alleged defect
of these systems. There are, it is said, powerful rival groups representing business and workers, but these are both 'producer' groups;
there is nobody in a position to speak for consumers and to press
their cause. The object of this article is to review the candidates for
the role of consumers' pressure group, to examine the prospects, and
to try to explain the causes of the difficulties.

The Representation of Consumers

A beginning may be made by dismissing some very weak claimants.
In its evidence to the Royal Commission on Trade Unions and
Employers' Organizations, the T.U.C. pointed out that trade
unionists were consumers as well as producers. When giving oral
evidence before the Royal Commission the Assistant General Secretary of the T.U.C., Mr Victor Feather, is reported as saying that
trade unionists were consumers sixteen hours a day and that the
consumer interest would be reflected by the General Council of the
T.U.C. itself.[1] This is amiable nonsense. The essential purpose of
trade unions is to protect their members in their working lives, not
their consuming lives. The whole structure and activity of the trade
union movement is focused on the employer-employee relationship,
and not on the supplier-consumer relationship. Nor have the unions

* Reprinted with permission from *The Political Quarterly*, vol. 39, no. 2, April–June
1968, pp. 181–94, and incorporating some revisions by the author. The author is
Senior Lecturer in Public Administration in the University of Birmingham. He is a
Member of Birmingham Consumer Group and Ordinary Member of the Consumers'
Association. He was formerly a research worker at P.E.P.

developed any particular expertise for the defence of consumers. For similar reasons—concentration on other things, and lack of expertise —the claim that local authorities are consumer bodies must be dismissed. Clearly there must be some other qualifications besides having consumers in membership, otherwise every organization under the sun would be a consumers' organization.

Claims are also sometimes made that knowledge and understanding of consumers' behaviour is in itself a qualification to act as a spokesman for their needs. Thus retail distributors and market researchers are thought, by their expertise alone, to be appropriate representatives of consumers. But it is scarcely a satisfactory claim. There may well be many occasions when the interests of distributors and consumers are in harmony, and in these cases collaboration —against manufacturers or governments—could be appropriate. In general, however, distribution is a form of production, and consumers may wish to criticize the quality of this service as of others. The interest of retailers and market researchers is in selling, and though they may serve as advisers and allies of buyers they are never adequate spokesmen for the interests of consumers.

There are, however, several organizations with serious claims as the representatives of consumers:

The Co-operative Movement

(a) The first and largest of these is the co-operative movement. The distinctive feature of this movement is its style of organization and its democratic principles of control, each member being entitled to play an equal part in determining its policies and in electing its management. There are some producers' co-operatives within the movement, but the main structure (now being recast) is dominated by the retail societies and their creations, the Co-operative Wholesale Societies. Employees are not excluded from membership of the retail societies (and in some situations take a large part in control), but the great majority of members are essentially customers. The practice of paying dividend to members according to the value of purchases emphasizes the primacy of the customers' position. It was in fact the work of Sidney and Beatrice Webb, in their *Consumers' Co-operative Movement* [2] and elsewhere, which led to the emphasis on the consumer character of the movement. The report of the Independent Commission in 1958 affirmed that:

> ... the Movement also has a wider duty to the consuming public as a whole.
> Being subject to no internal conflict between shareholders' interests and

consumers' interests, but viewing matters solely from the standpoint of the latter, it is especially well-placed to represent the consumer in all matters of public policy.[3]

The strength of the co-operative movement's claim to speak for consumers lies in the size and composition of its membership. Taken together the retail societies in Britain had in 1972 a total membership of over 12,000,000. Since usually only one member of a family joins, this probably means that over 50 per cent of the households in Britain are connected with the movement. Moreover, there is a large proportion of working-class members, a section of the community not prominent in other consumer organizations. The fact that co-operatives have well-established democratic systems for the articulation of their policies must be counted as an important asset, in spite of much apathy in parts of the process. The co-operative leaders have at least some constitutional basis for speaking on behalf of their members.

Unfortunately there are serious drawbacks to co-operative claims. It is sometimes said that ideological and political commitment is one of these. In fact the trade unions are also politically committed, and in practice the trade associations too: yet they are recognized as representative bodies. Nevertheless, membership of a co-operative implies acceptance (at least) of a particular way of trading, and this for the leaders is a matter of principle. Co-operative leaders represent co-operators, therefore, not consumers as such. It is true that the co-operative movement, including the Co-operative Party, has always insisted on its concern with general consumer issues, and has made proposals about consumer protection on a national scale. Non-members, however, cannot be regarded as an apathetic fringe, or as dissociating themselves from the organization of consumers, in the way non-members of a trade union may be regarded. They are rather non-co-operators; and they constitute a major section of the consuming public. In terms of trade, of course, the co-operatives' position is far from dominant—they account for under 10 per cent of retail trade. The co-operative movement cannot be accepted, therefore, as fully representative of consumers in general.

A second difficulty in the co-operative position lies in the productive activities and associations of the movement. The majority of co-operators are consumer-members; nevertheless, the bulk of the actual organization is productive in character. This is true, it must be noted, as much of the retail societies as of the C.W.S. Distributors are not consumers. The expert knowledge which becomes available is some advantage, but the necessary preoccupation with productive success and the intermingling at the professional

197

level of producer with consumer considerations must affect the clarity and the single-mindedness of the co-operative outlook. The co-operative movement has long participated in producers' trade associations, and in May 1967 it was announced that the Co-operative Union was participating in a new peak-level interest group, the Retail Consortium. In the confused world of economic interest groups, the consumer-aspect of problems has suffered from the lack of distinctive presentation of the consumers' viewpoint. In these circumstances, the relative 'purity' of a consumer-group is a matter of importance, and on this score the co-operative movement must rate poorly.

The Consumers' Association

(b) The most significant development in consumer affairs in Britain in recent years was undoubtedly the establishment of two comparative testing agencies. Only one of these, the Consumers' Association, now survives, contrary to the hopes of the Molony Committee.[4] The Consumers' Association was founded in 1956 by a few pioneers, and has thrived ever since. By 1972 it had over 600,000 associate members, essentially subscribers to its monthly journal *Which?* The control of the Association's affairs is in the hands of a Council of fifteen members, who are elected by the Ordinary Members. Until recently these were in practice chosen by the Council. In 1967 a scheme for 'democratizing' these arrangements was announced, by which the number of Ordinary Members was to be increased: in consequence the 230 enfranchised members of June 1967 had risen to 2,200 in 1972. A hundred or so of these usually attend the Annual General Meeting.

The basis for the recognition of a comparative testing agency in a representative capacity must lie in its expert knowledge of consumer attitudes, and in its clear attachment to the cause of consumers uncomplicated by other interests. In both these respects the Consumers' Association has strong qualifications. Its leadership and staff have long experience and great ability in dealing with typical consumer issues. The nature of its work ensures detailed and up-to-date knowledge of the markets for many commodities (especially 'consumer durables'), and of the ways in which the consumers' position needs protection and support. The constitution of the association ensures, moreover, that so far as it is possible, the consumer-aspect of affairs is the dominant consideration. There is a restriction on members of the Council:

No person shall be eligible to become or be a member of the Council of the Association if in the opinion of the Council he shall be directly engaged as a principal in the manufacture distribution and sale of goods or commodities to or in the rendering of services to the public or shall be directly engaged as a servant or agent in promoting the sales or use of such goods or commodities or services.[5]

Restrictions of a similar character were to be applied, by a 'screening' process, to the new Ordinary Members who became eligible under the democratization scheme; in practice there have been no exclusions.

No attempt to achieve complete independence and 'purity' can succeed, of course, since there is no such thing as pure consumer. However, some goods and services are more susceptible to comparative testing than others, and the rules of the Consumers' Association serve to exclude those closely concerned with production of goods or services likely to be tested. They do not exclude, of course, any interest in productive organizations since shareholders and employees remain eligible; but on balance the leadership of the Consumers' Association is as free from 'productive' entanglements as can be expected.

However, the Association does have some serious weaknesses. Its associate membership of 600,000 is small if one considers the size of the adult population which is, after all, the real consumer constituency. Its composition is believed to be overwhelmingly middle class. But in any case these associate members are mere subscribers, and for the Association's leaders to speak on their behalf would be as impertinent as is the claim of newspapers to speak for their readers. A claim to represent ordinary members would have more validity, but even the current enlargement of this group will leave it too tiny to expect recognition as a national peak-level interest group.

A second difficulty lies in the purpose of the Association, which is primarily that of comparative testing. It is necessary to the success of the Association for it to promote the use of its services, and to encourage the sales of *Which?* and other publications. This makes it adopt some of the techniques and attitudes of other organizations with a product to sell—large-scale advertising, for example, and hypersensitivity to criticism.[6] It could be argued that the Association should abandon its pretensions to represent anybody, and operate a research and testing service on a commercial basis. But it would be a serious loss to the consumers' cause if it were to do so, for it provides at present the main focus of independent consumer knowledge and thinking.

199

Leonard Tivey

The National Federation of Consumer Groups

(c) Consideration may also be given to the claims of the National Federation of Consumer Groups which brings together at the national level many local consumer groups. This was established in 1961 with the encouragement and support of the Consumers' Association.

In some ways the Federation and its member-groups can claim to speak for a more active section of consumers than any other organization. Local groups usually consist of subscribers to local consumer journals, but most of these publications are produced by voluntary effort. Consequently the groups contain a relatively high proportion of members who are involved in their work. In a situation where everyone has a bona fide consumer interest, those with a record of action in support of the cause have some right to be heard. If a grass-roots consumerist movement is sought, then the local groups provide it.

There are, however, disastrous weaknesses. There are now over 60 groups, with a total membership of perhaps 12,000. There are many areas with no group. They are all run by part-timers, and such expertise as may have been acquired is largely concerned with services, not manufactured products. Their financial resources are negligible, and the impact they make even on local communities is not always very great.

For many years the links of the Federation with the Consumers' Association were very close. In 1972, however, the financial support which had been given to the Federation headquarters was drastically reduced (there was never any money for the local groups themselves). In consequence the Federation is run part-time by its secretary in Birmingham. The vigour of the Federation and of many groups continues, and indeed they have now proved by their survival that the movement is not an ephemeral pastime; this in turn is leading to some official recognition as representative and nominating bodies. On major issues at national level the policies of the Federation are likely to put it in alliance with the Consumers' Association, but the possibilities of a distinctive role are emerging.

Specialized Consumer Organizations

(d) It is appropriate at this point to consider the role of a miscellany of consumer-type organizations with specific interests, as distinct

200

from the general concern of those discussed so far. One of these, the Patients Association, has had some success in the very difficult exercise of raising an independent voice for the consumers of medical services. The Advisory Centre for Education, with headquarters in Cambridge, aims to provide information and advice to consumers of educational services. A number of women's organizations, including Women's Institutes and Townswomen's Guilds, maintain their concern with some consumer matters. The Women's Advisory Committee of the British Standards Institution played a notable part in establishing the Consumer Advisory Council of the B.S.I., which launched the first journal giving comparative reports, *Shoppers' Guide*, in April 1957. The Citizens' Advice Bureaux deal with many types of inquiry; some of them are about consumer matters, and for dealing with these the Bureaux receive a Government subsidy. In another field, the motorists' organizations, and the Pedestrians' Association, have claimed to be spokesmen of road users. The Housewives' Trust is an active body which has achieved some recognition.

Ingenuity could no doubt extend the list: the National Union of Students could perhaps be regarded as an organization for consumers of educational services, though in fact, it has more of the characteristics of an occupational group. A list of organizations connected with consumer interests, put out by the Consumer Council, includes the National Marriage Guidance Council.[7] In general these miscellaneous bodies share the problems of the other bodies: some have unrepresentative constitutions, others are mainly preoccupied with non-consumer matters, and many have very small proportions of their clientèle in membership. Nevertheless their contribution is important, since they can pay continuous attention to services, like medicine and education, where the interests of consumers are particularly difficult to formulate and organize; and some of them help to spread consumer education to special audiences.

Governmental Bodies

In the history of consumer protection, of course, the part of the Government has been crucial: without legislation little could have been secured. In the matter of consumer representation there has also been initiative from Governments. A beginning was made in 1931 with the establishment of a consumers' committee under the Agricultural Marketing Act, to offer a countervailing influence to the producer-dominated Marketing Boards. The main development was in the nationalization Acts in the 1940s, which set up consumer, consultative or user committees in the publicly owned industries. These have been much-criticized bodies: nevertheless, they began, long before there was much public pressure, to formulate consumer attitudes to policies in their industries, and to provide a means whereby serious complaints could be taken up.

The Consumer Council

In the field of potential pressure groups, however, a more fundamental step was the creation in 1963 of the official Consumer Council, following the recommendation of the Molony Committee. This was concerned with consumers' education and with promoting action on their behalf. It was prohibited by regulation from dealing with individual complaints, from comparative testing and from legal action.

In the circumstances the Consumer Council took on the appearance of a major pressure group. The generality of its functions tended to give it a status appropriate to leadership and co-ordination, and it showed itself willing to undertake a campaigning role. It was never very well financed, however, and in 1971 the new Conservative government withdrew its grant and brought its career to an abrupt end. Perhaps this shows that an 'official' publicly-financed body can never be a free and effective pressure group. A body like the Bank of England can be a powerful independent force because it is recognized as having the City behind it. No one could be sure whether the Consumer Council (or, indeed, any consumer body) had much support or not. Certainly there was not the active demonstration of such support crucial for an active political influence. In 1972 there was another turn in the fortunes of the consumer movement, and for the first time a Minister was designated—Sir Geoffrey Howe became Minister for Industry and Consumer Affairs within the giant Department of Trade and Industry, with control of a considerable staff. Moreover, under the Fair Trading Act of 1973 a Director General of Fair Trading was appointed with very wide areas of concern. Practices he considers unfair can be referred to a Consumer Advisory Committee, and this in turn can lead to an order prohibiting the practice. Hence there is a consolidation of responsibility for consumer matters within the Whitehall machine—a form of 'clientelism' —and this brought a spurt of energy. The long-term development of this innovation could have importance for the policy-making process; at present it must be regarded as experimental.

A Consumers' Alliance?

The various bodies which might represent consumers have, therefore, many weaknesses and disadvantages. Some have few members
or resources; others are preoccupied with testing or distributive
activities. None of these are necessarily crucial in themselves—
certainly few would suggest that mass membership was an essential
prerequisite of political influence. In the pressure-group world,
however, the various consumers' organizations have yet another
drawback which is perhaps the most serious of all. Whatever claims
they have as spokesmen, they can scarcely be regarded as consumers'
leaders in the sense that they could negotiate on behalf of consumers,
or commit them to any kind of action. It is true that the leaders of
producers' organizations—trade associations and trade unions—
may not be able to 'control' their members, and that this lack of
ultimate sanction creates difficulties for their role in contemporary
methods of voluntary economic planning. Nevertheless, these
organizations can command the loyalties of their followers sufficiently to be accepted as bargainers on their behalf, as well as spokesmen for their needs. No consumers' organization is in a position to do
anything of the sort. As Miss Eirlys Roberts has written:

> The consumers' associations have not so far undertaken any collective
> action. They do not force manufacturers and shopkeepers to bring down
> prices, or put quality up, by boycotting goods which are too dear or not good
> enough. They do not oblige shops to keep open when it suits the customers,
> rather than the shopkeepers, that they should be open. They do not do so,
> partly because it was never their intention to do so. And, even if it had
> been, they have not the power to do so because, unlike a trade union, which
> consists of nearly all the workers in a factory or industry, consumer associa-
> tions consist of only a small part of all the consumers in the nation or in any
> locality.[8]

Co-operative societies may be in a position to collaborate (or to
refuse collaboration) with the Government or other bodies, by fixing
prices or dividends, for example. But these powers are essentially
those of producers; they do not involve consumer loyalties.

The concomitant of power and influence is, of course, recognition
—by Government, by official bodies, by other interest groups, by
Press and broadcasting authorities, and by public opinion. Recognition is both a result of effective power and influence, and a guarantee of continuing in that position. It is difficult to define the necessary
conditions: certainly there is no single essential. Some bodies may
achieve influence with few members, yet it is desirable to recruit a

203

high proportion of the clientèle. Absence of rivals or splinter groups is helpful. Resources, of money or expert knowledge or enthusiasm, are relevant factors. Opportunities for bargaining—as distinct from mere agitation or complaint—are of the greatest importance.

All in all, the consumers' movement lacks some of these key attributes. Some of the disadvantages may be overcome but many are likely to persist. An improvement might be made, however, if the various component organizations were to work together, ignoring each other's shortcomings and building on advantages. The co-operatives may not be single-minded consumers, but they have large numbers of working-class members and a long tradition of consumer protection. Though the Consumers' Association may have a small active membership and few popular roots, it has developed expert knowledge based specifically on consumer interests. Local groups, though weak in numbers and resources, provide some sort of active country-wide organization. The other bodies have narrow interests in themselves, but together serve to emphasize the consumer aspect of many public services.

An alliance of Consumers' Organizations would itself need to be loosely organized—a council, meeting occasionally, and a secretary perhaps; the basis for federation scarcely exists. Its function would be political, in the interest group sense, and its aims would be to secure representation for consumer attitudes in national policy-making, either by placing nominees on relevant councils and committees, or by informal contact with government departments and Members of Parliament. Existing bodies already attempt this, but an alliance might enjoy greater prestige and gain a better chance of recognition; and for any organized interest, recognition is a crucial stage in building up power and influence.

The Consumerist Ideology

Even an alliance is but one step forward, however, and it would do little to solve the problem of lack of control or influence over the supposed clientèle. In fact, the logic of a consumer interest group alongside sectional interests is not altogether clear, and some further exploration of the situation is necessary.

The doctrine of consumerism, at its simplest, is that there is a highly significant division of society, into producers and consumers; and that for one reason or another the consumer deserves support. This belief has been buttressed by more elaborate philosophies. For instance, one way of looking at the operation of nineteenth-century *laissez-faire* was to see in it the rule of the consumer: in a free market some might prosper and others not, but what was decisive was the ability to meet consumers' demands. The sovereignty of the consumer could be justified teleologically—'Consumption is the sole end and purpose of all production; and the interest of the producer ought to be attended to only so far as it may be necessary for promoting that of the consumer.'[9] It could also be justified democratically—since everyone is a consumer, the market could be represented as an arena for the exercise of the popular will. In the main the twentieth century has professed to see fallacies and exceptions in this analysis, too complex and controversial to elaborate here.

The moral precedence of the consumer is not to be found in Marxist-type socialist thinking. Instead of pity for the poor (a consumer category) there was a claim for justice for the workers, as the only true producers, and an expectation of power for the proletariat, a class defined in producer terms. In Britain, however, there was a current of socialist thinking which placed great importance on the consumer. The hostility of the Webbs to guild socialism and workers' control was in part the result of their preference for consumer control. In the main they saw the co-operative movement as the model of a desirable system, but, significantly, the principle was observed elsewhere:

> ... the municipality, and even the State itself, in so far as they undertook the provision of commodities and services for their citizens, were from the economic standpoint, also associations of consumers, based upon an obligatory instead of upon a voluntary membership.[10]

The principle of consumers' control was also vigorously advocated by Leonard Woolf in *Co-operation and the Future of Industry* (1919) and *Socialism and Co-operation* (1921);[11] and the brief history of guild socialism itself shows an increasing attempt to introduce consumer-representation into what was originally conceived as a producer-controlled movement.[12]

In a sense, both the *laissez-faire* outlook and these variants of Fabian socialism asserted the sovereignty of the consumer. In the *laissez-faire* version this was to be achieved through the operation of the free market; in the socialist versions a political system of control was required.

The hopes of the modern consumer movement seem to fall well short of the ambitions of sovereignty. The question of a major consumer pressure-group, or even of the consumer political party sometimes canvassed,[13] presupposes the existence of rival groups or parties, and of a government machine. The object of the movement is to remedy the weaknesses of the consumer, to put right an alleged imbalance: and that, nowadays, seems to be difficult enough. To appreciate the political problem facing the consumer movement, therefore, it is necessary to understand the root causes of the consumer's weakness.

A great deal is sometimes made of the fact that everyone is a consumer; but this truth only makes their underdog position more surprising than ever. The trouble is that everyone, or nearly everyone, is a producer as well, or a dependant of one. Moreover, the lack of parity between consumers and producers does reflect a genuine difference in the importance of the two aspects of life to most people. Property ownership apart, a person's productive activities are usually related to one job, from which there arises one income. On this single situation much is focused: a person's education, training and background lead up to it, and the amount of his purchasing power, the location of his home, the way he spends his days and his social class are determined largely by his occupation. It is therefore sensible for the individual to concentrate on securing satisfaction in this single situation. In contrast, an individual's activities as a consumer consist of a multitude of separate purchases, and even if many of these are not satisfactory, this can rarely be as significant for him as his productive role. It is unpleasant to get poor value for money, or even to be defrauded; but it is worse to lack skills or qualifications, to fail to have a badly wanted job, or not to get promotion.

The need for consumer protection arises, therefore, from an incoherence in the economic system, caused by the greater attention which the rational individual gives to his role as a producer compared with his role as a consumer. The need for protection is sometimes deeply felt, but has more often been perceived by intellectuals as a social requirement: in the main, it is wiser for an individual to concentrate on getting the right job than on getting the best goods. But though we may put our producer-roles first, it does not mean that we attach no importance at all to our consumer-roles, and may not wish to do something about them—or at least, some people wish to do something about them.

In the circumstances, it may be that a ready short-cut to the desired interest-group status lies in the narrowing of the consumer constituency. In a sense this tends to happen of its own accord, and it is of course accentuated by the necessary 'purist' rules of the Consumers' Association and similar bodies. The outcome would be a consumer movement, ignoring the co-operatives, representing middle-class non-commercial consumers. Indeed, it may already be right to regard much of the movement as essentially part of the growing political articulation of the professional middle class, as distinct from the industrial and commercial bourgeoisie. Further development on these lines would turn the movement into an undeniably sectional group, and would involve some drastic modification of its claims. At the same time it should be remembered that the most successful interests hitherto have been sectional, and in sectionalism there may be a basis for the consumer loyalties so far lacking. It may also be argued that a more effective movement could be based on the consumption of particular goods and services, in the way that trade unions are organized in particular crafts and industries. Thus the nationalized-industry consumer committee and the Patients Association would point the way, rather than the generalized Consumer Council or Consumers' Association. But this is mere speculation: the necessary bodies scarcely exist.

Finally, it may be observed that the general ideology of the consumer movement is very thin—especially for a group with universalist claims. A much deeper philosophy on matters of economic and social policy would be necessary if the movement were to compete at the levels of the C.B.I. and the T.U.C.; and although many pundits would be prepared to supply such an outlook ready made, its wide acceptance would involve years of maturation.

There is in fact a view, held on high authority, that a powerful consumer force exists in British politics, exerted mainly through the electoral machinery:

> The power of organized producers in a modern democracy is readily seen and widely recognized. Indeed, many fear that, overshadowed by these giants of the Collectivist economy, the consumer group, only poorly organized, or perhaps not organized at all, will be unable to bring its interests forcefully to the attention of Government. But this view neglects the function of the tightly-knit, competitive political party. Keenly on the scent of votes and pressed sharply by its rival in the chase, it probes every neglected thicket in the political landscape for its quarry.[14]

There is undoubted truth in this argument. Ruling politicians have done a good deal for consumer protection in recent years, perhaps from electoral motives. Yet the consumer may reflect, a little bitterly, that business men and industrial workers have powerful organizations, as well as votes, to promote their interests, and do not rest in a thicket, waiting for their needs to be sniffed out.

This brings back the opening problem of the article. The most powerful force, perhaps, for consumer representation is the growing need for it. The logic of the policy-making apparatus requires the responsible presentation of the consumer's case, in economic planning, in prices and incomes matters, and in social policy. The general implications of the analysis here presented are pessimistic: the prospects for consumer power are not rosy. Nevertheless, there is a place to be filled; it is probable that Governments would welcome growing consumer strength, if not exactly as an ally then as a counterweight to other pressures. Indeed, the revival of Government concern with consumer matters in 1972-3 can surely be explained by such motivation. But ultimately the best-disposed Government cannot recognize what is not there, and Consumer Councils and Ministers of Consumer Affairs are merely hopeful substitutes. The salvation of the consumer can only be achieved, in the pressure-group world, by consumers themselves. Only when people are prepared to act in support of their consuming interests will the activists become real leaders: and only then will there be any assurance of notice being taken of what they say.

Notes

1 Reported in *The Guardian*, 30 November 1966, p. 16.

2 S. and B. Webb, *The Consumers' Co-operative Movement*, Longmans, 1921.

3 Co-operative Independent Commission, *Report*, Co-operative Union Ltd 1958, p. 24.

4 Final Report of the Committee on Consumer Protection, Cmnd. 1781, 1962, p. 125, para. 393.

5 Consumers' Association, *Articles of Association*, clause 5.

6 See Colin Harbury, 'The Reluctant *Which?*' in *New Society*, 22 December, 1966.

7 Consumer Council, *Information for Consumer Education*, H.M.S.O., 1965, p. 46.

8 Eirlys Roberts, *Consumers*, Watts, 1966, p. 6.

9 Adam Smith, *The Wealth of Nations*, Book IV, Chap. VIII. This is a *non sequitur*—the second clause does not follow from the first.

10 Beatrice Webb, *My Apprenticeship*, Chap. VII.

11 See also Leonard Woolf, *Downhill all the Way*, Hogarth Press, 1967, pp. 85-8.

12 See, for example, G. D. H. Cole, *Guild Socialism re-stated*, Parsons, 1920.

13 In, for instance, Michael Young, *The Chipped White Cups of Dover*, Unit 2, October 1960.

14 S. H. Beer, *Modern British Politics*, Faber, 1965, p. 349. Professor Beer uses a very wide definition of 'consumer' in this context. See R. T. McKenzie, 'Parties, Pressure Groups and the British Political Process', *The Political Quarterly*, January 1958 (reprinted on pp. 276–88) for a similar view of the electoral sanctions of consumers.

Councillors and Interest Groups in Kensington and Chelsea*

John Dearlove

The majority of studies of local government in England have tended to be either detailed summaries of the statutes that have shaped the structures and functions of local authorities, or else they have been essays upon debatable problems of local government.[1] The heavy stress placed upon the importance of law, and upon the extent of central control,[2] has meant that there have not been systematic attempts to look at local authorities as policy-making bodies in their own right.[3] Instead it has been argued that local authorities act as 'agents' administering and executing policies the broad lines of which have been worked out by the Central Government.[4]

Even the more recent empirical case studies of particular local authorities have not centred discussion on the processes leading up to authoritative decision, and in spite of the fact that interest groups have been seen as assuming a critically important role in British national politics, there have been only scattered references to their activity in local politics.[5] Birch has pointed out that although 'the influence of pressure groups in national politics is well known . . . their activities on the local level appear never to have been studied',[6] and Sharpe writing more recently has noted that 'we have no systematic treatise on . . . local pressure groups'.[7]

Once a concern with local authority decision-making is put at the centre of a research inquiry, then the study of local interest groups becomes particularly important, as students of the political process have frequently seen interest groups as occupying a major role in the making of public policy because of their ability to influence the formal decision-makers.

I. The Research Question

My concern is with the relationship between interest groups and the

* Reprinted with permission from the *British Journal of Political Science*, vol. 1, no. 2, 1971, pp. 129–53.

council of the Royal Borough of Kensington and Chelsea, and although as a general question I am interested in the impact which groups have on council policy and with the response of the council to group demands and suggestions, I am *not* attempting to account for the policy decisions made by the council. Earlier work on interest groups seemed to argue that an explanation for the policy output of an authority structure was possible solely through a discussion of interest group activity. This view has been questioned,[8] however, and it is now recognized that in dealing with the more general question of policy-making a variety of other factors need to be taken into account that cannot be contained within the framework of a discussion limited to interest group activity.

Because my central concern is with the response of the council to interest groups, I take as a starting point the necessity of focusing on those who are the *subject* of group demands.[9] Early work on interest groups tended to focus more on the *interest groups* themselves and suggested that their influence was attributable to the pressure which they could exert upon formal decision-makers, who were invariably seen as passive, *papier maché* figures with a role limited to that of refereeing the group struggle. More recently it has been recognized that it is important to study the formal decision-makers who are the subject of group demands,[10] for as Zisk and associates have suggested, 'the predispositions of policy-makers act as filters through which interest group efforts to influence policy outcomes must pass. The accessibility of public officials to groups, and the degree to which they accommodate group requests, depends in part on these predispositions.'[11]

This more recent approach to the study of interest groups, suggests a more satisfactory way of accounting for the impact which they might have on authority structures, and in the following discussion there will be an attempt to outline the framework within which the majority group councillors respond to, and assess, and allow differential access to different groups and demands. The research represents an attempt to outline the categories used by councillors [12] when dealing with part of their 'psychological' environment [13] and hopes to suggest some of the factors which might allow certain groups and demands effective access. After the various categories that make up the framework have been outlined there will be a discussion of the inter-relationships among them in order to provide a less static picture of the scope for interest group activity within the councillors' normative framework. Before outlining the research findings, it needs to be remembered that the research is mainly based on interviews with councillors. There is no attempt to discuss particular cases of council activity in relation to interest groups in order to check whether or not the framework which was suggested to me was in fact used in practice. Clearly an analysis of case material would add to the discussion, but it lies beyond the scope of this particular paper which is confined to discussing the framework alone.

II. The Royal Borough of Kensington and Chelsea

It is not possible to say whether the area and authority chosen for study are typical or not, unless comparison is made with a specified sample of other local authorities. This is not my intention, but it is nevertheless important to note certain major features which characterize the area and authority, and which might affect the nature of the research findings reported in this paper.

The Royal Borough of Kensington and Chelsea is a London Borough that was created by the London Government Act 1963. It replaced the two Metropolitan Boroughs of Kensington and Chelsea that were created by the London Government Act 1899. Both Metropolitan Boroughs were overwhelmingly dominated by the Conservatives, and on the present council of the combined borough the Conservatives are still the major party. On the first council (1965–8) there were fifty-three Conservative and seventeen Labour representatives, and on the second council, elected in 1968, there were sixty-six Conservative and four Labour representatives. Moving out from the council to consider the area as a whole, 'one of the most distinctive features about the Royal Borough is the sharp contrast between North Kensington and the rest of the Borough'.[14] In North Kensington, there is a lower percentage of non-manual workers; more overcrowding; a greater deficiency of open space; and children are proportionately over-represented in that part of the Borough. The very distinctiveness of North Kensington when compared to the rest of the Borough, and the fact that North Kensington has tended to be Labour controlled,[15] has helped to contribute to the diverse pattern of interest group activity in the Borough.

It is impossible to say how many interest groups there are within the boundaries of the Royal Borough, until one has some notion of what one means by the term interest group. Almond[16] considers that there are four main types of structure that may be involved in the process of interest articulation: institutional interest groups, non-associational interest groups, anomic interest groups and associational interest groups. Like most students of interest groups I am concerned with the associational interest group, what Almond calls 'the specialized structures of interest articulation'.[17] Key gives the classic definition of this type of group when he states that 'political interest groups can be defined as "private associations" ... [which] promote their interests by attempting to influence government rather than by nominating candidates and seeking responsibility for the management of government'.[18] The problem with this definition, like that of Almond's, is that it tends to confine attention to those groups that are actually articulating demands to authority structures, and as such it tends to focus attention on those groups that are attempting to *change* the pattern of authoritative allocations. LaPalombara convincingly argues that it is also vital to consider as interest groups those structures that are involved in '*maintaining* an existing configuration of public policy. It is not merely for the future performance of authoritative functions that interest groups organize and intervene; many of them are vitally attuned to the preservation of the consequences of previous rule-making, rule-application, and rule-adjudication'.[19]

It is not really necessary to worry excessively about a precise definition of the term interest group;[20] it is enough to be aware that one is interested in structures that have an existence distinct from the formal authority structure, but at the same time have a certain involvement (or potential involvement) with that structure, either in preserving and defending existing outputs from it, or in attempting to urge change or innovation in the existing pattern. Neither is it important to provide a list of all the interest groups from within the area of Kensington and Chelsea which are (or might be) in some contact with the council; this would only be of interest if one wanted a descriptive catalogue of groups,[21] and this was not my concern.

III. The Research: Councillor Categories

In the summer of 1968, forty-seven Conservative councillors and aldermen from the Royal Borough of Kensington and Chelsea were interviewed for lengths of time ranging from forty minutes to four and a half hours [22] on a wide range of subjects relating to their activity as councillors. Among other things, however, there was a concern to explore certain dimensions of councillor thinking about interest group activity. In the year prior to that summer, regular attendance at council meetings, a close following of local issues, and unstructured interviews with councillors and interest group leaders, suggested that there were differing types, or categories, or assessments being made by councillors when they were considering groups, group demands, and external influence attempts.

First, it was apparent that councillors were making very different evaluations of the worthiness, reliability and helpfulness of the differing *groups* with which they came into contact. For example, at council meetings favourable references were made to the Kensington Housing Trust, the District Nursing Association, the North Kensington Playspace Group, and the Women's Royal Voluntary Service; more guarded references were made to the Notting Hill Social Council's Blenheim Project; and at the council meeting in January 1967, there was an outburst by the leader of the council against the Kensington and Chelsea Council Tenants Association when he pointed out that the council were 'not bad landlords [and] when we've had bad relations it's because the tenants are communist led and egged-on by one of their councillors'.

Second, as well as making differing assessments as to the worthiness and value of groups, it was also clear from debate at council meetings that councillors had preferences as to the *policies* which they felt they should, and should not, be pursuing. These policy predispositions frequently served as arguments which were used by councillors to reject policy lines that were urged on them by interest groups or the Minority Party. For example, a petition requesting the council to consider acquiring a block of flats in North Kensington was not acted on: councillors were not sympathetic to compulsory purchase or to 'attacks on private landlords'. One Labour councillor was aware of the policy predispositions of the Conservative councillors when he stated that although he was sympathetic to the use of compulsory purchase in this case: 'I'm not putting forward compulsory purchase as a sensible option to the Conservatives, as I know that their ideological bias stops them from taking such action' (Councillor Lawrence at Council Meeting 31 October 1967). The importance of these predispositions was not simply confined to housing matters, as when the council introduced its scheme for parking control in the southern parts of the borough although there were waves of resident protest (to which the council were sympathetic), but residents' demands that on-street parking for them should be free were not acted upon.

> I believe that the person who owns the car should pay for the cost of the scheme. We've split it [the cost] two-thirds to short-term parkers and one-third to residents and the balance of available places is the opposite. I think this is a fair balance. I don't think the residents should get it scot free, and it should never become a burden on the rates. (Councillor Brew, Chairman of Works Committee; Council Meeting 30 January 1968.)

214

Third, and finally, occasional reference was made to the *style* by which groups put across their demands for council action. For example, in the report of the Housing Committee to the council at the Council Meeting in May 1967, alarm was expressed at the sending of a petition by the Notting Hill Peoples Association, as it was considered that the issue had previously been resolved as a result of a private meeting between members of the Association and a few councillors. 'We regret ... that the Association felt the need to present a petition which reiterates opinions and suggestions already made' (Council Minutes, 2 May 1967, p. 267). In the period up to January 1969, there were four occasions on which 'disorder' by the public at a council meeting led to the mayor clearing the public gallery. The imposition of the sanction of clearance indicates something of the feeling of the majority group councillors to those instances of fairly anomic interest articulations, but statements by the mayor on these occasions suggest quite clearly the role which the public should fill at council meetings. 'Members of the public can attend and watch deliberations of their councillors—that is their right, but they may not participate or take part—that is for their elected representatives.' (The Mayor prior to the clearing of the public gallery, Council Meeting 31 October 1967.) Observation of council activity in the year prior to the summer of 1968 suggested that councillors thought about interest group inputs in terms of three categories, examples of which have been given above.

1 The source of the demand or suggestion. (The group or message sender)
2 The policy content of the group demand and its implications for council activity and resource commitment. (The demand or message content)
3 The style or method of articulation adopted by the demanding group. (The style of message presentation)

Interviews with councillors in the summer of 1968 included questions on these categories which, on the basis of previous observation, seemed to be important in their assessing groups and group demands. Although categories 1 and 3 were covered by direct questioning and there is clear information on 'good' (helpful) and 'bad' (unhelpful/ not helpful) groups, and 'proper' and 'improper' styles of group communication, it was not easy to see how systematic information could be collected on category 2—the policy predispositions. In fact there were general discussions with councillors on issues in the area, and their replies made it possible to build up something of a picture of councillors' views as to what the council should and should not

Table 1 *   Statements as to the Helpfulness of the Groups

	Very helpful	Helpful	Unsure	Not helpful
Kensington Housing Trust	23	11	0	0
Notting Hill Community Workshop	0	3	4	4
Kensington and Chelsea Arts Council	3	10	2	4
Kensington and Chelsea Inter-Racial Council	0	4	5	17
Ratepayers Association	1	4	0	2
Kensington and Chelsea Council Tenants Association	1	1	0	15
Kensington High Street Association	1	9	0	0
Neighbourhood Service Unit	0	7	4	2
Kensington and Chelsea Chamber of Commerce	5	12	1	0
Family Service Unit	13	6	0	0
Kensington Council of Social Service	3	3	1	0
Kensington Architectural Group	0	9	2	4
Campden Charities	16	7	0	0
District Nursing Association	11	10	0	0
North Kensington Playspace Group	5	11	1	1
Kensington Society	4	17	0	1
Task Force	4	8	1	0
Notting Hill Social Council	0	8	4	2
Women's Royal Voluntary Service	12	12	1	0
North Kensington Family Study	0	1	0	1

be doing. It has to be admitted, however, that this information is not as rigorous as that on groups and communication styles, and I am by no means clear as to how it would be possible to collect information on this subject more systematically.

A. The 'Good' and the 'Bad' Groups

Given the fact that I was concerned to see how councillors assessed the value of specific groups, it was clear that their attention had to be directed to a limited range of groups from within their area. A list of twenty groups was drawn up, which, on the basis of my past year's work in Kensington and Chelsea, was seen as constituting a reasonable cross-section of groups that had been fairly active and involved

* Table 1 provides a statement of all the evaluations made with respect to the listed groups and Table 2 on the basis of a weighting of the differing assessments provides a a list of the helpful (good) and the unhelpful (bad) groups.

Table 2   The 'Helpful' and the 'Unhelpful' Groups

Kensington Housing Trust	57
Campden Charities	39
Women's Royal Voluntary Service	36
Family Service Unit	32
District Nursing Association	32
Kensington Society	24
Kensington and Chelsea Chamber of Commerce	22
North Kensington Playspace Group	20
Task Force	16
Kensington and Chelsea Arts Council	12
Kensington High Street Association	11
Kensington Council of Social Services	9
Notting Hill Social Council	6
Kensington Architectural Group	5
Neighbourhood Service Unit	5
Ratepayers Association	4
North Kensington Family Study	0
Notting Hill Community Workshop	−1
Kensington and Chelsea Council Tenants Association	−12
Kensington and Chelsea Inter-Racial Council	−13

2 points for 'very helpful'   1 point for 'helpful'   0 points for 'unsure'   −1 point for 'not helpful'.

in the political process in Kensington and Chelsea at some point in the last three years either in assisting the council in the maintenance of existing policy or in urging change or innovation on the council.[23] The typed list was handed to councillors and they were asked the following question. 'Here is a list of groups which I hope is a reasonable cross-section of those in the Borough. I wonder if you could advise me as to how helpful you feel they are in making the Borough the sort of place you would like to see to live and work in—not just for their own members but for other people as well.'[24] Forty-four Conservative councillors were asked the question, and thirty-eight were prepared to make specific assessments.[25] Although eighty-six per cent of those asked the question were prepared to respond positively, no-one made assessments about all the groups on the list, and on average respondents made evaluative statements with respect to eight or nine groups on the list. In categorizing responses to this question, it was apparent that it would be necessary to have two categories of helpful response (helpful and very helpful) as several councillors wanted to make distinctions of degree in the groups that they considered as helpful. By and large, councillors were more sparing in referring to groups as not helpful (though they were less sparing in these judgments in interview than they were in speeches at Council Meetings). Finally, some respondents were unsure as to how to categorize particular groups, pointing out, for example, that although some things about the group meant that it could be considered as helpful in other ways this was not the case.

B. *What the Policy of the Council 'Should' and 'Should not' be*

So far this paper has concentrated on councillor assessments of a range of specific groups that are active in their area, the assumption being that councillors will be more ready to allow effective access to the groups which they consider as helpful than they will to the groups they consider as unhelpful. It is also important to realize that councillors are not indifferent as to the policies which they feel the council should and should not be pursuing, and just as the source of a demand will affect the chances of that demand gaining effective access, so the policy predispositions of councillors will also act as a screen which will affect their response to demands. The assumption in this case is that councillors will be more likely to allow effective access to a demand that does not run counter to their own policy predispositions than they will where the demand goes against their own view as to what they feel the council should be doing.[26]

The aim of this section is not to provide a total picture of the 'policy maps'[27] of all the councillors that were interviewed. The concern is to focus more narrowly on the chairmen of the first council (1965–8)[28] in order to gain some appreciation of what they saw as the proper role for government to assume.[29]

When chairmen of the first council were talking about issues with which the council had been involved in the past three years, and in which they themselves had assumed a major role, it was clear that a concern with the level of council expenditure and the 'needs of the ratepayers' was often uppermost in their minds. 'Value for money is behind council policy in everything we've done, and I should think that the percentage increase in the borough rate is probably the lowest in the whole of London.' '. . . this borough [is] . . . very highly rated and the individual ratepayer pays more per head than anywhere else in the country. One is conscious of this all the time, there are rich people in the borough, but there are poor as well, and a penny on the rates means a lot of pennies even on the average property.' Running alongside this predisposition there was a concern to stress the value of 'self-help', 'self-reliance', and 'voluntary collective' effort as opposed to government activity in the solution of 'public' problems. 'I'm a great believer in voluntary effort and in any community there's great scope for this. After all there's no need for the council to do everything.' 'I'm anti-authoritarian and power and property being centralized in the hands of authorities whether national or local. Where voluntary bodies are willing to do things, and can do things, and can do them as well as a local authority the only difference being that the ratepayer is saved money, then I'm all for it.'

The value of private collective effort was stressed by chairmen when commenting on the solution they would like to have seen in the case of Powis Square.[30] 'The solution we favoured in the past was that the inhabitants should form a committee and get the council to rate, but we couldn't get the residents to do this. Practically every square in South Kensington is run by the residents.' Not surprisingly a stress on the value of self-help and a reluctance to contemplate high levels of government spending meant that there was a stress both on the value of private enterprise and on the lack of desirability of government assuming a major role as provider and securer of life's amenities which could well necessitate attacks on the private sector and would certainly result in higher levels of government spending. The decision to buy Powis Square was one which the leader of the council found difficult to get through the party, as 'in general Conservative principles don't agree with acquiring property, especially for something like a playground. We believe that property is best administered privately.' When the Davies Investments empire collapsed there was a petition from inhabitants of a block of flats owned by the company urging the council to acquire the property themselves or else to help one of the housing trusts to acquire the block. The council were not prepared to contemplate acquisition themselves, and neither were they prepared to purchase compulsorily at the district valuer's price and to resell to one of the housing trusts that were only too keen to acquire the property. As a senior councillor put it: 'The liquidator has a duty to get the highest price for the property and we shouldn't deter him or interfere with him ... The people who have acquired the property are property experts and know what they are doing and should be left to get on with it.' During the first council the possibility of levying a rate on empty property was discussed, and although the Borough Treasurer presented a report which suggested the advisability of this, the council declined to rate, claiming in open council that it was not profitable. One senior councillor pointed out however that: '... there is another point of view which says that it's hard on a person with property who is trying to let it at the highest price to charge rates on it. . . . It seems a bit unfair.'

In terms of the Williams and Adrian typology of the proper roles for government to assume, it is clear that the dominant conception held by chairmen was one which saw government as limiting itself to maintaining traditional services.[31] There was a concern expressed that the general services used by all residents should be good, and refuse collection, street cleansing and street lighting were thought of as particularly important spheres of government activity and here there was a concern to offer a high standard of service. There was in fact a specific recognition of the problems of a particular type of resident—the car owners, the rate payers and those who were worried by traffic and aircraft noise and who were concerned to preserve the 'residential' nature of the borough. The overall orientation of the chairmen was, however, one which gave the council a fairly small role and which saw its activity as limited to the provision of statutory services. A chief officer stated: 'We don't make much use of permissive legalization, and that's policy. The council is keen on taking a view as to what is desirable and what is essential and every year it somehow comes about that only the essential is considered.' Councillors were conscious of the need to draw a 'balance between providing for the underprivileged, housing and welfare services, and seeing that the ordinary ratepayer is not overburdened and yet has good general services', but the concern with the rate level and the reluctance to consider government assuming more of an active role, meant that there was a lack of enthusiasm for seeing the local authority as a provider of services which would help secure life's amenities for all classes within the borough.

C. The 'Proper' and 'Improper' Methods of Communication to the Council

The following question was asked of forty-six Conservative respondents after there had been discussion of a number of issues in the area. 'If a group of constituents or an organized grouping has a particular idea which they want to put before the council in one of the sorts of areas we have been discussing, what is the proper or correct way for that idea to be presented to the council?' The assumption behind this question was that councillors would be more prepared to assess sympathetically a suggestion that was sent to them through a proper communication channel than they would where the style adopted was seen as improper or illegitimate.

The most notable feature of the collated responses (see Table 3) is that it was generally seen as best to go through the elected side of the council in a quiet, non-public way, rather than either through the officers, or through the use of the press or some form of demonstration which were frequently seen as undesirable attempts to apply pressure on the council.

There was considerable ambivalence expressed in assessments as to the legitimacy of petitions, and although fifteen councillors thought the petition *could* be used, only four councillors saw it as the

Table 3   The Assessments made by Councillors as to the Proper and Improper Methods of Group Communication to Them [32]

	The proper method (i) 'best' way (ii) only way	Other possible methods	Unsure	The improper method
Going through the ward representative	32	2	0	0
Contacting the chairman of the relevant committee	8	2	0	3
Petition	4	11	7	7
Contacting an officer	2	9	1	2
Raising the issue in the local press	0	1	2	6
Demonstration	0	1	1	18

best way of communicating a policy preference to the council, and only one respondent referred to this as the only way that could be used. Most councillors in pointing out that a petition could be used, usually went on to suggest that other ways were better. As a chairman on the first council put it: 'The way to do it by the book is to petition the council, but the correct way to do it is through the local councillor especially if he belongs to the majority party.' Although in 'theory' councillors saw petitions as an acceptable means of communication to the council, and although they felt there could be —as an alderman put it—'genuine' petitions, their experience with petitions led respondents to considering them as a form of pressure,[33] as an attempt to publicly force the council to move in a direction that was unacceptable to them. Petitions were acceptable where they presented diffuse bodies of opinion around one issue, like parking or pedestrian crossings, or traffic management schemes, but they were unacceptable where they came from organized groupings that were attacking the council and trying to urge it to change existing

221

commitments. Petitions where they represented a form of anomic interest articulation were acceptable; they were not acceptable where they were simply the style adopted by an associational interest group.

IV. The Research: The Inter-Relationships Among the Councillor Categories

So far the research that has been reported has been a descriptive account of certain critical dimensions of councillor thinking about interest groups and group demands. There has been no attempt to explain the pattern of responses that have been revealed. In this next section there is a specific concern to account for the councillors' differential assessments as to the helpfulness of the groups. This necessitates a consideration of the other two categories that have been identified, for councillor assessments of what council policy should be and of the proper methods of group communication affect the judgements which they make of groups in their area.

After councillors had identified *specific* groups as helpful or unhelpful, a number were asked a follow-up question which invited them to say what in general terms it was that led to their considering a group as helpful or unhelpful: 'In general terms what do you have in mind, what do you look for, when you identify a group as helpful or unhelpful?' Responses to this question can be divided into two categories. First, there were statements which suggested that groups were helpful because they provided information, represented ideas, and brought problems to the attention of the council. Second, there were statements which pointed out that helpful groups were those which were either working entirely independently of the council in providing some form of service, or else were offering some exchange to the council by providing a service with council assistance. The first set of statements referred to the value of groups as 'input' structures. The second set of statements referred to the value of groups as 'output' structures—as groups that were working alongside the council in some form of service provision. A new [34] North Kensington Councillor stressed the value of groups as input structures when she stated: '... groups exist as there is a need for them, but I don't know what I'd look for if I had to define a helpful group. If it comes up with ideas, or if it has information about the area or the people which we may not have, then it will be of great help.' Although new councillors and those representing North Kensington were generally more inclined to stress the helpfulness of groups in terms of their

222

being involved in the process of interest articulation, this view was not confined to those councillors, as senior and influential councillors also pointed to the value of groups as representers of opinion, but when they did this they were invariably more selective in specifying just what were the groups that were responsible and reliable in providing sound information and ideas. A senior South Kensington Councillor: 'One is very sympathetic to their suggestions and we look into them very carefully. Bodies like the Red Cross and the Women's Voluntary Service are responsible bodies and they won't put anything up without due consideration. The Kensington Society, the Chelsea Society, and the West London Architects are not fools, and when they put something up it merits attention and consideration. . . . They're responsible and live in the area.' Of course it was not the case that respondents answered by referring only to the input value of groups or to their output value, most in fact referred to both aspects of group activity when offering assessments as to the factors which led to their calling a group helpful: a North Kensington Councillor: '[a helpful group is one where] people are not only prepared to throw out ideas of what needs to be done, but also instead of just shouting, get down to doing something.' A senior South Kensington Councillor: 'They're helpful when they are prepared to give useful advice and guidance. Of course the Women's Royal Voluntary Service and the District Nursing Association are different, as they're actually doing a job of work.'

Information derived from a general open-ended question is inevitably difficult to code, but there is the strong suggestion that newer and less senior councillors, not occupying positions of formal authority on the council, were more inclined to suggest that helpful groups were those that were serving as input structures, and these councillors were fairly catholic in considering a whole range of groups as helpful in this way. Senior councillors and those who were chairmen—a role which automatically gives those position incumbents a major responsibility in the organization and running of council affairs—tended to stress far more the value of groups as output structures which helped the council in the administration and organization of council services. As a senior South Kensington Councillor put it: 'It is our policy to co-operate with groups. . . . Where voluntary bodies are willing to do things, and can do things, and can do things as well as a local authority, the only difference being that the ratepayers are saved money, then I'm all for it.' A chairman on the first council: 'The important thing to bear in mind is that a lot of these groups are doing things which, if they were not done by these groups would have to be done by us. A lot more would fall on the

Table 4   The 'Helpful' and the 'Unhelpful' Groups: The Differing
Assessments Made by Chairmen and Non-Chairmen

Chairmen (n = 9)		Non-Chairmen (n = 35)	
Kensington Housing Trust	14	Kensington Housing Trust	43
Family Service Unit	12	Women's Royal Voluntary	
Campden Charities	11	Service	29
Women's Royal Voluntary		Campden Charities	28
Service	7	District Nursing Association	26
District Nursing Association	6	Family Service Unit	20
Kensington Society	6	North Kensington Playspace	
Kensington High Street Association	5	Group	19
Kensington and Chelsea Chamber		Kensington Society	18
of Commerce	5	Kensington and Chelsea Chamber	
Task Force	4	of Commerce	17
Kensington Council of Social		Kensington and Chelsea Arts	
Service	3	Council	12
Kensington Architectural Group	1	Task Force	12
North Kensington Playspace		Kensington High Street	
Group	1	Association	6
Kensington and Chelsea Arts		Kensington Council of Social	
Council	0	Service	6
Notting Hill Social Council	0	Neighbourhood Service Unit	6
Notting Hill Community		Notting Hill Social Council	6
Workshop	−1	Ratepayers Association	5
Ratepayers Association	−1	Kensington Architectual Group	4
Neighbourhood Service Unit	−1	Notting Hill Community	
Kensington and Chelsea Inter-		Workshop	0
Racial Council	−3	North Kensington Family Study	0
Kensington and Chelsea Council		Kensington and Chelsea Council	
Tenants Association	−3	Tenants Association	−9
North Kensington Family		Kensington and Chelsea Inter-	
Study	(no ref.)	Racial Council	−10

ratepayers if these bodies weren't there.' Where chairmen and senior
councillors did refer to the input value of groups then they tended to
allow a more restricted range of groups as being legitimate representers of opinion.[35] This information derived from the general question
on helpful groups, is reflected in the councillors specific assessments
of individual groups. Table 4, which is a breakdown of the ratings
given in Table 2 into Chairmen and non-Chairmen columns, reveals
that Chairmen are more inclined to rate 'demanding' groups[36] as
unhelpful than are non-Chairmen.

'Demanding' groups will be less liked by the chairmen than by

Table 5   The Differing Assessments of the Helpfulness of the Demanding Groups made by Chairmen and Non-Chairmen [37]

	Chairmen		Non-Chairmen	
	Helpful	Not Helpful	Helpful	Not Helpful
Notting Hill Community Workshop	0	1	3	3
Kensington and Chelsea Council Tenants Association	0	3	2	12
Kensington and Chelsea Inter-Racial Council	0	3	4	14
Kensington Architectual Group	3	2	6	2
Notting Hill Social Council	2	2	6	0
Neighbourhood Service Unit	0	1	7	1
Kensington and Chelsea Arts Council	1	2	12	2
North Kensington Playspace Group	2	1	14	0
Total	8	15	54	34

the non-chairmen, because the acceptance of those groups would involve not only the imposition of an additional burden on the council but could also involve the possible reversal of existing commitments. Those councillors who have been on the council for a considerable length of time and have been (and still are) centrally involved in the making of decisions and the running of council services can be expected to be attached to past policy commitments and also particularly aware of the implications of policy changes and innovation, such that they do not regard the demanding groups as helpful. Table 5 is a crude attempt to test this proposition.

The ratio of helpful to not helpful assessments made by chairmen and non-chairmen with respect to the demanding groups does suggest that the chairmen are very much more critical of groups which challenge the existing pattern of council resource commitments. Although the position within the council occupied by respondents does seem to affect their assessments of groups, it is clear that this information does not account for the general pattern of councillor assessments in respect of the specific groups where there is a reasonable level of consensus as between the chairmen and the non-chairmen.[38]

The search for more inclusive explanations for the pattern of assessments suggests the importance of the policy predispositions of the councillors, as (not surprisingly) there does seem to be something of a match between the councillors' assessment of the helpful and unhelpful groups, and the councillors' conceptions as to the policies which they feel the council should and should not be pursuing. If one looks at the list of helpful and not helpful groups as perceived by the chairmen (Table 4) and then looks at this alongside the more impressionistic information on their policy predispositions it is clear that the groups that are regarded as helpful tend to be those whose activity and demands on the council are not such as to involve them in any clash with the policy predispositions of the chairmen. There is also a strong likelihood that the policy predispositions of the chairmen will be congruent with the actual pattern of the council's resource commitments. The chairmen are, after all, really the key decision-makers on the council and they are in a position where they are able to put their policy predispositions into practice. At the same time, however, the fact that chairmen have usually been on the council for a number of years prior to their occupancy of that role means that their policy predispositions will in large part be based upon the existing pattern of council policy and so when they are in a position to make policy decisions themselves they will tend to reiterate and continue the existing pattern.

Moving back to the question of the links between the assessment of interest groups and the councillors' conceptions as to the proper sphere of council policy, it does seem possible to divide the groups on the list into three categories,[39] depending on the implications which their activity and demands have for council policy. The activity of some groups is such as to involve demands on the council which clash with the councillors' conceptions as to what it is which they feel the council should be doing, whereas with other groups this is not the case.

1. *Output Groups*. These are groups that are not really involved in the making of demands on the council, but are rather assisting the council in the provision of some service. If they do make a demand on the council then they are in a position where they can offer something in exchange which is regarded as valuable by councillors. The housing trusts for example make considerable demands on the council for financial assistance but the council makes a profit out of loans to them, and in addition the fact that the housing trusts are involved in the provision of rented accommodation for working-class families means that some of the pressure is taken off the council for the provision of this service. There are five groups on the list that are in this category, and they are the groups that are regarded as most helpful by both the chairmen and the non-chairmen. The groups are: the Kensington Housing Trust, the Family Service Unit, Campden

Charities, the Women's Royal Voluntary Service, and the District Nursing Association.

It would seem that the chairmen's favourable assessments of these groups represents something of a reflection of their favourable attitude to the voluntary principle, low taxation, and private collective effort rather than government effort in the solution of public problems.[40]

2. *Input groups.* These are groups that are involved in making demands on the council, where an exchange is not offered. Input groups are of two kinds.

(a) Those input groups whose demands for council action do not run counter to the councillors' own predispositions as to what they feel the council should and should not be doing. These are the pressure groups that are seen by the chairmen as representing a legitimate public with a right to have a say and be consulted in the drawing up of policy proposals. Groups from the list in this category would include: the Kensington Society, the Kensington High Street Association, and the Kensington and Chelsea Chamber of Commerce.

It would seem that the chairmen's favourable assessments of these groups represents something of a reflection of their favourable attitude to 'private enterprise', the 'prosperity' of the commercial part of the borough, and the needs of a certain type of resident.

(b) Those input groups whose demands for council action run counter to the policy predispositions of the chairmen. These are the groups that either are, or have been, centrally concerned to reverse the council's present resource commitments, or which have sought to urge the council to take on new and extended commitments which would run counter to the chairmen's conceptions of what they should be doing. Groups from the list in this category would include: the Notting Hill Social Council, the Notting Hill Community Workshop, the Ratepayers Association, the Neighbourhood Service Unit, the Kensington and Chelsea Inter-Racial Council, the Kensington and Chelsea Council Tenants Association.

It would seem that these groups are regarded with disfavour because they not only seek to extend the sphere of council activity beyond that considered proper by most councillors, but, in addition, the fact that they often seek to reverse council policy means they are challenging long-standing commitments to which the chairmen in particular have become accustomed.

To observe that the chairmen's assessments of groups tend to be consistent with their policy predispositions is not to suggest that there is any causal connection between the two. Older pressure group theorists tended to argue that groups 'caused' the policies of authority structures, but it would be difficult to sustain this position in the case of Kensington and Chelsea, where in fact there is the strong suggestion that the relationship between groups and policies is the other way round, with the councillors' predispositions as to policies causing their favourable and unfavourable attitudes to certain groups. The councillors' assessments of groups sit within the framework of their policy predispositions which are not simply the residue of different group demands, but are a reflection of a more complex process, and in the case of chairmen and senior councillors are partly based upon and reflect their acceptance of the existing policy commitments of the council.

Looking at the usual pattern of the relationship between councillor assessments of groups, policies (or demands), and styles, one has a situation where the groups that are regarded as helpful are also the groups whose activities are not such as to involve the council in activity which would run counter to the councillors' (and particularly the chairmen's) own policy predispositions. In contrast, the groups that are regarded as not helpful are groups that raise demands for council action which run counter to the councillors' views as to the proper area of council activity. Additionally, it is clear that the groups that are regarded as helpful are also the groups whose style of communication to the council is proper, and there are no cases of the groups the council regard as helpful sending in petitions or demonstrating. The groups that are regarded as not helpful—the demanding groups—have *all* been involved in some form of public articulation of interest outside of the proper channels.

V. Overview

In section III, it was suggested that councillors thought about interest groups in terms of assessments as to the groups, their policies, and their styles. In section IV, it was suggested that there was a tendency for a certain pattern of assessments to go together. The helpful groups had acceptable policies and went about the process of demand presentation (if they are involved in this at all) in the proper way. In contrast to this, the unhelpful groups had policy positions that were unacceptable and they invariably had a style of demand presentation that was regarded as improper. This picture is a static one, however, and only applies in situations where no new groups are forming, and where the groups that do exist continue to pursue the same activities and use the same type of communication to the council.

If we were to deal fully with the dynamics of the situation, then two areas of enquiry would demand attention. First there may be changes over time in councillor assessment with regard to the specific categories. For example, councillors may change the assessment they make of specific groups, and they may also change their views as to the proper sphere of government and the proper style of demand articulation.[41] Although passing references will be made to the factors which affect the changing assessments councillors make of specific groups,[42] this particular problem will be ignored. Instead attention will centre on other possible *combinations* between the three assessment categories, besides the two[43] that have been identified as constituting the 'usual' patterns. There are factors which suggest that not all the six other combinations are really likely, and there is also a dynamic tendency for groups, particularly those that are regarded as unhelpful, to pass through a series of stages in terms of the demands and styles with which they are associated. Additionally, it will be suggested that there are factors which inhibit the likelihood that demands for policy change and innovation will be given sympathetic consideration by councillors.

A. The Unhelpful Groups

1. *The combination of unhelpful group with unacceptable demand and a proper communication style is unlikely.* Groups which are not too sympathetically regarded by the council, and which do urge the council to reverse commitments or innovate, invariably make a first attempt to gain access for their demand by the quiet more acceptable methods, but the fact that they invariably fail to gain effective access by these strategies pushes them into a more aggressive style of demand presentation. The situation was recognized by a North Kensington councillor when he referred to how groups should contact the council:

> 'You should get in touch with your councillor first, but if it's not council policy then a petition is necessary. Write to the press, march on the town hall and so on, but the initial thing to do is to actually make sure that the council do reject a thing before making it unpleasant. Most of the things that come up in petitions have usually been raised by quieter means but without much success.'

The impetus for the groups that are not liked and are urging unacceptable policies on the council to adopt an aggressive style of demand presentation does not only come from the problems they

229

experience in gaining access to the council by quieter means, but is also prompted by the nature of their support base and the particular ideology of the group leaders. These groups are usually deficient in resources and quite unable to attain their objectives without major council assistance and this means that they are dependent on the council in order to satisfy the aspirations of their members. At the same time, however, there is a strong suspicion of the council, particularly on the part of the rank and file support (and potential support) which means that the group members are suspicious of any attempt on the part of their leaders to go in for quiet means of demand presentation. Not only is there a certain pressure or expectation from the rank and file that there should be aggressive demand presentation, but additionally, the leaders' concern to demonstrate to their followers that they are active in the pursuit of group demands as well as their desire to recruit wider support for their case, means that it may be necessary for them to provide a focal point of political activity which not only demonstrates their activity, but also serves to mobilize wider support. On the one hand the leaders may not be allowed much social space by their followers in their patterning of group activity in relation to the council, and on the other hand there is the group leaders' desire for participatory politics and a widened support base. Both of these factors may lead the group away from a quiet style of demand presentation. Although a noisy demand style may not cause the council to reject the demand, it does predispose them to treat it unsympathetically, and in the absence of success, groups which are resting on a rather shaky and transactional support base may well tend to fold.

2. *There may be change to the combination, unhelpful group with acceptable demands and a proper communication style.* Although in the previous section it was argued that there are factors which inhibit groups regarded by the council as unhelpful and with unacceptable demands from adopting proper communication styles so that they tend to be forced back into the usual combinations, this is not the only possible development that may occur. Unhelpful groups failing to get their unacceptable demands met may in fact change the nature of their demands away from touchy political issues to ones where they have a greater chance of success as the predispositions of the councillors are less firm and fixed. In the context of Kensington and Chelsea, housing demands may be dropped and demands relating to playspace may be taken up, for example.

3. *There is no necessity for an unhelpful group with acceptable*

demands adopting an improper communication style. As was mentioned in section A(1) all groups usually make a first approach to the council through the proper communication channels, and it is only *after* their demand has been refused that they are forced to consider more public and improper methods of communication. Where a group changes its demands away from those that are unacceptable, it is liable to meet with success at the first approach through a quiet method, and as such there is no need for the group to contemplate aggressive style of demand presentation.

These represent the three possible combinations of assessment categories that might go with an unhelpful group, but it is possible that an unhelpful group might come to develop its activity in such a way that it turns away from seeking to get the council to innovate or change its resource commitments. Groups which start out seeking to urge the council to change or innovate in council policies in fact sometimes come *themselves* to be providing solutions to the problems they originally saw as being the responsibility of the council. The groups' involvement with the task, the leaders' sense of responsibility to their followers and clientèle, and the possible build-up of organizational resources means that there is a possibility that energy may be channelled into service provisions and away from input activity. In the context of Kensington and Chelsea, a group which sought to get the council to take a more active role in the provision of housing finished up forming a housing trust, and a group which sought to get the council to assume a wider responsibility for the provision of play facilities finished up providing additional facilities itself with a limited amount of council help.

Unsuccessful pressure groups can only sustain themselves for a limited amount of time, and unless they change their activities in some way there is a good chance that they will fold up. This is not the only possible development, however, as unhelpful groups, by associating themselves with different demands and articulation styles, may transform themselves into groups that are likely to be regarded more favourably by councillors. Finally, it is possible that unhelpful groups may turn from directing demands to the council to providing services themselves.

B. The Helpful Groups

The situation with respect to the helpful groups is almost the reverse of that of the unhelpful groups. Unhelpful groups are often forced to adopt improper communication styles and, if they are to survive, there are factors which *encourage* them to change the nature of their demands and the pattern of their activity. In contrast to this, the helpful groups do not need to adopt improper communication styles, and in their case there are factors which *discourage* them from transforming themselves in any way.

4. *A helpful group with acceptable demands does not need to rely on improper communication styles.* Groups that are well regarded by the council and are raising acceptable demands have no need to resort to pressure tactics. Groups of this kind are likely to be in close, and constant, communication with the council, and are assured of effective access through quiet methods. The point was recognized by a senior Chelsea councillor who stated, 'It would be inappropriate and unnecessary for the Kensington Society or the Chelsea Society to send in a petition; it's a once and for all thing and doesn't help establish an on-going relationship.'

5. *Helpful groups will be reluctant to take up unacceptable demands, even though they may be able to gain effective access for those demands by proper communication styles.* Groups that are well regarded by the council are usually aware that they have a good on-going relationship where they can expect that their demands will receive sympathetic consideration. These groups are conscious of their credit-worthiness with the council and they are usually concerned not to jeopardize that by either associating themselves directly with unacceptable demands or by entering into alliances with groups that are regarded by the council as unhelpful. The secretary of one of the leading housing trusts pointed to the importance of this when explaining the reluctance of the trust to involve itself with the Notting Hill Summer Project (N.H.S.P.).[44] 'We tried to help the N.H.S.P. but we realized we were in deep water and so we got out. We could have given a veneer of respectability to the organization, but it would not have helped us or the people in the area. . . . There is little difference between the Notting Hill Community Workshop and the Notting Hill Neighbourhood Services. I dislike their motives and distrust them, but then I distrust politicians of any ilk.' The Notting Hill Adventure Playground is another body which has a certain amount of goodwill with a number of councillors, and although at first it was closely associated with the N.H.S.P. there was always a certain wariness of the project on the part of the warden of the playground, and eventually he drew away. The housing trusts displayed a similar reluctance to involve themselves with the Notting Hill People's Association,[45] when it was seeking to urge the council to acquire property that was owned by Davies Investments Limited before its

collapse, in spite of the fact that they were in sympathy with their aims and with the report on housing conditions produced by that body.

6. *The pattern of helpful group with unacceptable demands and an improper style of communication, is not likely.* As was mentioned in section 5, helpful groups are conscious of their credit rating with the council and are, therefore, reluctant to involve themselves in any way with unacceptable demands. If they were to take up demands of this kind, however, they would not in the first instance at least, need to resort to improper means of communication with the council, as it is possible that their credit rating with the council would enable them to gain effective access by quieter means. It might be the case that the demand with which the helpful group was associated was so unacceptable that it was unable to gain effective access through quiet means of demand presentation even though the council were inclined to give it sympathetic consideration because it came from a reliable source. If the helpful group were sufficiently committed to the demand then it might in fact be prepared to adopt a more aggressive style of demand presentation, although in so doing it would probably realize that it would jeopardize all future relations with the council. I know of no cases of this in the recent history of interest-group activity in Kensington and Chelsea.

In terms of the changing patterns of relationship between the differing assessment categories, there is a twofold tendency which is important in limiting the possibilities of policy innovation and change being successfully introduced to the council by way of interest-group activity. First there is a possible tendency for unhelpful groups urging unacceptable demands to transform themselves into groups which are urging acceptable demands on the council. A failure to alter themselves in this way may mean that they will in fact cease to be in a position to survive as groups because the absence of tangible results may lead to support defection. Second, the reluctance of the helpful groups to take up unacceptable demands or to form alliances with unhelpful groups is important because it is precisely those groups that are in a position when they have a certain amount of credit with the council such that even unacceptable demands will be given sympathetic consideration and may well gain effective access.

The fact that helpful groups are not prepared to take up unacceptable demands, means that demands for change and innovation have to come either from new groups or from groups that are regarded by councillors as unhelpful, and it is precisely these sorts of groups which have difficulty in gaining access by proper and acceptable communication styles. The fact that unacceptable demands come from unhelpful groups and through improper communication channels means that councillors are provided with information which deflects them from considering the demands themselves on their merit. They can instead focus attention on the 'unreliable' and 'unrepresentative' source of the demand and on the improper way in which it was communicated, and so justify their not acting on the demand without ever really giving it any direct consideration.

VI. Concluding Remarks

One important facet of politics relates to the making of authoritative decisions, and as such, political scientists need to be centrally concerned with the behaviour of those who occupy roles in authority structures. Often those involved in modern political analysis have seen the study of the institutions of government as part of an older research tradition, and have focused attention more on the structures and processes that surround government.[46] There is some evidence to suggest that the institutions of government are once again receiving research attention,[47] but as Blondel notes, these 'must be studied from a "decision-making", not a legalistic point of view'.[48]

It is impossible for any decisional structure to respond favourably to all demands, or even to give equal consideration to them, and as such certain rules of thumb or 'decision rules'[49] are needed to guide and simplify the choice process. The categories of assessment that have been outlined in this paper can be seen as rules of thumb that are used by councillors in Kensington and Chelsea when considering demands that are directed to them. This research is based on the study of one local authority, and there is no reason to suppose that the rules used, and the patterns that have been identified, are the same as those in other governmental situations.[50] It is hoped, however, that the ideas outlined in this paper might stimulate further research which aims at looking at the relationship between interest groups and councillors in local government.

Notes

1 For similar comments on the nature of the literature on local government in England, see: Herman Finer, *English Local Government*, 2nd edition (London: Methuen, 1945), p. ix. William A. Robson, *The Development of Local Government*, 2nd edition (London: Allen & Unwin, 1948), p. 100. Joseph Redlich, *Local Government in England*, edited with additions by F. W. Hirst, 2 volumes (London: Macmillan, 1903), vol. 2, p. 377. Jeffrey Stanyer, *Country Government in England and Wales* (London: Routledge, 1967). pp. 8–12.

2 See particularly: William A. Robson, *Local Government in Crisis*, 2nd edition (London: Allen & Unwin, 1968). A West Midland Study Group, *Local Government and Central Control* (London: Routledge, 1956).

3 For similar comments see, W. J. M. Mackenzie, 'The Conventions of Local Government', *Public Administration*, xxviii (1951), pp. 345–56, pp. 348–9. L. J. Sharpe, 'In Defence of Local Politics', in L. J. Sharpe (ed.) *Voting in Cities* (London: Macmillan, 1967), 1–14, p. 2. For an example of a study which is an exception to the general rule see, Noel T. Boaden and Robert R. Alford, 'Sources of Diversity in English Local Government Decisions', *Public Administration*, xlvii (1969), pp. 203–23.

4 Richard Rose, *Politics in England* (London: Faber, 1965), p. 193. Robson, *Local Government in Crisis*, chap. IX. Leslie P. Green, *Provincial Metropolis* (London: Allen & Unwin, 1959), p. 156. Richard M. Jackson, *The Machinery of Local Government* (London: Macmillan, 1958), pp. 255–8. John J. Clarke, *Outlines of Local Government of the United Kingdom*, 20th edition (London: Pitman, 1969), p. 1.

5 Brief references to interest groups in Local Government in Britain appear in the following studies: 'Active Democracy—A Local Election', *Planning*, 261 (1947), pp. 1–20. L. J. Sharpe, 'The Politics of Local Government in Greater London', *Public Administration*, xxxviii (1960), pp. 157–72 esp. p. 169. The Greater London Group of the London School of Economics and Political Science (ch. W. A. Robson) 'Local Government in South East England', *Research Studies I. Royal Commission on Local Government in England* (H.M.S.O. 1968), esp. pp. 22, 32. Frank Bealey, Jean Blondel and W. P. McCann, *Constituency Politics* (London: Faber, 1965), pp. 380–2. L. J. Sharpe, 'Leadership and Representation in Local Government', *Political Quarterly*, xxxvii (1966), pp. 149–58. Maurice Broady, 'Community Power and Voluntary Initiative', in Maurice Broady, *Planning for People* (London: Bedford Square Press, 1968). Peter G. Richards, *The New Local Government System* (London: Allen and Unwin, 1968), p. 154. William Hampton, *Democracy and Community* (London: Oxford University Press, 1970), chap. IX.

6 Anthony H. Birch, *Small Town Politics* (London: Oxford University Press, 1959), p. 165.

7 Sharpe, 'In Defence of Local Politics', p. 1.

John Dearlove

8 See, for example, Joseph LaPalombara, 'The Utility and Limitations of Interest Group Theory in Non-American Field Situations', *Journal of Politics*, XXII (1960), 29–49, p. 36; Samuel H. Beer, 'Pressure Groups and Parties in Britain', *The American Political Science Review*, L. (1956), 1–23, p. 2. Oliver Garceau, 'Interest Groups Theory in Political Research', *The Annals*, CCCXIX (1958), 104–12, p. 106.

9 Of course any full discussion of the recipients of group demands in the context of Local Government in Britain would need to take account of the permanent officials of the authority as well as the councillors. In this research, however, attention is centred on the councillors, and the officers have not been interviewed to see how they assess groups and group demands.

10 The following studies all stress, in varying degrees, the importance of studying the formal decision-makers when dealing with the impact of interest groups on authority structures: Betty H. Zisk, Heinz Eulau, and Kenneth Prewitt, 'City Councilmen and the Group Struggle: A Typology of Role Orientations', *Journal of Politics*, XXVII (1965), 618–46. Lester W. Milbrath, 'Lobbying as a Communication Process', *Public Opinion Quarterly*, XXIV (1960), 32–53. Lester W. Milbrath, *The Washington Lobbyists* (Chicago: Rand McNally, 1963). John C. Wahlke, William Buchanan, Heinz Eulau, and LeRoy C. Ferguson, 'American State Legislators' Role Orientations Toward Pressure Groups', *Journal of Politics*, XXII (1960), 203–27. J. H. Millett, 'British Interest Group Tactics: A Case Study', *Political Science Quarterly*, LXXII (1957), 71–82. Oliver Garceau, and Corinne Silvermann, 'A Pressure Group and the Pressured: A Case Report', *American Political Science Review*, XLVIII (1954), 672–91. V. O. Key, Jr. 'The Veterans and the House of Representatives: A Study of a Pressure Group and Electoral Mortality', *Journal of Politics*, V (1943), 27–40. Lawrence D. Longley, 'Interest Group Interaction in a Legislative System', *Journal of Politics*, XXIX (1967), 637–58. Wilder Crane, Jr. 'A Test of Effectiveness of Interest Group Pressures on Legislators', *South Western Social Science Quarterly*, XLI (1960), 335–40. Andrew M. Scott, and Margaret A. Hunt, *Congress and Lobbies* (Chapel Hill, North Carolina: University of North Carolina Press, 1966). Heinz Eulau, 'Lobbyists: The Wasted Profession', *Public Opinion Quarterly*, XXVIII (1964), 27–38. Henry Teune, 'Legislative Attitudes Toward Interest Groups', *Mid-West Journal of Political Science*, XI (1967), 489–504. Raymond A. Bauer, Ithiel de Sola Pool, and Lewis A. Dexter, *American Business and Public Policy* (New York: Atherton Press, 1963). Robert J. Huckshorn, 'Decision-making Stimuli in the State Legislative Process', *Western Political Quarterly*, XVIII (1965), 164–85. Harman Zeigler, *Interest Groups in American Society* (Englewood Cliffs, New Jersey: Prentice Hall, 1964).

11 Zisk *et al.*, 'City Councilmen and the Group Struggle: A Typology of Role Orientations', p. 619.

12 The research represents an attempt to outline what Levi-Strauss would call a 'home-made model' rather than a 'constructed model'. See Claude Levi-Strauss, *Structural Anthropology* (New York: Basic Books, 1963), esp. p. 282. In Pike's terms the approach adopted relies on the 'emic' rather than the

'etic' standpoint, see Kenneth L. Pike, *Phonemics: A Technique for Reducing Language to Writing* (Ann Arbor: University of Michigan Press, 1947), pp. 8–20.

13 For a discussion of the terms 'psychological' and 'operational' environment, see Joseph Frankel, 'Towards a Decision-making Model in Foreign Policy' in William J. Gore and James W. Dyson, *The Making of Decisions: A Reader in Administrative Behaviour* (New York: Free Press, 1964).

14 Notting Hill Housing Service, *Interim Report: Notting Hill Housing Survey* (1968), p. 10.

15 The Parliamentary Constituency of North Kensington has consistently returned a Labour M.P. since 1945. Of the four wards in North Kensington, only one has been 'safe' Conservative, whereas two have been regarded as 'safe' Labour, and (until one was lost to the Conservatives in 1968) have only returned Labour councillors back until the inter-War period. The remaining ward in North Kensington has, in the eight elections since 1945, been won by Labour on five occasions, and the Conservatives on three occasions.

16 Gabriel A. Almond, 'A Functional Approach to Comparative Politics', in Gabriel A. Almond & James S. Coleman (eds.) *The Politics of the Developing Areas* (Princeton: Princeton University Press, 1960), pp. 3–64.

17 Almond, 'A Functional Approach to Comparative Politics', p. 34.

18 V. O. Key, Jr, *Politics, Parties and Pressure Groups*, 4th edition (New York: Crowell, 1958), p. 23.

19 Joseph LaPalombara, *Interest Groups in Italian Politics* (Princeton, Princeton University Press, 1964), p. 17. (my emphasis).

20 Truman considers that 'an excessive preoccupation with matters of definition will only prove a handicap', and he quotes A. F. Bentley favourably when he stated, 'Who likes may snip verbal definitions in his old age, when his world has gone crackly and dry'. David B. Truman, *The Governmental Process* (New York: Knopf, 1951), p. 23.

21 Some indication of the number of associational interest groups in Kensington and Chelsea is provided by the following information. In the council's estimates of 'grants to voluntary associations' for the year 1968–9 provision was made to some fifty or more organizations. The council provides representatives on over eighty 'outside bodies'. The list of 'organizations' and 'clubs and societies' drawn up by borough officials includes almost 200 groups. One organization active in North Kensington has calculated that there are some 150 groups and voluntary bodies active in that part of the Borough.

22 The Council of the Royal Borough is composed of sixty councillors and ten aldermen. Respondents were at first randomly selected for interview, but when it became apparent that shortage of time prevented the possibility of interviewing all councillors and aldermen as was intended, there was a special attempt to interview all chairmen and vice-chairmen. There was over a 90 per cent response rate among those contacted, and over 70 per cent of the Conservative representatives were interviewed (South Kensington

74 per cent, North Kensington 69 per cent, and Chelsea 64 per cent. 80 per cent of the aldermen were interviewed).

23 Two councillors specifically mentioned that the list was a good cross-section. One councillor felt I had drawn attention only to those groups that 'hit the headlines'. Three councillors felt I should have included certain other groups on the list, but only three additional groups were cited, Red Cross, Chelsea Society and the North Kensington Community Centre.

24 The term 'helpful' was chosen because it was seen as being a fairly neutral term which would allow councillors to talk about the groups they 'liked' and 'disliked'. In fact the question was seen by councillors as a chance for them to evaluate groups as 'good' or 'bad'.

25 Two new councillors said that they had been members for too short a time. One councillor said all were helpful and would not discriminate. One very senior councillor said that he did not know enough to answer. One senior councillor just did not want to distinguish. The Mayor would not answer as he pointed out that he had to avoid controversial opinions during his year of office, although he was advised that interviews would only be used in statistical form and that there would be no reference to specific respondents. One alderman said all groups were helpful except the 'political' ones which he would not identify. One new councillor said it was necessary to give 'context' and would not discriminate. In fact of the above eight, two did go on to offer specific assessments of the groups. Of course, not all the responses to this question consisted of evaluative statements as to the 'helpfulness' of the groups. Factual statements on the groups and on group activity were made, and questions were sometimes asked of the interviewer.

26 See the comment by Zeigler, *Interest Groups in American Society*, p. 276: 'Those groups whose goals do not conflict with legislators' perceptions of the public interest will be more effective than those groups whose goals do conflict with such perceptions.'

27 Heinz Eulau and Robert Eyestone, 'Policy Maps of City Councils and Policy Outcomes: A Development Analysis', *American Political Science Review*, LXII (1968), 123–43.

28 Chairmen were selected for special attention because they were the persons who were most influential and involved in the making, and maintaining, of council policy. One of the questions asked of respondents in fact sought to get them to identify those on the council who they saw as of particular importance in the making of major decisions. Most respondents answered by referring to the importance of the chairmen, and the chairmen of Housing, Works, and Planning Committees were singled out by some councillors as being of especial importance. The subject of 'The Influentials' is treated more fully in another paper. Chairmen of the first council were singled out for special attention, because the case material on group activity and council behaviour relates to the period of the first council from 1965 to 1968. All interview statements cited in this section were made by councillors or aldermen who were chairmen on the first council.

29 For a fuller application of this idea of differing conceptions as to the 'proper' role of government see: Oliver P. Williams and Charles R. Adrían, *Four Cities: A Study in Comparative Policy-Making* (Philadelphia: University of Pennsylvania Press, 1963), especially chapter I, 'The Study Approach'.

30 There had been continual concern on the part of groups in Notting Hill that Powis Square was not available as an amenity to residents. This concern culminated in a petition to the council requesting them to buy and run the square as a playspace. After delays and demonstrations the square was eventually acquired by the council.

31 Williams and Adrian, *Four Cities*. 'The typology characterizes four different roles for local government: (1) promoting economic growth; (2) providing or securing life's amenities; (3) maintaining (only) traditional services; (4) arbitrating among conflicting interests' (p. 23). The authors call type (3) 'caretaker government'.

32 Frequently councillors in replying to this question referred to the possibility of *more* than one method of communication being acceptable. Where councillors did mention the possibility of more than one method being used, they either volunteered or were prompted to suggest which method was 'best'. Not all councillors did consider that more than one method was proper, and these responses are added to those methods that were identified as best by those councillors who did refer to the possibility of using more than one method, to provide column one—'the proper method' to contact the council. The number of items in this column is, of course, equal to the number of councillors that were asked the question.

33 Frank Bonilla, 'When is Petition "Pressure"?', *Public Opinion Quarterly*, xx (1956), 39–48.

34 'New' refers to councillors that were first elected in 1968.

35 One of the questions asked of respondents sought to get them to assess the value they attached to various information sources that could have been used by them when making decisions. Generally councillors stressed the positive value of the information provided by the officers and other councillors, and stated that information provided by interest groups was usually regarded as suspect. The tendency to attribute particular value to 'internal' information sources and to be particularly suspicious of 'external' information sources was especially marked in the case of chairmen. 'The Information Sources' of councillors is treated more fully in another paper.

36 By 'demanding' groups, I refer to those groups which raise demands which, if met by the council, would cause the council to take on new commitments or else reverse existing commitments.

37 There is no weighting of the helpful statements. 'Very Helpful' and 'Helpful' assessments are both counted as one. 'Unsure' statements are, of course, not included.

38 See Table 4 for a comparison of chairmen/non-chairmen assessments of groups. It was not really the object of this paper to deal entirely with the differing

assessments of councillors on each of the dimensions of 'groups', 'policies' and 'styles'. It has been mentioned that the position on the council does affect councillor assessments of groups. There is no doubt that different councillors have differing views as to the policies which the council should and should not be pursuing, but this will not be dealt with here. Instead, attention has focused on the chairmen as it is they who are particularly important in the policy-making activities of the council. Interestingly there is no significant difference in chairmen and non-chairmen assessments of the 'proper' and 'improper' input styles.

39 Not all groups from the list are included in this categorization, as there are a number which it is more difficult to type in this way. Task force, for example, is an 'output' group, but it is regarded with rather less favour than certain of the other output groups because it is less 'established' and was more aggressive in promoting itself.

40 The chairmen's definition of what constituted 'public' problems would be rather more narrow than this statement would suggest, and an important part of their policy predispositions lies precisely in what they define as a problem which warrants 'public' as opposed to 'private' solution.

41 For example, when the Notting Hill Housing Trust was first formed in the early sixties, it was regarded with extreme suspicion, but this is now no longer the case and today it is regarded as a worthy and helpful body. In one sense the history of Western government could be written in terms of the expanding conceptions as to what government should be doing, and there is no doubt that in Kensington and Chelsea there has been a certain preparedness to contemplate government moving into new areas. Although I have not had information on this, I am inclined to suggest that in recent years councillors in Kensington and Chelsea have tended to become rather more intolerant of 'public' styles of demand presentation.

42 Councillor (and especially Chairman) assessments of the helpfulness of groups are based in part upon previous cases of council interaction with the groups. Assessments of a group will change if the nature of the interaction between the council and the group changes. For example an unhelpful group may come to be regarded as rather more helpful if it changes its demands and style, such that they are more acceptable to councillors.

43 The 'usual' combinations were identified as: (*a*) 'helpful' group with 'acceptable' demands and a 'proper' communication style; (*b*) 'unhelpful' group with 'unacceptable' demands and an 'improper' communication style. The other possible combinations of the three assessment categories are as follows: (*c*) 'unhelpful' group with 'unacceptable' demands and a 'proper' communication style; (*d*) 'unhelpful' group with 'acceptable' demands and a 'proper' communication style; (*e*) 'unhelpful' group with 'acceptable' demands and an 'improper' communication style; (*f*) 'helpful' group with 'acceptable' demands and an 'improper' communication style; (*g*) 'helpful' group with 'unacceptable' demands and a 'proper' communication style; (*h*) 'helpful' group with 'unacceptable' demands and an 'improper' communication style. The term 'acceptable' demand refers to the demands that fall within the

framework of the councillors' policy predispositions, whereas the term 'unacceptable' demands refers to those group demands which run counter to the councillors' conceptions of what they feel the council should be doing.

44 The project was organized by the Notting Hill Community Workshop and the Notting Hill Social Council and was centrally concerned with housing conditions and play facilities in North Kensington. The project was regarded with extreme suspicion by many of the leading councillors.

45 A body closely associated in the councillors' eyes with George Clark and the Notting Hill Community Workshop.

46 Jean Blondel *et al.*, 'Legislative Behaviour: Some Steps Towards a Gross National Measurement', *Government and Opposition*, v (1969–70), 67–85.

47 See especially the reference cited in Ralph Braibanti, 'External Inducement of Political-Administrative Development: An Institutional Strategy', in Ralph Braibanti (ed.), *Political and Administrative Development* (Durham N.C.: Duke University Press, 1969), p. 52, footnote 128.

48 Blondel, 'Legislative Behaviour', p. 68.

49 Otto A. Davis, M. A. H. Dempster and Aaron Wildavsky, 'A Theory of the Budgetary Process'. *The American Political Science Review*, LX 1966, 529–47, especially p. 543, and footnote 23.

50 Research in other contexts is to some extent suggestive of a similar pattern to that which has been identified in Kensington and Chelsea. In New York, for example, it has been noted how 'established' groups can gain access by 'low-keyed strategies', whereas the 'newcomers' (groups that are similar to the unhelpful, or demanding, grcups in Kensington and Chelsea) 'must rely on high pressure tactics'. See A. J. Bornfriend, 'Political Parties and Pressure Groups' in 'Governing The City: Challenges and Options for New York'. Robert H. Connery and D. Caraley (eds.), *Proceedings of the Academy of Political Science*, XXIX 1969, 55–67. Weiner in his discussion of interest group activity in India notes how the government likes output type groups and quiet methods of demand presentation and views with disfavour aggressive demanding groups (p. 188). Moreover it is also noted how certain group demands 'are overlooked on ideological grounds' (p. 215) Myron Weiner, *The Politics of Scarcity* (Chicago: The University of Chicago Press, 1962). For a more general discussion see William A. Gamson, *Power and Discontent* (Homewood, Illinois: The Dorsey Press, 1968).

Community Action*

Richard Bryant

Much of the current debate about community or social action tends to confuse two different interpretations of the term, with the general effect of muddling discussion and analysis.

(1) Community action may be used as a general term to denote any planned attempt to involve local groups or welfare publics either in voluntary self help schemes or as participants in the process of statutory policy making and service implementation. In this broad and eclectic interpretation community action can refer to a diverse range of initiatives,[1] such as neighbourhood self help groups, organizations representing consumer and client interests, protest or action groups focused around housing and income issues and statutory community programmes designed to improve the accessibility and take up of the social services. But whilst it may be useful, as a rudimentary and initial form of classification, to lump these various initiatives together, it is very deceptive to assume from this that they will share anything in common, other than a focus upon similar types of action settings, problems and groups.

Marris and Rein, in their study of American community action programmes, provide an illustration of the differences in approach which can exist.

> Community organization could be interpreted with a very different emphasis, according to the standpoint of the organizer. It could be used to encourage the residents of a neighbourhood to come to terms with the demands of a wider society, or conversely to force the institutions of that society to adapt more sympathetically to the special needs of a neighbourhood. Or it could be seen rather as a form of therapy, to treat apathy and social disorganization. And it might take an individual bias—promoting the social mobility of potential leaders, championing causes of personal injustice—or a communal bias more concerned with the neighbourhood as a mutually supportive community.[2]

* Reprinted with permission from the *British Journal of Social Work*, vol. 2, no. 2, Summer 1972, pp. 205–15.

The point being made here is a very simple one. To generalize indiscriminately about community action can obscure the differences, in terms of values, goals and strategies, which may exist between community groups.

(2) Community action may denote a particular approach to organizing local groups and welfare publics; an approach in which the political impotence or powerlessness of these groups is defined as a central problem and strategies are employed which seek to mobilize them for the representation and promotion of their collective interests. Some recent examples would include the claimants' and unemployed workers' unions, tenants' associations protesting about rent increases, the squatters' associations and the various neighbourhood-based groups which include representation as one of their goals. The central focus upon 'organizing for power' and political definitions of problems predisposes community action to use conflict as a strategy for achieving change and, as Peter Hodge has indicated, this acceptance of conflict as a purposive organizing and tactical force clearly distinguishes community action from other approaches to community work, such as community development.

> Community development is a process which aims to achieve change through consensus. It is client-centred and based on the self-determined goals of the community groups with which the worker is involved. . . . Community action is a parallel process but uses conflict to achieve change. The worker aims to verbalize discontent, articulate grievances, to form a pressure group with which to confront authority in a militant struggle for righting wrongs, gaining power, acquiring new resources and better services or amenities.[3]

It is with reference to this specific interpretation that the term community action will be used in this article.

Community Action—Key Features

When attempting to analyse the key features of community action it is necessary to distinguish between a range of related elements, each of which can contribute to the building up of a composite picture or model of community action. These elements include, at a minimum: settings, problem definitions, goals, strategies and the roles of local activists and professional change agents.[4]

Action Settings

The conventional setting for community action is a geographic locality, where issues relating to housing and the physical environment provide the initial stimulus for the growth of collective initiatives. For example, initiatives which develop around rent increases, lack of recreational amenities, slum clearance and urban renewal programmes. However, it would be misleading to assume from this that community action is exclusively based upon geographic settings or that the activities of locality-based groups are narrowly restricted by the physical boundaries of a particular housing estate or neighbourhood. Community action can develop on the basis of functional interests which unite people who have no direct geographic links— as is often the case with organizations representing welfare clients and claimants[5]—and the activities of local groups do at times transcend their immediate geographic boundaries. Thus a tenants' association protesting about rent increases may, if it is effectively organized, attempt to take action at a variety of political and administrative levels, including, on occasions, the level of national government. The very fact that formal political powers are normally located outside localities means that community groups will mobilize beyond their initial geographic base and operate in extra-territorial spheres.

Problem Definitions

The assumptions which underlie community action invariably imply the existence of a conflict of interests between community groups and the public or private institutions which exercise a decision-making influence over their life situations.

This conflict definition of problems and issues can take a variety of forms, ranging from a 'them and us' frustration with the apparently entrenched and insensitive nature of public authorities, to a more politically sophisticated analysis in terms of the exploitation and powerlessness of local groups. Rather than being the product of a mindless form of 'conflict mongering', as some critics of community action have implied, these conflict definitions invariably represent rational expressions of the built-in tensions and inequalities which can exist between community groups, particularly those representing groups in poverty and ethnic minorities, and established private and public institutions. Just as in industrial relations it is naïve to speak of a harmony of interests between employer and employees, so it is equally simple-minded to assume, in the field of community relations, a natural consensus of interests between, for example, council tenants and housing authorities, privately rented tenants and their landlords, and welfare claimants and the various agencies which administer benefits and services.[6] Community action merely makes explicit the tensions and inequalities which may exist in various situations, and, as previously noted, it is the recognition and purposive use of conflict which help to distinguish community action from other approaches to community work.

Goals

The material or task goals of community action vary widely in scope and ambition, ranging from the relatively modest aim of winning new recreational facilities for an area to seeking basic changes in housing and welfare policies which, if they were completely realized, would entail fundamental changes at the level of national government. Underpinning these material objectives is a second set of organizational or process goals, which relate to the creation and maintenance of the organizational structures through which community action is mobilized. Included in these organizational goals are such tasks as fund raising, recruitment of members, publicity and information services, the forging of coalitional links with other community organizations and the devising of procedures through which members can participate in the planning of collective policies. The importance of these organizational goals should not be under-valued, for community action is rarely sustained over the long term in a spontaneous manner. Even in crisis situations, where the force of circumstances can act as an immediate stimulus to collective action, organizational goals are needed to consolidate and sustain any spontaneous activism which may be generated.

Strategies

It is in relation to strategies and tactics that the conflict assumptions of community action are made particularly explicit. Two general sets of strategies may be distinguished—bargaining strategies and confrontation strategies.[7]

Bargaining strategies are conventionally employed in situations where negotiation is possible between the various interests involved and the framework for action is defined by the institutionalized processes of formal and pressure group politics. The tactics adopted by community groups, operating in bargaining situations, may embrace the lobbying of councillors, M.P.s and prestigious public figures, petitions, and information and publicity campaigns directed at the mass media. In contrast, confrontation strategies are employed in situations where a polarization of interests exists and the conventional processes of political representation are viewed, by community groups, as being unproductive or dysfunctional for the

245

pursuit of their ends. The accommodated conflict of the bargaining situation is replaced by an open conflict or warfare situation and recourse is likely to be made to tactics of an extra-parliamentary and extra-legal nature;[8] for example, street demonstrations, sit-ins, muck-raking campaigns, rent strikes, the takeover of private property and, on occasions, the threat and use of physical violence. Although the use of confrontation strategies can create divisions, on both tactical and ideological grounds, within community groups[9] it would be too simple to equate directly bargaining and confrontation strategies with a theoretical choice between 'reformist' and 'revolutionary' models of social change. The local circumstances which prevail will tend to shape decision making about tactics and during the history of an initiative a mixture of strategies might be employed, which embrace both those of bargaining and confrontation. Thus a community group may be forced to adopt confrontation tactics after all the conventional political options have been unsuccessfully exhausted,[10] while a group might only achieve a bargaining position after a period of open conflict has established its credibility as a force to be reckoned with.

The Role of Local Leaders and Professional Change Agents

The distinction between the roles of local leaders and professional change agents is one which has tended to become blurred in some of the recent community-work literature, and an exclusive concentration upon 'professional approaches' can create the impression that all community work and community action is dependent upon the intervention of professional workers.[11] A local leader is someone who has a natural claim, because of a particular life situation and status, to hold a position in a community organization or interest group. They may be residents on a council estate, claimants of welfare benefits, unmarried mothers or old age pensioners, who occupy a leadership position in organizations representing council tenants, welfare claimants, unmarried mothers, etc. In contrast, a professional change agent is someone who has no natural claim or status in relation to a local group but works with the group in order to provide certain specialist services and resources. He is invariably an 'outsider',[12] in both status and class terms, who is either paid by a sponsoring body or has made a personal choice to associate with a community group. Confusion between local leaders and professional change agents is unfortunate because it distorts the basic differences which should exist in terms of roles and functions. The local leader is essentially a spokesman, advocate and publicist for his organization. He represents a community organization to external institutions and provides a reference point for the communication of local views and grievances. On the other hand the professional change agent is a resource person and consultant, who provides services and information which would not normally be available or accessible to local groups.[13] Although the professional may, on occasions, assume formal leadership roles, for instance in relation to local groups which have no tradition of self organization, his distinctive contribution is defined by the supportive aids and expertise he is able to command because of his outsider status. It does not rest, as is the case with the contribution of local leaders, upon the status he has as a natural member of a group or organization. When outsiders assume leadership roles, on a permanent basis, they invariably undermine the credibility of community groups.

What Does Community Action Achieve?

Any attempt to assess the effectiveness of community action is fraught with difficulties, primarily because we lack at the moment any systematic body of research into the activities, achievements and failure of community groups. Whereas British sociologists have devoted considerable attention to studying local social systems, comparatively little attention has been paid to documenting and examining the processes through which local groups engage in organized action.[14] Thus any attempt at assessment must be very partial and impressionistic.[15]

Material Results

In terms of achieving material or concrete results the effectiveness of community action is likely to be dependent upon a variety of factors; especially the nature of the issue or set of issues at stake, the financial and organizational resources the local group can command, the degree of popular involvement in on-going initiatives, the influence and sanctions local groups can exercise and the coalitional links which exist between the local group and other community and political organizations. Of all these factors the decisive one, in terms of deciding material effectiveness, tends to be the 'nature of the issue' which is the focus for action. Is the issue one which requires major policy and political changes for the achievement of a successful outcome, or is it one which merely requires a modification in local administrative procedures and practices? For example, we can compare a campaign which is concerned with protesting about increases in council house rents, with one which is focused upon improving the collection of dustbins and waste upon council estates. An initiative directed at rent levels will often raise policy questions which directly involve the policies of both local and national governments, particularly when the local government is implementing national government directives, as will be the case with the Conservatives' new Fair Rents policy. In such a situation the effectiveness of community action will ultimately depend upon the mobilization of broad-based political forces which are capable of having an impact in the national political arena. In contrast, a campaign about the dustbins, whilst it may arouse intense local passions and controversy, is not normally a 'big issue' which requires action at a variety of political levels and the reversal of major policy decisions for the achievement of a successful solution.

As a rule community groups lose the battles on the big issues but may win, as a result of their initiatives, secondary or 'spin-off' gains. Hampton provides an example of this in his study of politics in Sheffield.[16] The 'big issue' which provided the stimulus for community action was the introduction of a rent rebate scheme for council house tenants, which provoked considerable opposition from the city's tenants' associations. The tenants' action did not prevent the implementation of the scheme, but did effect a number of secondary concessions.

> The opposition to the rent rebate scheme did not succeed in forcing the withdrawal of the schemes, but the alterations made in response to the protests indicated that the tenants' campaign was effective. Both groups on the city council changed their policy during the course of the dispute. The Labour group made three major revisions to the scheme and these resulted in a rate contribution of over £600,000 to the housing revenue account. The Conservatives changed their mind about the 'lodger tax' and allowed for a rate contribution to the housing revenue account.[17]

More generally we can note how community campaigns, representing the interests of groups in poverty, whether they be welfare claimants or homeless families, have succeeded, at times, in winning local reforms, without effecting any significant policy change at the level of central government.[18] The 'big issues' which are raised by community groups and which transcend local solutions require, for effective action, the mobilization of forces in the national political arena. As Coates and Silburn have observed:

> Direct action on the many grievances of the deprived members of the population is a crucial lever to the development of their self-respect and

social understanding but it is not a sufficient remedy for their problems, which demand overall solutions such as can be only canvassed by nationally structured political and social organization. Unless a serious effort is made at this level, it is unlikely that basic change will take place.[19]

Coates and Silburn also make the important point that the political impotence of community groups in the face of big issues is a critical reflection on the existing policies and organization of the British Labour Movement. For, in theory, the Labour party and the unions could provide the agency through which the demands of community groups might be given a national expression. In relation to this observation it is worth noting that, on the few occasions when community campaigns have made an impact upon central government policy, these campaigns have invariably been fused with broader-based political and union action, as was the case with the Govan (Glasgow) rent strike, which contributed to the passing of the first Rent Control Act of 1915.[20] The relationship between local and national action is obviously crucial in determining the effectiveness of community action, but questions relating to the means and ideologies of working for structural change are ones which tend to divide community activists. The positions taken on these questions vary widely. They range from the quasi-populist view that community groups themselves can provide a collective and independent agency for national action, to the more mainstream socialist view that coalitional links must be forged between community groups and the traditional organizations which represent working-class interests.[21]

Qualitative Change

An exclusive emphasis upon the material achievements and failures of community action can direct attention away from the qualitative changes, in terms of attitudes, self image and the acquisition of new skills, which can also result from an involvement in community action. A number of reports on community action initiatives have drawn attention, albeit on the basis of impressionistic evidence, to examples of qualitative change. For instance, Radford in a commentary upon the King Hill campaign pointed out:

> During 1965 not only the atmosphere but the attitudes and behaviour of the people in King Hill changed visibly. For the first time people were being encouraged to make decisions for themselves, and there was this tremendous feeling we were together, doing something important. Self-respect blossomed with the realization that they were capable of organization and that they could fight injustice. . . .[22]

249

Changes of this nature, which essentially express the unleashing of new human potentials, can prove as threatening to politicians, administrators and social workers as the material demands community groups make. Groups and individuals who previously have been defined as 'passive' or 'apathetic' may emerge through an involvement in community action as being active and organized, challenging conventional wisdoms and the competence of established institutions and official personnel. One of the central lessons which can be drawn from recent American experience is that community action does not, if it is a genuine expression of popular feeling, necessarily conform to the models of 'participation' embodied in statutory programmes. Fundamental conflicts, which often reflect contrasting sets of cultural and class values, can occur between official conceptions of 'participation' and actual expressions of 'participation in action'.

> Beneath the rhetoric of the Johnson Administration's brief and romantic interlude with the poor was a deep-rooted distrust of the poor themselves, manifested when the poor—and particularly the Negro poor—choose to believe the rhetoric of participatory democracy and act on that belief. The poor as aggressors or as rude initiators of action, unresponsive to benevolent control, ungrateful and distrusting, and even violent, are less appealing to indulgent political leadership than the humble and apathetic poor.[23]

However, as a precaution against over-simplified generalizations, it is relevant to note here that community action rarely involves, on a regular basis, the mass of a particular community or group. Except perhaps in times of crisis, the day-by-day involvement tends to be limited to a hard core of activists, whose work might be supplemented by a wider circle of occasional participants. The mass of a community or group are likely to have a relatively passive involvement; they may attend the occasional public meeting but will not usually be regular contributors to the on-going processes of organization and detailed policy decision making. The American community organizer Alinsky has remarked, with typical candour, that a 2 per cent involvement on a regular basis is the most any community organization can hope to achieve. This question of the different levels and intensity of participation is likely to have some implications for the qualitative changes which may result from community action. One may speculate that the changes which do occur may well be limited to those individuals who are members of the activist core of community organization.

Community Action and Statutory Authorities

The revival of interest in community action, which has been particularly marked since the mid-1960s, is one strand in a broader trend which also embraces new developments in statutory welfare planning.[24] Community work, which has been for so long the Cinderella of the social work services, is currently undergoing a period of unprecedented expansion. The growth points in this expansion include the newly reorganized social work departments, the government's urban aid and community development programme, the local work of the Community Relations Commission, the linking of youth and community services and the growth of new training courses for professional community workers. One question, which naturally arises in relation to these developments, is whether community work in statutory agencies will embrace the conflict strategies of community action as well as the more traditional, and less contentious, consensus strategies of community development and community organization. From the evidence we currently have available it would appear that community action does not figure on the statutory agenda. Conflict, whether as a purposive strategy or as a natural consequence of promoting social change, has been carefully limited and circumscribed.

Holman has indicated the basic limitation which exists—statutory authorities will not, as a rule, sponsor projects which threaten to promote dissent against themselves:

> ... there is no evidence that local authorities could tolerate, let alone promote any strategies which lead to direct conflict with themselves. On the contrary, Tower Hamlets got rid of an employee who stimulated clients to protest. Wandsworth withdrew financial support from a voluntary body which mildly criticized council policy; Brighton would not renew a lease for slightly unorthodox work with beatniks, and few councils will grant aid to community action groups. In other words, local authorities will run services for people, will finance voluntary community work which reflects their own methodology, but will encourage nothing that creates conflict even where it is the only hope of change.[25]

Holman and others have strongly urged statutory authorities to adopt more flexible policies and to stretch their boundaries of conflict tolerance. But even if changes were to occur, it is still questionable whether the goal of client participation in the formal structure of the social services could be effectively realized. The American experience provides a sobering precedent for such proposals.[26] As a number of studies have indicated, client participation in welfare organizations, to begin to be meaningful in decision-making terms, requires access to the informal processes of power and not merely membership of committees which exercise consultative and 'rubber stamping' functions. Almost by definition the life situation and status of the client pre-empts access to these informal processes and as a consequence there is always likely to be a credibility gap between the rhetoric and reality of client participation in policy making. A 'we participate, they rule' situation could simply function to reinforce tensions rather than promote new collaborative relationships. While these observations do suggest that statutory community work is of limited potential when viewed within a strictly community action framework, they should not be interpreted as meaning that statutory community work developments will not yield results in other, less controversial directions—for example in extending the existing limited boundaries of preventative social work.

The Future of Community Action

The future of community action, like its past, is likely to be more directly determined by local circumstances, the existence of natural leadership and responses to national and local government policies, than by formal developments which occur within the field of social and welfare planning. The limitations of local groups and welfare publics in the face of 'big issues' and the lack of those supportive resources which middle-class pressure groups take for granted, will, one suspects, only be overcome in the long term through a radical realignment in the politics and organization of the British Labour Movement. Perhaps it is to the trade unions, rather than the social work departments, that community action theorists and activists should be directing their attention.

Notes

1 Cf. Lapping, A. (ed.) '*Community action*', *Fabian Tract 400*, 1970; and Adeney, M., *Community Action—Four Examples*, The Runnymeade Trust, 1971.

2 Marris, P., and Rein, M., *Dilemmas of Social Reform*, Routledge & Kegan Paul, 1967, p. 169.

3 Hodge, P., 'The future of community development', in Robson, W. A., and Crick, B. (eds.), *The Future of the Social Services*, Penguin Books, 1970, pp. 69–70.

4 Cf. Rothman, J., 'Contemporary community organization in the United States', *International Review of Community Development*, 23–4 (December 1970), pp. 219–33.

5 Cf. Silburn, R., 'The potential and limitations of community action', in Bull, D. (ed.), *Family Poverty*, Duckworth & Co. Ltd., 1971, p. 142.

6 For examples of conflict in the community field see Hampton, W., *Democracy and Community*, Oxford University Press, 1970; Rex, J., and Moore, R., *Race, Community and Conflict*, Oxford University Press, 1967; and Dennis, N., *People and Planning*, Faber & Faber, 1970.

7 Cf. Warren, R. L., 'Change by conflict', *Canadian Welfare* (May–June 1968).

8 For examples see Rose, H., *Rights, Participation and Conflict*, Child Poverty Action Group, poverty pamphlet five, 1971.

9 For example see Rustin, M., 'Community organizing in England—Notting Hill Summer Project 1967', *Alta, University of Birmingham Review* (Winter 1967–8), pp. 189–211.

10 Cf. Radford, J. 'From King Hill to the Squatting Association', in Lapping, A. (ed.), op. cit.

11 For example, the Gulbenkian Report on Community Work makes only a passing reference to locally initiated and self-organized developments. Cf. The Calouste Gulbenkian Foundation, *Community Work and Social Change*, Longmans, 1968.

12 Cf. Gans, H. J., *The Urban Villagers*, The Free Press, 1962, Ch. 7.

13 For example see Bryant, R., and Bradshaw, J., *Welfare Rights and Social Action: The York Experiment*, Child Poverty Action Group, poverty pamphlet six, 1971.

14 Compared with the American literature there is, at the moment, a shortage of British Case Study material on community action initiatives and the functioning of community organizations.

15 This section draws upon Bryant, R., 'Approaches to community work', M.Ph. Thesis, York University, 1970 (unpublished).

16 Hampton, W., *Democracy and Community*.

17 *Ibid.*, p. 276.

18 For discussion of these limitations see Silburn, R., 'The potential and limitations of community action'.

19 Coates, K., and Silburn, R., *Poverty: The Forgotten Englishman*, Penguin Books, 1970, pp. 233–4.

20 Cf. Macdonald, I., 'Housing—the struggle for tenants' control', *International Socialism* (Summer 1968).

Richard Bryant

21 For example, compare the views of Coates and Silburn op. cit., with those expressed by Jan O'Malley, 'Community action in Notting Hill', in Lapping, A. (ed.), op. cit.

22 Radford, J., 'From King Hill to the Squatting Association', in Lapping, A. (ed.), op. cit., p. 42.

23 Clark, K. B., and Hopkins, J., *A Relevant War Against Poverty*, Harper & Row, p.v.

24 Cf. Holman, R., 'Combating social deprivation', in Holman, *et al.*, *Socially Deprived Families in Britain*, National Council of Social Services, 1970.

25 Holman, R., 'The wrong poverty programme', *New Society* (20 March 1969). Also see Poppleston, G., 'The ideology of professional community workers', *The British Journal of Social Work*, Vol. 1, No. 1 (April 1971).

26 See, for example, Clark, K. B., op. cit.

Groups and Political Participation *

S. E. Finer

Definition

By 'political participation' I stipulate: *sharing in the framing and/or execution of public policies.* Participation in one's family affairs, one's workplace, the collective or village fields and the like are not political participation except in so far as the policies adopted there are in some clear way related to policies propounded for or administered on behalf of *the public as a whole.* Participation in one's local government would qualify, since there is a clear legal and political linkage between this and policies propounded for and administered on behalf of the public as a whole.

Among the new states, some allegedly exist where most inhabitants are concerned solely in their domestic routines without these in any way regarding the public policies, i.e. the government of the entire society. It seems unlikely that any state lives down to this absolute condition, though a large number may approximate to it and it is better to consider a state of this kind as being to some degree fictive —an 'ideal type' rather than a factual description. The point is, however, that the political culture of such states has been styled *parochial* by Almond and Verba:[1] i.e. it is a culture in which the population neither know nor pass judgement on the policies of the government of the society as a whole. The society in which they do both is styled by Almond and Verba a *participant* one. In the 'parochial' state, though the sphere of the 'public' has been expanded as local communities have been amalgamated into a larger territorial unit, the mentality of the population still remains wedded to the domestic concerns of these local communities. In so far as this occurs in real life, these populations are certainly participants—in their family or village affairs; but they are not—on my definition— *political* participants. The same is true in a modern industrial state

* Reprinted with permission from G. Parry (ed.), *Participation in Politics*, Manchester University Press, 1972, pp. 59–79.

which, by and large, *is* of the participant type, in so far as we look at the activities of groups of people who, let us say, are intensely concerned in their tennis club without this having the remotest bearing upon policies propounded by the government for the society as a whole. These tennis club members certainly participate; but they do so in their tennis affairs. They do not participate *politically*.

Theories of the Relationship of Groups to Government

Four main views have been put forward as to the desirable relationship of groups to the government. They may be characterized as:

1. *Groups as Opponents of the Government*

This is the anti-despotic thesis, whether the despotism be that of Louis XV or of something called *mass society*. It argues the necessity of *corps intermédiaires* which should be powerful enough to focus the loyalties of members and act as an organizational centre for airing their grievances, and interpose a veto on the activities of the despot. This chain of thought runs from Montesquieu[2] to Kornhauser[3] *via* de Tocqueville.[4]

2. *Groups as Substitutes for the Government*

In its most extreme form, Anarchism, the argument runs that society should consist exclusively of the free interaction of freely forming and freely dissolving self-governing and voluntaristic societies, the coercive apparatus of the State disappearing in this process. A less extreme view would accord this coercive apparatus some limited co-ordinative or other (e.g. educational) functions (e.g. G. D. H. Cole's *Social Theory*). This tradition runs from the Anarchists proper, through Syndicalism and Guild Socialism, incorporates the views of the ethical pluralists (Figgis, Maitland, Duguit and the early Laski) and is to be found in much writing of the contemporary New Left.

3. *Groups as Extensions of the Government*

The underlying theory here is the alleged inability of such folk as workmen, doctors, farmers and the like—in short of occupational groups—expressing worthwhile views on anything but their occupational concerns; hence the devising of arrangements by which they can express such views to the Government, in its capacity as the representative of the State, which for its part reposes on some transcendental principle of authority like the Nation, the Volk, or 'the interests of the toilers'. In so far as there is any coherent theory along these lines, it is the theory of the Corporative State worked out *ex post facto* by the acolytes of Mussolini, and introduced into Italy in 1927; and later adopted, with modifications, by the Nazis in 1934.[5]

4. *Groups as Intermediaries between Public and Government*

Theories of this type—which we may call pluralistic theories—are *ex post facto* rationalizations of a situation alleged to exist in liberal-democratic industrialized states. The existence of pressure groups having at long last been ascertained, these are justified as a desirable and even a necessary ancillary to the primary circuit of representation, viz. *parliamentary* representation.

Theoretically, it would be possible to satisfy the institutional requirements of total political participation by arranging for continuous consultation of the electorate on all matters by those it has elected, including officials—for these would have to be elected also. Indeed, it is possible to conceive of this as a practical and not just a theoretical possibility today, since in principle the electorate could be consulted by television on all matters of public dispute: and then, at the end of the debate, the matter could be put to referendum by the taking of a public opinion poll.

This conception, that political participation could be achieved and fulfilled by continuous consultation of the electorate by its elected representatives, is the ideal of the eighteenth-century Radicals (and their posterity, the Chartists). The reformers of Wilkes's day demanded manhood suffrage, annual parliaments, and the exaction of pledges from M.P.s. When parliamentary reform finally arrived, however, no such state of affairs came about. Instead of parliaments being elected each year—which would have produced an electioneering atmosphere *in perpetuo*—long intervals were interposed between one election and its successor. (In England, until 1911, the statutory interval was no less than seven years. Even today, it is five.) Instead of mandated delegates, the doctrine of the 'representative' was propounded by Edmund Burke, and has become part of the constitutional dogma of not only England but of the parliamentary states of the Continent where the Constitutions expressly forbid the '*mandat impératif*'. As for the public election of officials, the only large democratic state where this principle survives in any substantial form is the U.S.A.; in Europe, new representative institutions were grafted on to the well established bureaucratic tradition —even in England, despite the late bureaucratization of this state.

At the same time, huge private industrial corporations, and relatively bureaucratized parties and interest groups, not to speak of the public bureaucracy itself, have come on the scene and interposed themselves significantly and visibly between the individual citizen and the legislature. Thus, the diminution of the original eighteenth-century political-participation plan, coupled with the intermediation of huge bureaucratized associations between voter and legislature has created two major difficulties: (a) those that lie in their governments being elected for a long period on a vague mandate and (b) those that derive from the details of policy being entrusted, not merely for execution but often for initiation, to appointed officials.

In these circumstances, it is argued that if the policy is to be effective (at the least) or democratic (at the most) it is necessary that groups that represent the interested publics be in constant contact with the elected representatives on the one hand (in order to supply or contest the details of their programmes) and, on the other hand, with the officials appointed to advise such governments and to execute their final decisions. Thus the electoral arrangements become arrangements only for the general orientation of public policy, while the group-dialogue with the elected government supplies the necessary secondary contacts for filling in the detail.

It is not my intention to examine the philosophical or logical merits of these four viewpoints, still less to ask by what they are ultimately justified—whether by reason of their instrumentality to further and more ultimate aims, or to the development of the human personality; the more so since the latter and more difficult operation is already being performed by other contributors to this symposium. I am setting myself a simpler task but one which in my simplicity I consider logically prior to either of these enquiries. It seems to me that it is idle to argue the toss about the desirable role of groups *vis-à-vis* the government if it can be shown that such a role is probably or definitely impracticable. My object, then, is to enquire into the practical likelihood of groups being able to play any of the roles assigned to them in these theories.

The Preconditions for Effective Political Participation *Via* Groups

These seem to me to number four:

1 Unlimited freedom of speech, association and access to the
   government.

2 Unlimited freedom of individuals to join and quit the groups.

3 A perfect leader/member responsiveness inside groups.

4 A perfect (i.e. 100 per cent) membership of the groups.

If would-be participants have no groups to join; or if they enter a group which is not permitted to speak its mind; or if they find that their group, however free in other respects, will never be consulted by the government—then *pro tanto* avenues of participation are wholly or partially cut off. This is why the *practice*—as embodied in Fascist Italy, Nazi Germany, and Soviet Russia—of approaches of the third type (corporativist) eliminates them *in limine* as effective vehicles of participation.

But again: even if groups do exist which are free to speak and are consulted by government, but individuals are not free to join them, or having joined, to quit them—then again their representative quality is thereby impugned. For in such cases, the minorities inside such groups would be excluded from contact with the government by the decision of the majority faction. A perfect responsiveness of the leadership to their members' views is also required; for the leaders are the vehicles by which these views are conveyed to the government. And finally, the smaller the proportion of eligibles who join groups, the smaller the extent of popular participation *via* groups (by definition). Likewise, the feebler the members' concern to express their views to the government *via* these groups, the more distorted the viewpoints expressed by these groups are likely to be.

Preconditions: How Far the Evidence Suggests They are Met

1. *Unlimited Freedom of Speech, Association and Access*

All governments impose some constraint upon what is said, where it is said, and how it is said; and likewise on what associations are or are not lawful. The law is far more accommodating on these matters in the western liberal democracies than in any other type or régime in the world, however; if only because no prior authorization for the establishment and no concurrent supervision of the running of the group is required there (with trivial and mostly professional-body exceptions), whereas the licensing of such bodies is the rule in the Communist states and, with exceptions, in most of the largely authoritarian states that remain over.

Access is formally guaranteed by the U.S. constitution; and in practice is an underlying assumption of all other liberal-democratic states also.

259

It is in *practice* that one might have to qualify these *legal* freedoms. As for access—to get it out of the way first—it is notorious that some important social groups are denied access to government departments on ideological grounds in certain liberal-democratic régimes; e.g. the leftist trade unions in Japan and Italy.

More importantly, however, it is argued that although the law permits groups to form and express themselves freely in the liberal democracies, this freedom is restricted by the socio-economic culture of these societies and notably in two ways: (a) social conditions make it harder for manual workers to aspire to membership or leadership of groups than for the white collar groups; (b) the cultural environment being dominated by capitalist values effectively brain-washes the masses into demanding what they don't want and not demanding what they do, so that true needs are not expressed in groups, and false needs are.

As to the first, this is quite true, but, it would appear, widely so; for the same gap is found in non-capitalist countries. (In 1958 the proportion of children of manual working class parents in universities was higher in the U.K. than in the U.S.S.R.) As to the second, it simply reflects in portentous language the truism that all societies are culture-bound and therefore conform neither to the folkways and mores of other and preferred societies, nor to the imaginary ones of Bacon, More or Campanella. It can be argued, however, that there is more likelihood of new values receiving some institutional expression where the legal freedoms exist, than in the socialist systems where they do not.

2. *Unlimited Freedom to Enter and to Quit the Groups*

Once again, legal freedoms may be qualified by socio-economic constraints. It may again be alleged that the legal system of the western liberal democracies are freer in this respect than those of authoritarian régimes, but even in them the existence of restricted societies is often recognized by the law (e.g. among the professions). Socio-cultural restrictions may be very real; it may be morally impossible or at least very difficult to enter, say, a particular religious confession or to leave it. In practice this is most valid for some readily indentifiable ascriptive groups like ethnic ones.

3. *Leader-responsiveness*

The only model fit to observe here is the western-liberal democratic model. Where, as in all the Communist or authoritarian states, the leaders of groups are appointed by the government, any correspondence between their views and those of their members is entirely fortuitous.

The western paradigm is, in short, the nearest to the anarchist/new leftist model that so far exists. But there is ample evidence that on many issues and in most associations the distance between the leaders and members may be very wide, e.g.

(a) *Political issues in trade unions*

Paradoxically, it is precisely on wide public issues, e.g. foreign policy, that the views of leaders and members diverge very widely in the British trade unions. It seems curious that when Arthur Deakin was the General Secretary of the T.G.W.U.[6] its members were, to all appearances, staunch rightists, and that the moment he was succeeded by Cousins and Cousins by Nicholas, and Nicholas by Jones, they all became staunch Leftists. It is an attested fact that, whereas no national leaders of any union are known to be paid-up members of the Conservative Party, between one third and one quarter of their followers are known to vote Conservative. It is equally true that, whereas the T.U.C. condemned the Suez operation, B.I.P.O. polls showed that over half the population of the country supported it and that this support was strongest among the wage earners.

(b) *Apathy and activism in British associations*

The proportion of activists is small in associations. In Britain, the activists in political parties have been estimated at about 150 per constituency, amounting to some 0·5 per cent of the total electorate, and not more than 1·5 per cent of the membership of the parties.[7] Almond and Verba give the following percentages for those claiming ever to have been officers in associations of which they are members.

Table 1   Percentage Members Claiming to have held Office in Various Associations by Nation

Nation	% total population	% organization members
U.S.A.	26	46
U.K.	13	29
Germany	7	16
Italy	17	23
Mexico	8	34

Source: Almond and Verba (1963), Table X.7.

S. E. Finer

At the same time relatively few members bother to vote for leaders, and even fewer attend branch meetings. The following figures apply to some associations in the U.K.

Table 2 Electoral Participation in Selected Associations in Britain

Association	% participation
T.G.W.U.	20–40
N.U.R.	32
E.T.U.	30
Co-op Societies	10·12—0·23

Source: Finer (2nd ed. 1966) pp. 124–7.

Table 3 Branch Attendances in Selected Associations in Britain

Association	% attendances
Civil Service Clerical Assn.	5–7
Co-op Societies	3·29–0·04

Source: ibid.

Some evidence supports the view that the leadership has less discretion in employers' associations than it does in trade unions and co-operative associations. This is not practical to quantify, since few matters are put to the vote. But inspection of the decision-making process does suggest that unless the leaderships accommodate to the feelings of the rank and file, the latter, being firms and associations, are likely to vote with their feet and found a rival association.

The above relate only to interest-groups proper, i.e., to groups defending a material stake in society. Promotional groups exist to press a cause on behalf of society as a whole. It would be of great interest and importance to have data for the promotional groups. One would surmise that since these are committed to a cause, and often deliberately confront the government, the leadership is more responsive and the rank and file more active in these associations. So far, no data exist.

(c) Qualifications to apathy and the leader/responsiveness
     conclusions

It is observable, though, that in trade unions, where an issue appears to be of vital concern to members, the degree of active participation increases and leader responsiveness to rank and file is

262

enhanced. The example of the B.M.A. in 1965 is instructive. Since 1960 the impatience of the rank and file G.P.s had been growing and this was evidenced by the large membership of two breakaway unions, the M.P.U. and the G.P.A. which, by 1965, had some 9,000 members, equivalent to almost one half of the total G.P.s represented by the B.M.A. in its negotiating capacity. In 1965 the G.P.s' impatience with the government pay award boiled over and a revolt against the leaders occurred. The latter then belatedly covered their tracks and, in a *volte-face*, broke off their connections with the government and took the opposite line of advising their members to tender resignations to the N.H.S.; 18,000 out of 22,000 did so. This example is of general application: *in a matter of direct concern to members, rank and file are more active and leaders forced to respond to them.*

4. *Perfect Membership*

(a) *Primary density*

This means its member/potential-member ratio.

Compared with the general population, this is low. Compared with the groups perceived as 'involved in political affairs' it is even lower. Tables 4 and 5 show that three-quarters of the Americans are not even passive members of politically involved groups; that four-fifths of British and German people are not: and that over nine-tenths of Italians and Mexicans are not. Nor is that all. Suppose we equate the fact of being or having been an officer in an association with 'activism'; and suppose now we apply the averages of activism so defined (and to be found in Table 1) to all politically involved groups (excepting political parties which are not included here). In that case, only 12 per cent of Americans have ever been an officer of a politically involved organization, only 6 per cent of the British, 3 per cent of the Germans, 4 per cent of the Mexicans and a mere $1\frac{1}{2}$ per cent of the Italians.

Thus, even in the liberal-democracies with a long experience and toleration of participation and access to the government, the number of people who are even passive members of politically involved groups is small, and the number of activists tiny.

(b) *Secondary density*

This signifies the total membership of organizations actively engaged in a political issue/the total electorate.

Primary density overrates the degree of participation at any point of time because the figures are an average of membership of associations which have been *at any past time* involved in a political issue;

Table 4   Membership in Various Types of Association, by Nation

Organization	U.S.	U.K.	Germany	Italy	Mexico
Trade unions	14	22	15	6	11
Business	4	4	2	5	2
Professional	4	3	6	3	5
Farm	3	0	4	2	0
Social	13	14	10	3	4
Charitable	3	3	2	9	6
Religious*	19	4	3	6	5
Civic-political	11	3	3	8	3
Co-operative	6	3	2	2	0
Veterans'	6	5	1	4	0
Fraternal†	13				
Other	6	3	9	6	0
Total per cent members	57	47	44	30	24
Total number of respondents	970	963	955	995	1,007

* This refers to church-related organizations, not to church affiliation itself.
† U.S. only.

Source: Almond and Verba (1963). Table X.2.

Table 5   Respondents who Believe an Organization of Theirs is Involved in Political Affairs, by Nation

	% of Total population*		% of organizational numbers*	
United States	24	(970)	41	(551)
Great Britain	19	(963)	40	(453)
Germany	18	(955)	40	(419)
Italy	6	(995)	20	(291)
Mexico	11	(1,007)	46	(242)

* Numbers in parentheses refer to the bases upon which percentages are calculated.

Source: Almond and Verba (1963), Table X.5.

the numbers involved in a particular issue at a particular moment of time are likely to be very much smaller.

The only way to establish *secondary* density is by a case study of an issue: i.e. by identifying the groups involved and calculating the numbers involved. I take a favourable example: the great Transport Act of 1947, a mammoth Act, affecting the consumers, the unions, the shippers, traders, hauliers and docking and canal interests and in some respects the municipal corporations. In the case of the unions we only know the names and the numbers in the unions concerned—not the numbers of members who were interested; so our figures are nominal and are certain to be far larger than in actual fact. Particularly is this true of the T.G.W.U. which was only peripherally affected by the measure, viz. in its docker and haulier sections. At the other extreme, the actual number of individuals in the employers' association—the F.B.I., N.U.M., A.B.C.C., and traders' co-ordinating committee is, in absolute terms, small. Even if all had been actively and personally concerned, they would have run only into some thousands.

In respect, however, to other affected parties—notably the road hauliers, the Railway Stockholders Union, and the like—we can, if we are concerned with activism, take as our guide the number of persons who variously petitioned Parliament against the Act. The number here was 805,000. This number is superior to the sum of the membership of the Road Haulage Association and of the Railway Stockholders Union, which were 15,000 and 60,000 respectively. I shall therefore take the larger figure to establish the more favourable case.

We find then:

Trade Unions: N.U.R., T.G.W.U., A.S.L.E.F., R.C.A.		
approx.		1,800,000
Stockholders	23,000	
Traders using transport	23,000	
Another group using transport	164,000	
Signatures collected by the R.H.A.	595,000	
Total petitioners		805,000

The total membership and petitioners involved in the entire operation was well less than three millions. In fact it was just 10 per cent of the total electorate—and this is an outside estimate. Careful inspection of the press for the entire period shows that the general public outside these categories was totally uninterested in the Bill.

These conclusions are borne out by what Almond and Verba themselves have to say on the discrepancy between what they call 'subjective' competence (i.e. the belief that one ought to or could influence central and local government policies), and their actual participation. In the U.S.A. 77 per cent of the respondents replied that they '*could* do something' about a local regulation; but only 33 per cent of even these say thay have actually *tried* to do something. In England 78 per cent replied that they *could* do something about a

265

local regulation: only 18 per cent of even these tried. Fifty-one per cent of the American respondents reported that the ordinary man *ought* to play some part in the affairs of his community: when asked what they did in their free time, only about 10 per cent of these respondents mentioned such activities.[8]

Efficacy and Scope of Participation *Via* Groups

To summarize the conclusions I derive from the above:

1. Juridically, the scope for political participation *via* groups is far greater in the western liberal-democracies than in any other type of régime.

2. In socio-economic terms no evidence can be adduced for thinking that this scope is less than elsewhere, and I would personally hazard the guess that it is far greater.

3. Yet, the secondary density of participating associations (even in the very favourable example I chose) is low.

4. The primary density of politically involved associations is low.

5. The proportion of activists in these associations is describable only as 'fractional'.

From this I tentatively conclude that:

(a) *If* (this is a very iffy 'if', and the matter is taken up in the concluding paragraphs of this paper)—if the low levels of participation *via* groups is any indication of some persistent trait of human nature; or, to put it another way—if these low levels of participation are due to some root causes which are permanent and unrelated to the structure, the location, and the purposes of the group in its societal context—then the Type 2 theories, of anarchistic provenance, seem utopian.

(b) The Type 4 theories (i.e. of the groups as intermediating bodies) conform more to the actual state of affairs; but one sees how limited is the proportion of potentially affected persons who participate at all, let alone participate actively *via* their associations.

(c) The same is true for the Type 1 theories, but the more limited claims that these make for the role of the groups bring them closer to the actual state of affairs, as far as the current evidence reveals this.

But even these conclusions relating to the Type 4 and Type 1 theories must be qualified; and this for two reasons. In the first place the primary density of groups varies as between one potential clientèle and another, and as between one society and another. In short, participation *via* groups is not evenly distributed over an entire society but highly concentrated in some of its sectors and sparse in others. In the second place, the ability of the groups to participate, or alternatively, the extent to which government is prepared to entertain a relationship with them, is not directly related to their primary density, which is only one of many variables which may induce a government to engage in a relationship with a group. Among the other variables are the wealth of a group; its organization; its social prestige; its possession of some scarce skills or special knowledge; its latent support among an electorate; and above all on the leverage it can exert on society by its ability to impair or halt some social processes which the government and/or public hold to be essential.

I conclude that if we were to regard the existing state of affairs as the consequence of some necessary and permanent rather than adventitious factors, we should have to say that the theories which receive most support are the simple Type 1 theories which need claim little more for groups than a certain veto power. Type 4 theories receive the next best body of support subject to the qualifications given above, that the group system always gravely distorts the relation between the numerical distribution of interests and the extent of participation permitted to the organization of such interests. While the Type 2 theories seem utopian on the showing of the existing data on apathy, it still remains to inquire as to whether this apathy is not due to structural and other factitious causes, which, given a different set of arrangements, could be modified if not abolished.

The Subjective Aspect of Participation

Are individuals participants unless they are persuaded that they are participants? By the same token: if folk are persuaded they are participating, does that in itself make them participants?

I regard this as of supreme importance. I am not at all sure I know the answer. I would merely like to offer two observations.

1. On my definition, a member may agitate till he is blue in the face about matters that merely concern his group; he would not be a *political* participant. To be this, the issue must be one that directly affects government policy and is seen so to affect it. The second definitional point is that even if an issue arises which does affect government policy but the member is apathetic, then, again, he is not politically *participant*. Two conditions must be met for political participation *via* groups, viz:

267

(i) The issue affects government policy (or is thought to).

(ii) The member is active in his group in this matter.

It will be seen that four possible situations arise. The member is active but the matter doesn't affect the government: hence participation, not political participation. Again: the member is inactive though the matter directly affects government policy. Here there is no participation, political or otherwise. Thirdly, the issue neither affects the government, nor is the member active in it; total passivity. Fourthly—and it seems to me the only relevant consideration here: the issue affects the government and is seen to, *and* the member is active in his group over the issue. This alone is political participation *via* the group—a direct confrontation or support for government policy through the medium of the group. This was certainly how the Railway Stockholders Union, the Road Haulage Association and the Mainline Railway Companies saw the issue in 1947, just as the three Railway Unions did. I would suggest that for *interest* groups proper the number of these occasions is relatively rare. Among *promotional* groups they are likely to be more frequent; the activities of the Campaign for Nuclear Disarmament or the Movement for the Abolition for Capital Punishment may serve as examples. But nobody has counted the number of occasions in a year still less over a period of years on which such groups are active, nor has anybody compared one state with another in this respect. Such an enterprise might prove very rewarding indeed.

There remains to consider a social aggregate of a type which for certain analytical purposes might not qualify as a 'group' within the context of the discussion so far: I refer to crowds, mobs, sit-ins, demonstrations, and the like. Clearly, if a sit-in is concerned with public policy, then those who take part in the sit-in are engaged in *political participation*. It is when we ask what kind of groups are these, and how far they are assimilable to the kinds of groups discussed so far, that a puzzle arises.

One part of this puzzle is spurious. If a trade union, or a number of *groupuscules*, or the members of a political party march along the streets, sit-in at Trafalgar Square, or throw stones at the police, all we are describing is the *mode* by which *institutionalized* groups are trying to affect public policy. A problem only arises in connection with meetings which are fortuitous, *ad hoc* and, for the most part made up of private individuals who have not hitherto been united in a common enterprise and are unlikely to be so united again—at least, for some time to come. About such meetings one or two things can be said which serve to distinguish them from those institutionalized and structured groups, with a fair duration through time, about

268

which the bulk of this paper is concerned. The first point is that the secondary density of such demonstrations etc., is very low; because definitionally, the population which is eligible to take part in such demonstrations is the entire public, while the tens of thousands who fill Washington, or Trafalgar Square, however impressive their numbers seem, form a minute fraction of the entire nation. The second point is that, such participation is very intermittent indeed, since many participate in a demonstration only one or twice in a lifetime. (Those who do demonstrate with any degree of regularity tend to be members of a permanent or semi-permanent group which regards the demonstration as a standard mode of activity.) Now the action taken by such crowds of demonstrators may be very effective, either in calling the government's attention to a grievance, or in provoking reactions which may—as in France, in 1968—lead to far-reaching political changes (albeit not necessarily of the kind the demonstrators wanted). The third point is that the effect ceases there. For, if the crowd decides to remain in permanent being, it *pro tanto* ceases to be a crowd—it becomes a structured and purposeful organization; and, if the crowd does intend to do more than provoke a change in government, if it wishes to govern in its own right, then it will *have* to remain in being. Whereas the groups with which the four theories of 'group participation in politics' are concerned are all *institutionalized* groups, it is the essence of the crowd or of the spontaneous demonstrations that they are non-institutionalized: that they are *anomic*. For this reason, the only one of the four theories of group participation into which spontaneous demonstrations and the like could possibly fit is Type 1; where groups are regarded as anti-despotic devices.

2. Let me now make a second observation on the *subjective* aspect of participation. It is always easy, and very tempting, to use some existentialist argument about the defeated being as much a part of the outcome as the victors; or to argue that 'nothing is quite lost'; or to say that so complicated are the interactions which lead up to the decisions ultimately taken by a government, that 'the true legislators of mankind are undiscoverable'. It may well be true that in our modern societies the decision-making process is so complicated that the slightest action here, there, and elsewhere, has a bearing on the outcome; and on these grounds seek to persuade persons that they have in some way or another 'participated'.

I do not believe that this would convince anybody that he has in fact participated. I believe, on the contrary, that to achieve participation it is not enough to be able to establish objectively that such and such a personal activity (or, *note well*, personal in-activity) must have had an effect; but that the individual concerned must himself *feel* that he had exerted some influence. In short: for someone to feel that he is a participant, it would not be sufficient that such and such an outcome were produced, but that they should *be seen to have been produced in a certain way*—that a causal connection between the individual's action and the final outcome is manifest, and manifest *to him*.

A colleague points out: 'But in Tanzania the public's failure to react to certain government projects had a political effect.' The only rejoinder worth making is simply—I am not surprised! More pertinently, another colleague asks: 'Can non-attendance, or non-activity in a group not be participation of some kind, in certain circumstances?'

First, let me distinguish. There is a true non-participation, and a false non-participation. The latter can take either of two main forms. To begin with: it may well be that the membership of a group accept, without *apparent* reaction, the activities of their leaderships on their behalf. But, as the emphasis supplied to the word is intended to suggest, this may be only an *apparent* failure to react. It may well be that the membership is satisfied with what is being done, and sees no reason to react. While this type of pseudo-non-participation is analytically distinguishable from true non-participation it may be very difficult to demonstrate empirically. In principle, it can be done however—by questionnaire and survey methods. The second major type of pseudo-non-participation is where the member of a group quite deliberately abstains from the activities of the group with the intention of producing a certain effect on its policies; akin, for instance, to deliberately abstaining from the vote in order—so one hopes—to throw the election to one side rather than the other.

But we are left with genuine non-participation: which is as much as to say, the individual does not react at all, and does not act at all for this reason and this reason alone. He may be ignorant. He may be unmindful. He may be uninterested. The essential definition of non-participation is that this individual neither thinks nor cares and therefore does not act about the policy being put forward. The mere (and obvious) fact that his inactivity and indifference has an objective effect on the policy outcome cannot be regarded as his 'participation' in that outcome. This would be saying that since his non-participation has affected the outcome, his non-participation is participation. Let us take an example; some obscure civil servant drafts a Statutory Rule relating to the sale of a certain poison in chemists' shops. Nobody —not one soul among the public, or the pharmaceutical profession, or the M.P.s—reacts to this decision in any way. The rule made by the civil servant thereby attains the force of law. Are we really to say that in these circumstances, where only one man in the entire population took action, the absolute *non*-reaction of the entire remainder of the population (which certainly affects the outcome) is the same as their participation in it? If an entire country is put to sleep while a law is passed, and wakes up to find it in operation, have they participated? And: would they *agree* they had participated?

To repeat, participation requires not only that such and such an outcome be produced, but that the concerned individual must *feel* that it has been produced, in some way or another, as a result of his own efforts. The causal connection between his activity and the outcome must be clear to him.

Now if this is so, it can only be achieved by *overt* contact, *overt* knowledge of the effects of one's activity—even if that effect were negligible. It seems to be commonplace that those outside the decision-making group usually dispute the rationality of the conduct of the decision-making process and feel that if they had been present the outcome would have been different.

Now, given the very limited number of cases of even politically engaged groups which are involved in a direct relationship to government policy; the limited extent of leader-member responsiveness; the limited extent of primary and secondary density; it would seem that the only way in which the *subjective* requirements for total participation can be met is by conducting all public business in a goldfish bowl. This would undoubtedly cause anybody who became engaged by what he saw to enter into argument at any time and for any length of time with those charged with making a decision and with all the others who, like himself, felt engaged to participate in the process, albeit with different views. The long round of discussions so entered into would unquestionably make the participants *feel* they were participants in a way which today, as I have demonstrated, is limited to narrow circles of narrow publics.

If this is what is entailed—and much new leftist writing, and new leftist activity in universities suggests to me that it is—difficulties of a technical and moral character will arise. The technical difficulty is simply the problem of getting the decisions made in time, the procedure being tiresome and cumbersome to a degree. This being so, those who are charged with responsibility for getting the decisions will, if experience be any guide, seek the short cuts by proceeding behind the scenes and 'fixing' meetings in advance. To borrow an American analogy; the fixing of election candidates will lead to the demand for a primary election; the effort to engineer this will lead to an informal pre-primary election; and from there to the still more

271

informal processes of fixing the slate for the pre-primary. In this plethora of elections, pre-election committee meetings and pre-pre-election meetings, the voter loses interest. If this is so, and if in addition 'participation' entails 'goldfish-bowl' decision-making, as I have outlined, then its chances are unrealizable, and 'political participation' becomes just a glittering word to enchant and harness the masses.

Towards Increasing the Degree of Participation

This is not quite the end of the argument; for it is not logical to argue that because current levels of group participation in politics are low and show marked evidence of apathy and lack of interest, levels of group participation cannot be improved. To prove this demands that we demonstrate that this low level of participation is due to some inherent and immutable factor or factors in human nature. But there always remains the possibility that these low levels of participation are adventitious and due to environmental factors and that if these were suitably modified the levels of participation might rise. In order to investigate this it is advisable to distinguish two sets of questions: the first enquiring into what might be likely to improve group participation levels in the existent political and social structure, and the second enquiring into what effects these political and social structures may be deemed to have on the levels of participation.

The first is fairly easily answered owing to the data deployed in Almond and Verba's *The Civic Culture*, together with the tables (at p. 70) of Kornhauser's *The Politics of Mass Society*. The two sets of data concur: social participation increases with the level of education, and with socio/economic status. (In the Western societies which these works deal with, these two variables are of course associated.) It *might*, therefore, be inferred by some that more education and higher per capita incomes are ways in which hitherto non-participant groups can be made more participant. To demonstrate this with any conviction, however, it would be necessary to run a time-series; and this, to my knowledge, has not so far been attempted. It may be relevant, however, to point out that although the per capita income of the average American is more than double that of the Briton, and although, too, something like one quarter of the American relevant age group has received higher education compared with a small fraction of the corresponding age group in Britain, the proportion of participants to non-participants in the two societies (as recorded by Almond and Verba, at p. 264 above), is not so markedly different. This suggests that structural and other characteristics may have an effect on participation, and it is precisely arguments of this kind that British 'participationists' deploy. 'Only change society', say they, 'and so-called human nature—and with it levels of participation—will change also.'

It seems to me that their negative arguments are more convincing than their positive ones. By negative arguments I mean the criticism they direct at the data relating to low levels of participation in existing groups. For instance: we know that the levels of voting for officers and on more general matters in the British trade unions is very low. But, it is fairly argued, a Trade Union is a unifunctional organization: it exists to defend its members' standard of living and conditions of work. Therefore it will necessarily occupy only a fractional part of its members' attention—that part which happens, at a moment of time, to be actively engaged in such bread and butter questions. If the worker were a member of a multifunctional organization, like a kibbutz, he might be expected to show more interest on more occasions. Again: it is argued that the structure of an organization may well contribute to apathy. Certainly it is significant that the N.U.T., where meetings are often held on school premises and where ballots are organized by schools, displays a considerably higher turnout in electing its officers than the traditional union branch, which is divorced from work-place, and based on locality.

Both points are valid. A third point strikes me as dubious. This is the argument that participation in one sphere acts as a school for participating in other spheres; local government is a school for participation in central government, and participation in workshop affairs is a school for both. The argument is largely based on the well attested association (cf. Almond and Verba at pp. 284ff, Tables XI. 4 and XI. 5) that those individuals who are participants in one sphere tend to be participants in others. Certainly. But the question is why? Is it because participation in one sphere leads to a taste for participation elsewhere, or is it that participants are self-selected types who will tend to be active in whatever organizations they find themselves, and who will seek out more and more organizations to be active in? In a very ably argued contribution, Mrs Pateman [9] argues that participation at workshop level increases the participatory capacity. Alas, since she is honest, she includes among her other findings certain figures which cast doubt on this proposition. In the John Lewis Partnership, devised to encourage participation, 'the level of interest in, and knowledge of, the representative institutions is low' (p. 79). Likewise with the Scott Bader partnership (p. 81). And in her investigation of the Yugoslav Workers' Councils she confesses that

273

—as in our own country—'women tend to be under-represented and skilled and highly skilled workers over-represented' (pp. 99–101).

Suppose then that by increasing the educational and the socio-economic levels of the population and by structuring groups in ways which it has been suggested would evoke more of their members' attention, more of the time, and more easily—suppose that by doing all this the levels of group-participation in politics were to rise? What would be the role of the groups in this reconstituted democracy?

Clearly, they would be able to play, even more advantageously than now, the anti-despotic role assigned them in theories of Type 1. And, equally clearly, they would be able to play, even more advantageously, the role of intermediaries assigned them by theories of Type 4. Remains the question: would these reconstituted and revitalized groups be able to act as substitutes for government along the lines suggested in Theory 2? It appears to me that even the minimalist theories of this kind assume a permanent, widely spread, self-conscious interest in public affairs; and whether this does indeed exist is extremely open to question. No existing evidence can be said to prove that it does not exist: precisely because this evidence is culled from structural situations which, the Group 2 theorists *allege* (but do not prove), prevents the growth of such a permanent interest. But at the same time it cannot be said that the existing evidence proves that this permanent self-conscious interest in public affairs *does* exist, but in latent form, hemmed in by constrictive institutions, and only waiting to be liberated from these to bound joyfully into full participation. Either way—whether we accept the evidence of the existent, or we reject the existent in order to create our evidence—we are indulging in an act of faith.

Notes

1 Almond and Verba, *The Civic Culture*, Princeton University Press, 1963, and Little Brown, Boston, 1965.

2 Montesquieu, *L'Esprit des Lois* (numerous editions).

3 Kornhauser, *The Politics of Mass Society*, Routledge, London, 1960.

4 Tocqueville, *Democracy in America* (numerous editions).

5 Paoloni, *Sistema Rappresentativo del Fascismo*, Naples, 1937.

6 The following abbreviations are used:
    ABCC—Association of British Chambers of Commerce
    ASLEF—Association of Locomotive Engineers and Firemen

BIPO—British Institute of Public Opinion
BMA—British Medical Association
ETU—Electrical Trades Union
FBI—Federation of British Industries*
GP—General Practitioner
GPA—General Practitioners Association
MPU—Medical Practitioners Union
NHS—National Health Service
NUM—National Union of Manufacturers
NUR—National Union of Railwaymen
NUT—National Union of Teachers
RCA—Railway Clerks Association
RHA—Road Haulage Association
TGWU—Transport and General Workers Union
TUC—Trades Union Congress

7 Rose, *Politics in England*, Faber, London, 1965.

8 Almond and Verba, p. 483.

9 Pateman, *Participation and Democratic Theory*, Cambridge University Press, 1970, chs. IV and V.

* Now the Confederation of British Industry.

275

Parties, Pressure Groups and the British Political Process *

R. T. McKenzie

Samuel Beer, perhaps the ablest American student of British politics, has commented: 'If we had some way of measuring political power, we could possibly demonstrate that at the present time pressure groups are more powerful in Britain than in the United States.'[1] The realization that this may be the case appears to have grown rapidly in Britain in recent years and, in most quarters, the reaction to it has been gloomy;[2] indeed, among many publicists the gloom has given way to outright despair. Thus, according to Paul Johnson, assistant editor of the *New Statesman*, 'Acts of policy are now decided by the interplay of thousands of conflicting interest groups, and cabinet ministers are little more than chairmen of arbitration committees. Their opinions play virtually no part in shaping decisions which they subsequently defend with passion. ... When everyone's wishes count, nobody's opinions matter.'[3]

There are no doubt many explanations of this despairing (and, I would argue, belated) recognition of the powerful role played by interest groups in Britain. There can be no question that their activities and their influence have increased in recent decades. This surely was inevitable; once it had been largely agreed by all parties that the governments (national and local) should collect and spend over a third of the national income, tremendous pressures were bound to be brought to bear to influence the distribution of the burdens and benefits of public spending on this scale. And further: a new and powerful factor was injected into the equation when the trade unions, since the second world war, won recognition (in Sir Winston Churchill's phrase) as an 'estate of the realm'. The highly articulate middle class (by whom, and for whom, so many of our journals of opinion are written) developed an acute sense of claustrophobia as they watched the giants around them, organized business, labour, the farmers, and the rest, struggling among them-

* Reprinted with permission from *The Political Quarterly*, vol. 29, no. 1, 1958, and incorporating minor revisions.

selves (and often with the government of the day) for an ever larger share of the national income.

An Unexplored Field

These developments since the second world war provide reason enough for the new and acute awareness of the role of pressure groups in Britain. But in addition it must be noted that the standard accounts of the British political system (whether in the school tests, or in the academic journals) had done little or nothing to inform even the comparatively well-educated section of the British community about the realities of the sort of pressure politics which has always been a major factor in political life in this country. An American writer on this subject quotes a British information officer lecturing in America in 1954 as saying that there is 'a complete absence of pressure groups and lobbies in Britain'.[4] Unfortunately such a remark cannot be dismissed as a misguided effort in national propaganda; it was no doubt an honest expression of a widely accepted myth about the British political system. Thirty-five years ago Sir Ivor Jennings demonstrated the vitally important part played by pressure groups in the parliamentary arena: 'Much legislation', he wrote, 'is derived from organized interests ... most of it is amended on the representation of such interests, and ... often parliamentary opposition is in truth the opposition of interests'. (*Parliament*, p. 503.) But, strangely, no scholar for twenty years took the cue, even though the first book on the role of groups in the political process, A. F. Bentley's *The Process of Government* (Fisher Unwin), had appeared in 1908.[5] Indeed, it was only in the late 1950s that learned articles began to appear on the problems of definition and methodology and on the activities of particular interest groups. If the scholars and serious publicists have been so remiss, perhaps even the well-informed citizen can be forgiven for harbouring the illusion that pressure groups are a uniquely foreign political phenomenon accounting for the 'pathological state of American democracy' and the *immobilisme* of France.

The Respective Roles of Pressure Groups and Parties

A starting point in clarifying the situation in this country is to examine the respective roles in the British political process of political parties and of pressure groups. One source of confusion about the role of party has arisen from Burke's much quoted observation that a party is 'a body of men united for promoting by their joint endeavours the national interest upon some particular principle in which they are all agreed'.[6] This remark has been leaned on much too heavily; it provides no explanation at all of the *function* of party in a democratic society; and even as a *description* of parties it is misleading because it places far too great a stress on the role of principle (and by implication, on the role of ideology and programme).

Yet some exponents of democratic theory, starting, it would appear, from Burke's definition, have implied that political parties serve (or ideally ought to serve) as the sole 'transmission belts' on which political ideas and programmes are conveyed from the citizens to the legislature and the executive. According to their ideal political model, a group of citizens first organize themselves into a political party on the basis of some principle or set of principles; they then deduce a political programme from these principles and their candidates proceed to lay this programme before the electorate; if the party secures a majority in Parliament it then implements the 'mandate' given it by the electors. If issues arise not covered by the 'mandate', then it is for the M.P.s to use their own judgment in deciding what to do; they are to deliberate, one gathers, in a kind of vacuum in which no external pressures (either from the constituencies or from organized interests) play upon them.

According to this democratic model, it is the exclusive function of the parties to canalize and to transmit the will of the citizenry to their elected representatives who then proceed to transmute it into positive law. The existence of organized groups of citizens, standing outside the party system and pressing the legislature and the executive to adopt certain specific policies, is either ignored or treated as an unfortunate aberration from the democratic ideal.

This conception of the democratic process is, in fact, completely inadequate and grossly misleading even if one applies it in this country, where parties are based on rather more specific sets of principles than they are in many other countries. (Although even in Britain it would not be easy to list the respective 'sets of principles' on which the members of the Conservative, Labour, and Liberal Parties 'are all agreed'.) Max Weber offered a better working definition of parties when he described them as 'voluntary associations for propaganda and agitation seeking to acquire power in order to ... realize objective aims or personal advantages or both'. The 'objective aims' may be of greater or lesser importance in providing the basis of association and the motive force for the activity of a particular party. But there is little doubt that it is the 'collective pursuit of power' which is of overriding importance. It is obvious too that during the pursuit of power, and after it has been achieved, parties mould and adapt their principles under the innumerable pressures brought to bear by organized groups of citizens which operate for the most part outside the party system.

I would argue that the basic functions of parties in the British political system are to select, organize, and sustain teams of parliamentarians, between whom the general body of citizens may choose at elections. The 'selection' and 'sustaining' of the teams is mainly the job of the party outside Parliament; the 'organization' of the teams (and the allocations of roles, including the key role of party leader and potential Prime Minister) is the function of the party within Parliament. It does not matter whether the party is organized on the basis of a set of principles on which all its members are agreed, or whether, alternatively, it represents merely an organized appetite for power. In either case parties play an indispensable role in the democratic system by offering the electorate a free choice between competing teams of potential rulers. In Britain, the parties do profess their loyalty to differing sets of principles and these help to provide an element of cohesion for the parties themselves, and they have the further advantage of offering the electorate a choice, in very broad terms, between differing approaches to the social and economic problems with which governments must deal.

None the less, elections in this country are primarily rough-and-ready devices for choosing between rival parliamentary teams. Under our electoral system (with its disdain for the principles of proportional representation and its penalization of minor parties) the winning team of parliamentarians rarely obtains half the votes cast. (Indeed only three governments in this century have managed to do so.) And even when, as in 1951, the winning party, the Conservatives, obtains fewer votes than their Labour opponents, no one challenges their right to rule the country.

Pressure Groups as a Corrective to Electoral Anomalies

It is, in part, one suspects, because of the tacit recognition of the enormous and legitimate role played by organized interests that the public acquiesces in the apparent anomalies of our electoral system. It did not much matter that a Conservative government took office in 1951, having obtained fewer votes than the Labour Party which it ousted; the Conservatives would be less sympathetic to the aspirations of the principal supporters of the Labour Party (the trade unions), but the new government was bound to be aware that they could not administer the economic affairs of the country unless they paid very close attention to the demands and the opinions of the trade unions. The trade unions for their part showed no disposition to sulk in their tents when the party of their choice was defeated in the election (although it had obtained more votes than the victors). The trade unions could not expect to play a dominant role in determining the policies of the new government; but they could be confident that most of the channels of communication between the trade unions and the newly elected executive would remain open and that their views would carry great weight with the new administration.

I have suggested that any explanation of the democratic process which ignores the role of organized interests is grossly misleading; I would add that it is also hopelessly inadequate and sterile in that it leaves out of account the principal channels through which the mass of citizenry brings influence to bear on the decision-makers whom they have elected. In practice, in every democratic society, the voters undertake to do far more than select their elected representatives; they also insist on their right to advise, cajole, and warn them regarding the policies they should adopt. They do this, for the most part, through the pressure-group system. Bentley, in the first trail-blazing analysis of pressure groups written sixty years ago, no doubt over-stated his case when he argued that individuals cannot affect governments except through groups; therefore, Bentley claimed, the 'process of government' must be studied as 'wholly a group process'. But there can be no doubt that pressure groups, taken together, are a far more important channel of communication than parties for the transmission of political ideas from the mass of the citizenry to their rulers. It is true that a larger proportion of the electorate 'belongs to' political parties in this country than in any other democracy. (The Conservative and Labour Parties together claim a membership of over nine million, rather more than one in every four of the voters.) But the number of *active* members who do the work of the parties in the constituencies, who draft the resolutions debated in party conferences and so forth, is not more than a few hundred per constituency. This stage army of the politically active, numbering a hundred thousand or so in each party, invariably claims to speak in the name of the millions of inactive members of the party and, indeed, on behalf of the twelve or thirteen million who normally vote for each party at an election. Further, they alone choose the candidates for their respective parties, and this is of course a vitally important function, since nomination is tanta-mount to election in two-thirds or three-quarters of the constituen-cies in Britain. But it is perfectly clear that when most citizens attempt to influence the decision-making process of their elected representa-tives, they do so through organized groups which we call 'interest groups' or 'pressure groups'.

The Articulation of Group Demands

David Truman, in *The Governmental Process*, defines interest groups as 'shared-attitude groups that make certain claims upon other groups in the society'.[7] And he adds that when they make their claims through or upon any of the institutions of government, they may be called '*political interest groups*'. In popular parlance they become '*pressure groups*', which is an acceptable enough term, so long as the word 'pressure' is not permitted to carry a too pejorative connotation. Pressure groups differ from parties in that they seek to influence the policy decisions of politicians (and administrators) without themselves seeking to assume direct responsibility for governing the country.[8] And the *pressure groups system*, in the lan-guage of the sociologist, is the set of institutional arrangements in any society which provides for the 'aggregation, articulation, and transmission' of group demands, when these demands are made through or upon governments.

Three Categories of Pressure Groups

Many attempts, some of them very elaborate, have been made to classify pressure groups. But a very simple and workable threefold classification is possible: first there are the *sectional groups*, which include all those whose basis of association is the common economic interest or vocation of their members (e.g., the Federation of British Industries, the National Farmers' Union, the Trades Union Congress, the National Union of Teachers, etc.). Their principal function is to advance the interests of their members and to provide them with a variety of services; but inevitably, in the course of their work, they spend a great deal of their time attempting to influence the decisions of elected representatives in one or another of the organs of govern-ment.[9] Secondly, there are the *promotional groups*; they are not usually organized on the basis of a common economic or vocational interest, but are devoted to the advancement of a particular cause

281

such as prison reform, the abolition of capital punishment, the defence of animal welfare, the strengthening of Sabbatarian legislation, etc. These first two categories include almost all groups which are of major political significance within the pressure-group system. But it is possible to designate a third category: *all other groups* which are not included within the first two. This may seem an odd method of classification, but it is very nearly true that every group within a society, however non-political its purpose, occasionally attempts to influence public policy. For example, a Ramblers' Association 'comes alive politically' on the rare occasion on which Parliament discusses Bills dealing with land use or national parks.* The philatelists' associations admittedly would rarely be classified as pressure groups, yet they too no doubt occasionally make representations to governments with respect to the policies pursued in issuing stamps. It is difficult indeed to think of any groups which would not under certain circumstances attempt to bring pressure to bear on the elected decision-makers.

David Truman and others have devised another category to which they attach considerable importance: *potential interest groups*. An example of what they have in mind is the category of people, largely unorganized, who are deeply devoted to maintaining the 'rules of the game' by which political democracy is sustained. When interest groups or political parties seriously transgress these (largely unwritten) rules, then this potential interest group is likely to spring into life. The first indications of its existence might take the form of letters to *The Times* drawing attention to certain dangerous developments in the eyes of the letter writers. Subsequently, if the situation is considered serious enough, *ad hoc* organizations would no doubt be set up to recruit support for those who shared the anxieties of the founders. A specific example of such a potential interest group taking tangible form occurred when the B.B.C. announced its decision to reduce the hours of broadcasting on the Third Programme. It soon became apparent that we had amongst us, perhaps without realizing it, a potential pressure group devoted to the defence of high standards in sound broadcasting. Indeed, the more one contemplates the British political scene, the more extraordinary it seems that students of the political process in this country should have so largely ignored the role of pressure groups. There can be few countries in the world in which the inhabitants so readily and so frequently organize themselves into groups for the purpose of influencing or changing the minds of their elected representatives.

* For a different interpretation of the Ramblers' Association, see p. 167. (Ed.)

Political Affiliation or Neutrality?

Certain of the great sectional groups choose to work through one or other of the great political parties in addition to bringing external pressure to bear on them. Thus, a large proportion of the trade unions are directly affiliated to the Labour Party and a number of unions also sponsor Labour candidates. But, as was noted above, the Trades Union Congress as well as individual unions reserve the right to deal directly with governments, whether Labour or Conservative. The relations between the business community and the Conservative Party are more obscure, in part because the Conservatives do not permit direct affiliation of organized groups, and also because they do not publish their accounts.* It can be taken for granted, however, that business men, as individuals and in groups, provide the greater part of the Conservative Party's revenue.[10] Yet the great associations representing the business community, such as the Federation of British Industries (superseded in 1965 by the Confederation of British Industry), expect to be and are intimately consulted by Labour governments. The Federation explained its own purpose in these words: '*whatever the government in power,* [the Federation] seeks to create conditions in which each firm has the maximum opportunity to turn its own ideas and resources to the best account in its own and the national interest'.[11]

Certain other associations, such as the National Union of Teachers, have also sponsored individual candidates for one or other or both parties. But, as the experience of the National Farmers Union suggests, most interest groups in recent years have tended to avoid a too close association with a particular party. This is partly no doubt because both parties, during their terms of office since the second world war, have shown their willingness to serve, up to a point, as brokers reconciling the interests of rival pressure groups.

There is no doubt widespread fear that parties will in fact degenerate into nothing more than brokers serving competing interest groups; and it is this fear which underlies much of the hostile comment on the activities of pressure groups, and which inhibits a realistic evaluation of the positive and legitimate function of these groups in the political process. It may well be that much writing on pressure groups too casually assumes a happy state of equilibrium. (Bentley argues that 'the balance of group pressures

* The Companies Act of 1967 now requires the disclosure of political contributions by companies. (Ed.)

is the existing state of society'.) There is no doubt that governments which indulge in 'piecemeal surrender to interest groups' become incapable of devising a coherent social policy. In the extremity, of course, government action could become merely the resultant of the forces that play upon the decision-makers.

The Experience of Sweden

But the danger can easily be exaggerated. Sweden can be described even more aptly than this country as 'a pluralist society' yet it is far from the 'pluralist stagnation' which some critics of the interest-group system fear. Gunnar Heckscher (who is both a professor of politics and a Conservative member of the Swedish Parliament) recently commented that 'it is now regarded as more or less inevitable' in Sweden that certain of the powerful interest groups 'should exercise a power almost equal to that of Parliament and definitely superior to that of the parliamentary parties'.[12] Yet he does not see in this situation any really serious ground for concern; nor is there, he says, any demand in Sweden that action should be taken to curb the powerful organizations. Heckscher attributes the comparatively good health of the Swedish body politic to the 'strong sense of responsibility among group leaders' and the 'politics of compromise' which govern the relations between the great groups themselves, as well as their relations with governments.

Despite the political and social tensions in contemporary Britain, surely much the same comment can be made about the situation in this country? Vague as the phrase may be, the concept of the 'national interest' is still to the forefront in the course of almost every big sectional dispute in this country. Business, Labour, the farmers, the university teachers, still consider it expedient to argue their case, at least in part, in the terms of the national interest. Governments may from time to time give in to one or other of the great pressure groups, also in the name of the 'national interest'. But they also on occasion stand out boldly against the claim of pressure groups on the ground that to give way would be to *betray* the national interest.

The Effect of Pressure Groups on Government

If governments may have appeared in recent years to be more pusillanimous than heretofore, it may be in part because since 1950 we have been living in an unusual period of knife-edge parliamentary majorities; and during such periods governments are bound to spend a good deal of time peering over their own shoulders. It is too often forgotten that a uniform 1 per cent shift from one party to another means a turnover of eighteen seats, and hence a drop of thirty-six in the ruling party's majority. (Thus if at the 1959 election the Conservatives had suffered a net loss of two in every hundred of those who supported them in 1955, then their government would have been defeated.) One of the most effective ways of minimizing the influence on governments of at least some pressure groups, if this is considered urgently necessary, would be to provide one party or another with a sweeping parliamentary majority.[13]

There are of course other grounds for concern, quite apart from the possibly inhibiting effect of the pressure-group system on governmental decision-making. Many fear that the powerful groups are becoming more powerful and the less well-organized groups relatively weaker. Samuel Eldersveld, writing of the situation in the United States, discussed the possibility that the interest-group system is resulting, not in increased political competition, but in imperfect competition, leading to oligopoly.[14] And he adds that the 'diversification of power sources [in America] means that the decision-making process is more indirect, non-public, and obscure'. The same fears are often expressed in Britain. Are there not a very few great interest groups, it is suggested, whose leaders form a kind of inner circle of 'oligarchs' which deals frequently and intimately with senior ministers? And is it not the case that this handful of people decide the fate of the whole community, which is, for the most part, unaware even of the issues they are deciding? Again, it would be foolish to ignore evidence of the trend in this direction; equally foolish to ignore the countervailing forces. Certainly it is true that the leaders of big business, big labour, and the farmers have greater ease of 'access' to senior ministers, whichever party is in office. But it would be inaccurate automatically to equate 'access' with 'influence'. (To take a slightly frivolous example it seems likely that a Conservative government would be more willing to defy the trade unions and a Labour government the business organizations, than either of them would be likely to defy the Sabbatarian groups, which are not thought to have very ready access to ministers.) And further, it must be remembered that intimacy of contact involves the recognition of mutual responsibilities. Ministers may explain the situation to interest-group leaders frankly and then ask their co-operation 'in the national interest'.

R. T. McKenzie

The Unorganized, Inarticulate Sections

There remains, however, the problem of the ill-organized (or even unorganizable) sections of the community. Is there not danger that they will be either ignored or trampled upon by the really powerful interest groups? Certainly the danger is real. But it is the politicians' ultimate worry to see to it that the 'little men' (each of whom has as much political influence in the polling booth, at least, as anyone in the land) do not revolt against their policies in such numbers as to bring about their electoral ruin. This surely is one ultimate safeguard of the ill-organized. Indeed, it is arguable that in the long run governments are at least as frightened of the unorganized consumers (in their capacity as voters) as they are of the highly organized economic interests. None the less there is an area of public policy in which the absence of organized groups represents a serious problem. Thus, for example, governments under pressure from shop employees and certain categories of shop-owners, may contemplate further restricting shop hours; there is no one to speak for the shoppers. Or again, governments may be fearful of liberalizing licensing hours because of the pressures they would set in motion against themselves from the highly organized temperance forces; there is no organized body to speak for the drinkers. Here, it seems to me, the public opinion polls have a legitimate and important role to play. The evidence they can produce of the shoppers' attitude to proposals for restricting shop hours, or the drinkers' attitude to licensing laws, should be *one* of the factors taken into account by the decision-makers, in addition to the views of the organized interests, in arriving at their policy decisions.

But with reservations such as these, it seems to me reasonable to conclude that the pressure group system, with all its dangers, is both an inevitable and an indispensable concomitant of the party system. It provides an invaluable set of multiple channels through which the mass of the citizenry can influence the decision-making process at the highest levels. Is it possible that the widespread uneasiness about pressure groups in Britain today is really a result of the shift in the balance of power between the classes? In the paper quoted above, Eldersveld remarked that in 'the fluid politics' of America there is no longer 'a decisive ruling class' but rather a set of 'multiple élites'. The same development has obviously occurred in this country; and it is clear that the new élites are struggling to assert their strength in part through the pressure-group system.

Notes

1 Samuel H. Beer, 'Pressure Groups and Parties in Britain', *The American Political Science Review*, March 1956, p. 3.

2 Thus even so well informed an observer as W. J. M. Mackenzie concludes that the dominant role of organized groups in British public life means: 'We are gradually shifting back into a situation in which a man is socially important only as a holder of standard qualifications and as a member of authorized groups, in fact into the new medievalism which was the promised land in the days from the younger Pugin to William Morris.' W. J. M. Mackenzie, 'Pressure Groups in British Government', *British Journal of Sociology*, June 1955, p. 146.

3 P. Johnson, 'The Amiable Monster', *New Statesman*, 12 October 1957, p. 468. In the same vein, Bernard Hollowood has remarked that 'Parliament has become the abused referee of the big power game and ... the unhappy millions on the terraces are powerless, almost voiceless spectators', in 'The Influence of Business and the City', *Twentieth Century*, October 1957, p. 253.

4 Cited in F. C. Newman, 'Reflections on Money and Party Politics in Britain', *Parliamentary Affairs*, Summer 1957, p. 309.

5 Since this essay was written several books devoted to the study of interest groups in Britain have appeared, including S. E. Finer, *Anonymous Empire*, Pall Mall (London, 1958); J. D. Stewart, *British Pressure Groups*, their role in relation to the House of Commons, Clarendon Press (Oxford, 1958); Allen Potter, *Organised Groups in British National Politics*, Faber (London, 1961).

6 *Thoughts on the Present Discontents*, Oxford University Press, World's Classics (ed.), Vol. II, p. 82.

7 D. B. Truman, *The Governmental Process*, Knopf (New York, 1962), p. 37.

8 It is admittedly comparatively easy to make this distinction in a preponderantly two-party system of the sort that exists in Britain and the United States; but it is more difficult in certain Continental countries, where minor parties, which would elsewhere be content to function as pressure groups, offer candidates at elections even though they have no prospect, or even expectation, of winning full responsibility for governing the country. And of course it is arguable that in this country the Scottish and Welsh Nationalists are little more than pressure groups seeking to publicize their cause by offering candidates at elections. For a further discussion of this question see Allen Potter, 'British Pressure Groups', *Parliamentary Affairs*, Autumn 1956, pp. 418–19.

9 These sectional interest groups are the organizations, in Franz Neumann's phrase, 'by which [social] power is translated into political power'. *The Democratic and the Authoritarian State*, Free Press of Glencoe (Glencoe, Ill., 1957), p. 13.

10 It is important to remember, however, as F. C. Newman has pointed out that

in the case of both parties, 'it is the programme that attracts the money, the money does not structure the programme', in 'Reflections on Money and Party Politics in Britain', *Parliamentary Affairs* (Summer 1957), p. 316.

11 *The F.B.I., what it is, what it does*, p. 1 (italics mine). For a very valuable examination of the structure and functioning of the F.B.I., see S. E. Finer, 'The Federation of British Industries', *Political Studies* (February 1956), pp. 61–84.

12 G. Heckscher, 'Interest Groups and Sweden', a paper presented to the *International Political Science Round Table*, Pittsburgh, 7–14 September 1957 (duplicated), p. 8. See also his 'Pluralist Democracy; the Swedish Experience', *Social Research* (December 1948), pp. 417–61. It should be noted, in connection with Heckscher's remark quoted above, that there are five parties in the Swedish Parliament, and in such circumstances it is perhaps less surprising than it would be here to remark that certain of the great sectional groups are more powerful than the parliamentary parties.

13 The Conservatives in the 1959 election secured a majority of 100 and in the course of that Parliament did act more boldly than hitherto in, for example, attempting to introduce an incomes policy despite trade union hostility; in promoting the Beeching plan for the reorganization of the railways, despite much resistance in the rural areas; and in the sponsorship of legislation to abolish resale price maintenance against the strong resistance of the small shop-keepers who traditionally support the Conservative Party.

14 S. J. Eldersveld, 'American Interest Groups', a paper presented to the *International Political Science Round Table*, Pittsburgh, 7–14 September 1957 (duplicated).

British Pressure Groups: Conclusions*

J. D. Stewart

1

There are a few people who wish to dismiss pressure groups out of hand as bad in themselves. That, however, is unrealistic, for whenever society has developed to that degree of complexity that makes groups of people conscious of sectional needs, pressure groups exist. But criticism of the part pressure groups play in political systems has normally been directed at their influence. The custom has been to assert that groups have too much influence rather than too little—to attempt to build barricades against their further growth rather than to ease their path. But if it is possible to assert that groups have too much influence, there is presumably some level below which it would be unfortunate if the influence of groups were to fall.

It is not easy to place an exact meaning on the term 'group influence'. Since groups compete against each other, it is clearly not a conception which can be reached by adding up the totals of group achievement. The failure of a trade union to secure an act limiting the working day is balanced by the success of an employers' association in its efforts to prevent this.

The use of the term 'group influence' and the assumption that in some political systems it is greater than in others, rests upon the premiss that there are other elements in the process of decision-making. Group influence is high when all that is involved in a decision by the governmental process is a trial of strength between groups.

There are many elements that can enter into the process of decision-making—the members of the legislature, the party, the government as the party in action, and the government as the continuing executive of the state. Where these or any of them form

* Reprinted from *British Pressure Groups: Their Role in Relation to the House of Commons*, 1958, Chapter X, pp. 238–44, by permission of The Clarendon Press, Oxford.

289

decisions without considering the representations or activities of the groups, then group influence is low.

For any one decision it is difficult, if not impossible, to say what are the important elements. It is often possible to identify that part of the process of government which formally took the decision, but not to single out the factors which led to that decision being taken.

If it is impossible to make a final analysis of any individual decision, it is not necessarily impossible to say of a political system that group influence is high or low. The activities of the groups themselves, the particular institutional structure, and the cumulative effect of many decisions, enable the tendency of the system to be seen and make probable what on one decision must remain only a possibility. In analysing a political system it is possible to show at what points group activity is directed, and the extent to which those points have the resources and the authority to resist group influence.

An individual member of a legislature, unprotected by party discipline, is not likely to have much authority to resist the influence of pressure groups, although he may have the resources to do so.

A political party, purely concerned to obtain power, lacks the resources to resist pressure groups even though it may have the authority to do so.

Authority is dependent upon the power for independent action possessed by the person or institution, resources upon their willingness and their ability to evolve their own standards and policies.

It would be foolish to attempt to define an optimum level of group influence. Yet there are certain situations which I suggest should be regarded as dangerous. A system which does not give to the government the resources from which to come to a decision on group demands and the authority to enforce it, is dangerous because it is turning the process of decision-making into a struggle between pressure groups, the result of which does not derive from clear judgement upon their demands. A positive outlook is required from within the process of government. It is desirable that in making decisions upon group representations, there be brought into play considerations deriving from a wider view of the political scene than is possible to individual groups. There will never be agreement on what is the national interest, but that there are interests other than those closely concerned in an issue is generally agreed. A group exists to express the views of those closely concerned. But in any decision all are concerned, however remotely.

On the other hand, a system of government which did not recognize the part that groups have to play would be equally dangerous. The views of those closely concerned should play an important part in any decision that is taken. Any difficulty a group finds in expressing these views or bringing them to the attention of the government blocks up the channels of communication upon which the government, if it is responsive to opinion, must depend. Though the government should always feel itself able to overrule the groups, a system in which the government overrules an opinion passionately held by a group, without backing from the rest of society, is lacking in tolerance. The group should always be able to appeal from such intolerance.

A balance is required and each system has its own problems in arriving at it.

2

The British system of government might appear to have found a satisfactory balance. In one sense it has. The basic point of decision upon a group's demand is the government, which gains authority both from its position as the party in action and from the power and knowledge that has been built up in the ministries.

The power of the party rests upon so much wider a basis than that of any one group, that the support of that group is not vital to it. It is able to appeal to people beyond the interests into which they divide their lives and to obtain from them a loyalty which gives it strength to challenge the groups.

The party has the authority to resist the group. But it also appears to have the resources. If the only object of the party were to gain power, then it would merely need to act as a broker between competing groups. If, however, the party seeks to gain power for a purpose then it has the resources as well as the authority to resist the groups. Party policies may themselves have been modified by groups, but at the moment of decision they belong to the party. The virtue of a party decision as opposed to a group decision is that the party, in making its decision, can be assumed to have considered more factors than the group. It derives from a view of society, not merely from the view of a group in society.

The ministries also have authority, apart from the party. They can use party discipline even without party theory. In the departments a wealth of knowledge has been built up which should ensure that the government brings to the groups' representations a positive attitude. In the machinery of government there is the means to relate each department's problems to wider issues.

The government has the authority and resources to challenge the groups.

Lest it be thought that the groups are placed in too weak a situation, it should be remembered that the system provides safeguards. Groups have ample opportunity to make their views known. The machinery of consultation is particularly well developed, despite occasional defects. The place of most groups is recognized. Their representatives sit upon government committees. There are long and healthy discussions between groups and government.

There are further safeguards should the groups be treated unfairly. The government accepts the appeal to Parliament or to public opinion in that a decision may be modified in the light of the group's impact there.

3

Along these lines runs the theoretical justification of the position of pressure groups in the British system of government. There are, however, indications that there are certain dangers, and that the system may not be working as well as this analysis makes out.

Over a large field of political activity there is no party viewpoint. This may be inevitable, since many of the problems are essentially group problems.

Professor S. H. Beer has suggested that there has been a weakening in the philosophies of the parties which tends to give more influence to pressure groups:

> From this tactic and these shaping forces results not a politics of class or of social philosophy, but a kind of pressure politics. The term is inexact as applied to British politics if it is suggested that policy is made simply by groups pushing an inert government or party this way and that, for it is often the government or party which in the competition for electoral support teaches the group what its rights and interests are and excites it to demand them.[1]

An analysis of the 1955 Labour Party election manifesto might seem to give some justification to this point of view. But it is not necessary to accept his full criticism to see that the party does not always bring a positive outlook to pressure group demands. This may not be due to a change in the nature of the party so much as a change in the nature of the problem. The growth of group issues in politics may have overwhelmed the party.

An added burden is thrown upon the ministers and ministries who are expected to evolve their own standards to judge upon and between the representations of pressure groups. Their authority remains unimpaired, but that they have the resources to achieve this without the aid of party standards is doubtful. They are expected to judge every issue empirically, or, if it is preferred, upon its merits. The result of the empirical approach to politics depends upon the attitude with which one starts. To judge a question on its merits depends upon one's conception of merit.

In forming this attitude and this conception the most potent influences outside the department are the groups, and on many issues they are the only outside influences there are. In many cases there will be one or two groups only. For the system tends to give weight to a few dominant groups.

The minister or ministry with which the group is concerned is likely to develop an attitude that is largely sectional. It would be a strange Ministry of Agriculture that did not try and do its best for agriculture and it is only too easy to drift into the attitude of thinking the best for agriculture to be what the farmers through the N.F.U. consider it to be. In any ministry the thoughts and arguments that are heard from outside sources come largely from pressure groups. Civil servants and politicians whose daily routine involves contact with the groups, hearing their viewpoints and their problems, obtaining information from them and co-operating with them on committees, may come to accept the standards of the group as their own. There is a danger that departments may become mere pressure groups within the government.

It is probably too much to expect civil servants or even ministers always to impose a mental control on the representations of groups in an attempt to weigh these views against some conception of the national interest. What is necessary is that there be acceptable ideas besides those of groups in the fields in which there are no party views. The contribution that an individual group can make could be rendered more valuable by a challenge. The construction of a ministry will determine the extent to which the views of a group are challenged by other groups. But group battles are not the only thing needed to prevent the Minister of Agriculture from being merely a Minister for Agriculture.

The *Manchester Guardian* has written of the discussion on local government reform:

> It is of course right and proper that the Minister should consult such bodies in advance and that in formulating his own proposals he should bear in mind the divergencies of views between them. But it would be gross dereliction of duty on his part to leave all initiative to them, to accord them a right of veto or to use their constitutional inability to compose their differences as an excuse for government inaction. For in this matter the local

authority associations do not represent the wishes of local electors or the interests of local government; they stand for nothing but the defence and promotion of the particular forms of local authority, whose obsolescence has made reform so urgently necessary.[2]

It is not necessary to accept the full censures of the *Manchester Guardian* on these associations to see the point it is making. There are other views on local government, besides those of the associations, besides those of local authorities. There is a danger that close contact with these associations may make a department place too much importance on their views. It is from this attitude that any possible veto from an association derives its force. Where the groups with which a ministry is closely concerned are divided in opinion, the ministry is very reluctant to act.

The problem of finding the national interest cannot be solved by a minister concerning himself with an abstract ideal. There can be no agreed national interest. But there can be a viewpoint derived from other considerations than those advanced by the groups closely concerned in the problem.

The clash between the sectional and national interest of which theorists talk is difficult to grasp. The sectional interest, as represented by the group, is clear; the national interest is not. But the impossibility of establishing the national interest does not absolve the government from its task. Two things at least are required of it. These are to try to find out whether there are other viewpoints on an issue besides those of the groups immediately concerned, and to attempt to evolve other criteria of judgement than the ones they advance. The government is given by our political system the authority to impose its conceptions of national interest. What the system cannot give is the initiative to do so.

4

These are the dangers that exist in our system of government. It is well to be aware of them. Such awareness is in itself an important factor in meeting the dangers. However, they should not cloud our judgement of the value of pressure groups in our present system of government. Consideration of these dangers may modify the justification of the pressure group's role given earlier in this chapter, but will not destroy it. They are dangers that must be guarded against, but we should be exaggerating their importance if we were to proceed from that to a wholesale condemnation of the part pressure groups play in our system, which, as has been shown, is often a valuable one.

Pressure groups are necessary to the government of our complex society. The coherent expression of opinion they render possible is vital. They have become a fifth estate, the means by which many individuals contribute to politics. Without them discontent would grow and knowledge be lost. It is important that the system of government be such that their role can be carried out with responsibility.

Notes

1 S. H. Beer, 'The Future of British Politics', *Political Quarterly*, vol. 26, no. 1, pp. 38–9.

2 *Manchester Guardian*, 2 March 1955.

Bibliography

Several standard texts on British government and politics include sections on pressure groups. The following are useful in this respect:

HANSON, A. H., and WALLES, G., *Governing Britain*, Fontana/Collins, London, 1970.

PUNNETT, R. M., *British Government and Politics*, Heinemann, London (2nd ed.), 1971.

ROSE, R., *Politics in England*, Faber, London, 1965.

STACEY, F., *The Government of Modern Britain*, Clarendon Press, Oxford, 1968.

WALKLAND, S. A., *The Legislative Process*, Allen and Unwin, London, 1968.

The following bibliography includes not only studies of British pressure groups but also includes some American literature, where this is relevant to the theoretical issues discussed in Part I. It excludes articles reprinted in this volume.

Abbreviations:
A.P.S.R.   *American Political Science Review*
P.Q.   *Political Quarterly*
P.S.   *Political Studies*

ALLABY, M., *The Eco-Activists: Youth Fights for a Human Environment*, Charles Knight, London, 1971.

ALLEN, V. L., *Power in Trade Unions*, Longmans, London, 1954.

ALLEN, V. L., *Trade Union Leadership*, Longmans, London, 1957.

ALLEN, V. L., *Trade Unions and the Government*, Longmans, London, 1960.

ALMOND, G. A., 'Research Note: A Comparative Study of Interest Groups and the Political Process', *A.P.S.R.*, vol. LII no. 1 (March 1958), pp. 270–82.

ALMOND, G. A., and COLEMAN, J S., *The Politics of the Developing Areas*, Princeton U. P., Princeton, 1960.

Bibliography

ALMOND, G. A., and POWELL, G. B., *Comparative Politics: a Developmental Approach*, Little Brown, Boston, 1966.

BARKER, A., and RUSH, M., *The Member of Parliament and His Information*, Allen and Unwin, London, 1970.

BARNES, H. E. (ed.), *An Introduction to the History of Sociology*, University of Chicago Press, Chicago, 1948.

BARNETT, M. J., *The Politics of Legislation: The Rent Act 1957*, Weidenfeld and Nicolson, London, 1969.

BARR, J., 'The Amenity Protesters', *New Society*, 1 August 1968.

BARR, J., 'Environment Lobby', *New Society*, 5 February 1970.

BARRY, B. M., *Sociologists, Economists and Democracy*, Collier-Macmillan, London, 1970.

BEER, S. H., 'Group Representation: Britain and the United States', *Annals of American Academy of Political and Social Science*, vol. 319 (September 1958), pp. 130–40.

BEER, S. H., *Modern British Politics*, Faber, London, 1965.

BEER, S. H., 'Pressure Groups and Parties in Britain', *A.P.S.R.*, vol. L no. 1 (March 1956), pp. 1–23.

BEER, S. H., 'The Representation of Interests in British Government', *A.P.S.R.*, vol. LI no. 3 (September 1957), pp. 613–50.

BENTLEY, A. F., *The Process of Government* (ed. P. Odegard), Belknap Press, Harvard, 1967.

BOCOCK, J., 'The Politics of White Collar Unionization', *P.Q.*, vol. 44 no. 3 (July–September 1973), pp. 295–303.

BRENNER, M. J., 'Functional Representation and Interest Group Theory: Some Notes on British Practice', *Comparative Politics*, vol. 2 no. 1 (October 1969), pp. 111–34.

CASTLES, F. G., 'Business and Government: A Typology of Pressure Group Activity', *P.S.*, vol. XVII no. 2 (June 1969), pp. 160–176.

CASTLES, F. G., *Pressure Groups and Political Culture*, Routledge, London, 1967.

CASTLES, F. G., 'Towards a Theoretical Analysis of Pressure Politics', *P S.*, vol. XIV no. 3 (October 1966), pp. 339–48.

CHRISTOPH, J. B., 'Capital Punishment and British Party Responsibility', *Political Science Quarterly*, vol. LXXVII no. 1 (March 1962), pp. 19–35.

CHRISTOPH, J. B., *Capital Punishment and British Politics*, Allen and Unwin, London, 1962.

COATES, R. D., *Teachers' Unions and Interest Group Politics*, University Press, Cambridge, 1972.

CRICK, B., *The American Science of Politics*, Routledge, London, 1959.

DAMER, S., and HAGUE, C., 'Public Participation in Planning: A Review', *Town Planning Review* (July 1971), pp. 217–32.

DAVIS, M., 'British Public Relations: a Political case study', *Journal of Politics*, vol. 24 no. 1 (February 1962), pp. 50–71.

DAVIS, M., 'Some Neglected Aspects of British Pressure Groups', *Midwest Journal of Political Science*, vol. VII no. 1 (1963), pp. 42–53.

DEAKIN, N., 'The Politics of the Commonwealth Immigrants Bill', *P.Q.*, vol. 39 no. 1 (January–March 1968), pp. 25–45.

DENNIS, N., *People and Planning*, Faber, London, 1970.

DENNIS, N., *Public Participation and Planners' Blight*, Faber, London, 1972.

DION, L., 'The Politics of Consultation', *Government and Opposition*, vol. 8 (Summer 1973), pp. 332–53.

DOWLING, R. E., 'Pressure Group Theory: Its Methodological Range', *A.P.S.R.*, vol. LIV no. 4 (December 1960), pp. 944–54.

DOWNS, A., *An Economic Theory of Democracy*, Harper & Row, London, 1957.

DOWSE, R. E., and PEEL, J., 'The Politics of Birth Control', *P.S.* vol. XIII no. 2 (June 1965), pp. 179–97.

DRIVER, C., *The Disarmers*, Hodder and Stoughton, London, 1964.

ECKSTEIN, H., 'Group Theory and the Comparative Study of Politics', *in* ECKSTEIN, H., and APTER, D. (eds.), *Comparative Politics: A Reader*, Free Press, New York, 1963, pp. 389–97.

ECKSTEIN, H., 'The Politics of the British Medical Association', *P.Q.*, vol. 26 no. 4 (October–December 1955), pp. 345–59.

ECKSTEIN, H., *Pressure Group Politics: The Case of the British Medical Association*, Allen and Unwin, London, 1960.

EHRMANN, H. W., *Interest Groups on Four Continents*, University Press, Pittsburg, 1958.

FIELD, F., 'A Pressure Group for the Poor', in BULL, D. (ed.), *Family Poverty*, Duckworth, London, 1971, pp. 145–57.

FINER, S. E., *Anonymous Empire*, Pall Mall, London (2nd ed.), 1966.

FINER, S. E., 'The Anonymous Empire', *P.S.*, vol. VI no. 1 (February 1958), pp. 16–37.

FINER, S. E., 'The Federation of British Industries', *P.S.*, vol. IV no. 1 (February 1956), pp. 61–84.

FINER, S. E., 'Interest Groups and the Political Process in Great Britain', in EHRMANN, H. W. (ed.), *Interest Groups on Four Continents*, University of Pittsburg Press, Pittsburg, 1958.

FINER, S. E., 'The Political Power of Private Capital', *Sociological Review*, vol. 3 no. 2 (December 1955), pp. 279–94; vol. 4 no. 3 (July 1956), pp. 5–30.

FINER, S. E., *Private Industry and Political Power*, Pall Mall Pamphlet no. 3, London, 1958.

FINER, S. E., 'Transport Interests and the Roads Lobby', *P.Q.*, vol. 29 no. 1 (January–March 1958), pp. 47–58.

FULFORD, R., *Votes for Women*, Faber, London, 1957.

GARCEAU, O., 'Interest Group Theory in Political Research', *Annals of the American Society for Political and Social Science*, vol. 319 (September 1958), pp. 104–12.

GHOSH, S. C., 'Pressure and Privilege: the Manchester Chamber of Commerce and the Indian Problem, 1930–34', *Parliamentary Affairs*, vol. XVIII no. 2 (Spring 1965), pp. 201–15.

GOLEMBIEWSKI, R. T., 'The Group Basis of Politics; Notes on Analysis and Development', *A.P.S.R.*, vol. LIV no. 4 (December 1960), pp. 962–71.

GRAZIA, A. DE, 'Nature and Prospects of Political Interest Groups', *Annals of the American Academy of Social and Political Science*, vol. CCCXIX (September 1958), pp. 113–22.

GREGORY, R., *The Miners and British Politics 1906–14*, Oxford University Press, London, 1968.

GREGORY, R., *The Price of Amenity*, Macmillan, London, 1971.

GROVE, J. W., *Government and Industry in Britain*, Longmans, London, 1962.

HAGAN, C. B., 'The Group in Political Science', *in* YOUNG, R. (ed.), *Approaches to the Study of Politics*, Atlantic Books, London, 1958, pp. 38–51.

HALE, M. Q., 'The Cosmology of Arthur Bentley', *A.P.S.R.*, vol. LIV no. 4 (December 1960), pp. 955–61.

HAMPTON, W., *Democracy and Community; A Study of Politics in Sheffield*, Oxford University Press, London, 1970.

HARRISON, M., 'Political Finance in Britain', *Journal of Politics*, vol. 25 no. 4 (November 1963), pp. 664–85.

HARRISON, M., *The Trade Unions and The Labour Party Since 1945*, Allen and Unwin, London, 1960.

HERRING, E. P., *Group Representation Before Congress*, John Hopkins Press, Baltimore, 1929.

HINDELL, K., 'The Genesis of the Race Relations Bill', *P.Q.*, vol. 36 no. 4 (October–December 1965), pp 390–405.

HINDELL, K., and SIMMS, M., *Abortion Law Reformed*, Peter Owen, London, 1971.

HOWARTH, R. W., 'The Political Strength of British Agriculture', *P.S.*, vol. XVII no. 4 (December 1969), pp. 458–69.

HUGHES, J., and POLLINS, H., *Trade Unions in Great Britain*, David and Charles, Newton Abbot, 1973.

JAY, A., *The Householder's Guide to Community Defence Against Bureaucratic Aggression*, Jonathan Cape, London, 1972.

JENKINS, P., *The Battle of Downing Street*, Charles Knight, London, 1970.

KIMBER, R., and RICHARDSON, J. J. (eds.), *Campaigning for the Environment*, Routledge, London, 1974.

KIMBER, R., and RICHARDSON, J. J., 'The Role of All-Party Committees in the House of Commons', *Parliamentary Affairs*, vol. XXV no. 4 (Autumn 1972), pp. 339–49.

LAPALOMBARA, J., *Interest Groups in Italian Politics*, Princeton University Press, Princeton, 1964.

LAPALOMBARA, J., 'The Utility and Limitations of Interest Group Theory in Non-American Field Situations', *Journal of Politics*, vol. XXII, 1960, pp. 29–49.

LAPPING, A., 'Who's for Fluoride?', *New Society*, 9 October 1969.

LATHAM, E., *The Group Basis of Politics*, Cornell University Press, Ithaca, New York, 1952.

LATHAM, E., 'The Group Basis of Politics: Notes for a Theory', *A.P.S.R.*, vol. XLVI no. 2 (June 1952), pp. 376–97.

LIEBER, R. J., *British Politics and European Unity: Parties, Élites and Pressure Groups*, University of California Press, Berkeley, 1970.

MACKENZIE, W. J. M., 'Pressure Groups in British Government', *British Journal of Sociology*, vol. VI no. 2 (June 1955), pp. 133–48.

MACKENZIE, W. J. M., 'Pressure Groups: The "Conceptual Framework"', *P.S.*, vol. III no. 3 (October 1955), pp. 347–55

MACRIDIS, R. C., 'Interest Groups in Comparative Analysis', *Journal of Politics*, vol. 23 no. 1 (February 1961), pp. 25–45.

MANZER, R. A., *Teachers and Politics in England and Wales*, Manchester University Press, Manchester, 1970.

MILLETT, J. H., 'British Interest Group Tactics: A Case Study', *Political Science Quarterly*, vol. LXXII no. 1, March 1957, pp. 71–82.

MILLETT, J. H., 'The Role of an Interest Group Leader in the House of Commons', *Western Political Quarterly*, vol. IX no. 4 (1956), pp. 915–26.

MONYPENNY, P., 'Political Science and the Study of Groups: Notes to Guide a Research Project', *Western Political Quarterly*, vol. VII no. 2 (June 1954), pp. 183–201.

MOODIE, G., and STUDDERT-KENNEDY, G., *Opinions, Publics and Pressure Groups*, Allen and Unwin, London, 1970.

MULLER, W. D., 'Trade Union Sponsored Members of Parliament in the Defence Dispute of 1960–61', *Parliamentary Affairs*, vol. XXIII no. 3 (Summer 1970), pp. 258–76.

NETTL, J. P., 'Consensus or Élite Domination: the Case of Business', *P.S.*, vol. XIII no. 1 (February 1965), pp. 22–44.

NOEL-BAKER, F., 'The Grey Zone—the Problems of Business Affiliations of M.P.s', *Parliamentary Affairs*, vol. XV no. 1 (Winter 1961–2), pp. 87–93.

ODEGARD, P. H., 'A Group Basis of Politics: A New Name for an Old Myth', *Western Political Quarterly*, vol. XI no. 3 (September 1958), pp. 689–702.

OLSON, M., *The Logic of Collective Action*, Harvard University Press, 1965.

PARKER, R. S., '"Group Analysis" and Scientism in Political Studies', *P.S.*, vol. IX no. 1 (February 1961), pp. 37–51.

PARKIN, F., *Middle Class Radicalism*, Manchester University Press, Manchester, 1968.

PARRY, G., (ed.), *Participation in Politics*, Manchester University Press, Manchester, 1972.

PENNOCK, J. R., '"Responsible Government", Separated Powers, and Special Interests: Agricultural Subsidies in Britain and America', *A.P.S.R.*, vol. LVI no. 3 (September 1962), pp. 621–33.

PLATT, D. C. M., 'The Commercial and Industrial Interests of Ministers of the Crown', *P.S.*, vol. IX no. 3 (October 1961), pp. 267–90.

PLOWDEN, W., *The Motor Car and Politics 1896-1970*, The Bodley Head, London, 1971.

Political and Economic Planning, *Advisory Committees in British Government*, Allen and Unwin, London, 1960.

Political and Economic Planning, *Industrial Trade Associations*, PEP/Allen and Unwin, London, 1957.

POTTER, A., 'Attitude Groups', *P.Q.*, vol. 29 no. 1 (January–March 1958), pp. 72–82.

POTTER, A., 'British Pressure Groups', *Parliamentary Affairs*, vol. IX no. 4 (Autumn 1956), pp. 418–26.

POTTER, A., 'The Equal Pay Campaign Committee', *P.S.*, vol. V no. 1 (February 1957), pp. 49–64.

POTTER, A., *Organised Groups in British National Politics*, Faber, London, 1961.

PYM, B. A., 'Pressure Groups on Moral Issues', *P.Q.*, vol. 43 no. 3 (July–September 1972), pp. 317–27.

Report from the Select Committee on Members' Interests (Declaration), HC. 57, 1969.

Report of the Royal Commission on Trade Unions and Employers' Associations 1965-68 (Chairman, Lord Donovan), Cmnd. 3623, H.M.S.O., London, 1968.

Report of the Committee on Intermediaries, Cmnd. 7904, 1950.

RICHARDS, P. G., *Parliament and Conscience*, Allen and Unwin, London, 1970.

RICHARDSON, J. J., 'The Making of the Restrictive Practices Act, 1956—A case study of the Policy Process in Britain', *Parliamentary Affairs*, vol. XX no. 4 (Autumn 1967), pp. 350–74.

RICHARDSON, J. J., *The Policy Making Process*, Routledge, London, 1969.

ROBERTS, B. C., *Trade Union Government and Administration in Great Britain*, Bell, London, 1957.

ROBERTS, G. K., *Political Parties and Pressure Groups in Great Britain*, Weidenfeld and Nicolson, London, 1970.

ROSE, G., *The Struggle for Penal Reform*, Stevens, London, 1962.

ROSE, R., *Influencing Voters*, Faber, London, 1967.

ROSS, G. W., *The Nationalization of Steel*, MacGibbon & Kee, London, 1965.

ROTHMAN, S., 'Systematic Political Theory: Observations on the Group Approach', *A.P.S.R.*, vol. LIV no. 1 (March 1960), pp. 15–33.

SCHATTSCHNEIDER, E. E., *The Semi-Sovereign People: A Realist's View of Democracy in America*, Holt, New York, 1960.

SELF, P., and STORING, H. J., *The State and the Farmer*, Allen and Unwin, London, 1962.

STEWART, J. D., *British Pressure Groups: Their Role in Relation to the House of Commons*, Oxford University Press, 1958.

STRAUS, G. R., 'Pressure Groups I have known', *P.Q.*, vol. 29 no. 1 (January–March 1958), pp. 40–7.

STREAT, SIR R., 'Government Consultation with Industry', *Public Administration*, vol. XXXVII no. 1 (Spring 1959), pp. 1–8.

TAYLOR, R., 'Arthur F. Bentley's Political Science', *Western Political Quarterly*, vol. V no. 2 (June 1952), pp. 214–30.

TIVEY, L., and WOHLGEMUTH, E., 'Trade Associations as Insterest Groups', *P.Q.*, vol. 29 no. 1 (January–March 1958), pp. 59–71.

TRUMAN, D., *The Governmental Process*, Knopf, New York (2nd ed., 1971).

TUTTLE, E. O., *The Crusade Against Capital Punishment in Great Britain*, Stevens, London, 1962.

VIJAY, K. I., 'Some Reflections on the Study of Pressure Groups in Great Britain (1955–70)', *Sociological Analysis*, vol. I no. 3 (June 1971), published by the Dept of Sociological Studies, Sheffield University.

WALLER, I., 'Pressure Politics', *Encounter*, vol. XIX no. 2 (August 1962), pp. 3–15.

Bibliography

WILSON, H. H., *Pressure Group: The Campaign for Commercial Television in England*, Secker and Warburg, London, 1961.

WILSON, H. H., 'Techniques of Pressure: Anti-Nationalisation Propaganda in Britain', *Public Opinion Quarterly*, vol. XV no. 2 (Summer 1951), pp. 225–43.

WILSON, J. H., 'Public Relations and Parliament', *Public Relations* (April 1962), pp. 5–8.

WOOTTON, G., 'Controlling Lobbyists: Lessons from America', *The Times*, 3 December 1968.

WOOTTON, G., 'Ex-Servicemen in Politics', *P.Q.*, vol. 29 no. 1 (January–March 1958), pp. 28–39.

WOOTTON, G., *Interest Groups*, Prentice Hall, New Jersey, 1970.

WOOTTON, G., *The Politics of Influence*, Routledge, London, 1963.

Addendum

BENEWICK, R., and SMITH, T. (eds.), *Direct Action and Democratic Politics*, Allen and Unwin, London, 1972.

BLANK, S., *Industry and Government in Britain: The Federation of British Industries in Politics, 1945–65*, Saxon House/Lexington Books, 1973.

COUSINS, P. F., 'Voluntary Organisations as Local Pressure Groups', *London Review of Public Administration*, vol. 3, pp. 22–30.

DEARLOVE, J., *The Politics in Local Government*, Cambridge University Press, 1973.

FINER, S. E., 'The Political Power of Organised Labour', *Government and Opposition*, vol. 8 no. 4 (Autumn 1973).

GRANT, W. P., and MARSH, D., 'The Confederation of British Industry', *Political Studies*, vol. XIX no. 4 (December 1971), pp. 403–15.

GRANT, W. P., and MARSH, D., 'Government and Industry: A New Pattern of Representation?', *Public Administration Bulletin*, no. 14 (June 1973), pp. 10–20.

HEINEMAN, Jr., B. W., *The Politics of the Powerless: a study of the Campaign Against Racial Discrimination*, O.U.P. for the Institute of Race Relations, 1972.

KIMBER, R., RICHARDSON, J. J., and BROOKES, S. K., 'British Government and the Transport Reform Movement', *P.Q.* (April 1974).

MAY, T., and MORAN, M., 'Trade Unions as Pressure Groups', *New Society*, 6 September 1973, pp. 570–3.

RYAN, M. C., 'A Pressure Group Prepares for Europe: The Country Landowners' Association, 1961–72', *Parliamentary Affairs*, vol. XXVI no. 3 (Summer 1973), pp. 307–17.

TAYLOR, R., 'The T.U.C.: a study in influence', *New Society*, 9 August 1973.